Research Methods in Business Studies

FOURTH EDITION

Research Methods in Business Studies

PERVEZ GHAURI

Professor of International Business
King's College London
London, UK

KJELL GRØNHAUG

Professor of Business Studies
Norwegian School of Economics and Business Administration
Bergen, Norway

**Financial Times
Prentice Hall**
is an imprint of

Harlow, England • London • New York • Boston • San Francisco • Toronto
Sydney • Tokyo • Singapore • Hong Kong • Seoul • Taipei • New Delhi
Cape Town • Madrid • Mexico City • Amsterdam • Munich • Paris • Milan

Pearson Education Limited
Edinburgh Gate
Harlow
Essex CM20 2JE
England

and Associated Companies throughout the world

Visit us on the World Wide Web at:
www.pearsoned.co.uk

First published 1995
Fourth edition published 2010

ISBN: 978-0-273-71204-6

British Library Cataloguing-in-Publication Data
A catalogue record for this book is available from the British Library

Library of Congress Cataloging-in-Publication Data
Ghauri, Pervez N., 1948–
    Research methods in business studies / Pervez Ghauri, Kjell Grønhaug. – 4th ed.
      p. cm.
    Includes bibliographical references and index.
    ISBN 978-0-273-71204-6 (pbk. : alk. paper)   1. Management–Research.   2. Business–Research.
I. Grønhaug, Kjell.   II. Title.
    HD30.4.G49   2010
    658–dc22

                                                                              2009050942

ARP impression 98

Typeset in 9.5/12.5pt Stone Serif by 35
Printed in Great Britain by Ashford Colour Press Ltd

Contents

Part I Challenges and ambiguities of business research

Part II The research process

List of figures

List of screenshots

List of boxes

List of tables

Supporting resources

Visit **www.pearsoned.co.uk/ghauri** to find valuable online resources

For instructors
- PowerPoint slides that can be downloaded and used as OHTs

For more information please contact your local Pearson Education sales representative or visit **www.pearsoned.co.uk/ghauri**

Preface

We are very pleased to present the fourth edition of our book on Research Methods. The first edition of this book, published in 1995, received considerable recognition and attention, mainly from scholars in the United Kingdom, Scandinavia and the Netherlands.

The second and the third editions, published in 2002 and 2005, were used in several American and Asian schools, in addition to many European schools, and have been translated into the Chinese, Portuguese and Estonian languages. The third edition in particular was widely praised for its direct and concrete approach to research methods not only for business studies but also for social sciences in general. Over the past fifteen years, we personally received many positive comments on the accessibility and directness of the text from our colleagues and the students who used it. But at the same time we also received a lot of feedback on what was missing in the book, and valuable input on how it could be improved.

About a year ago the publisher approached us for a possible fourth edition and at that time we started a more systematic collection of comments from the colleagues who have been using the book. The publisher also sent the third edition to ten anonymous reviewers and asked for their comments as to the strong and weak points of the book and their recommendations as to how it could be improved. We have thus received an abundance of comments on the previous editions, how the book should be improved, and what a fourth edition should include. In this respect, we would like to thank the following colleagues for their valuable advice and comments: Jose-Pla Barber, Peter Buckley, Tamer Cavusgil, Jeremy Clegg, Ulf Elg, Philippe Gugler, Amjad Hadjikhani, Saba Khalid, Jean-Paul Lemaire, Ulrike Mayrhofer, Niin Nummmela, Rebecca Piekkari, Stefan Schmid, Rudolf Sinkovics, Carl-Arthur Solberg, Roger Strange, Veronika Tarnovskaya and Sari Wahyuni.

Following the comments from above-mentioned colleagues, we have worked on the fourth edition and have considerably changed and, hopefully, improved it. Not only have we added a new chapter and about 50 pages of new text, we have also reorganized the whole book. It is now divided into three parts: (I) Challenges and ambiguities of business research; (II) The research process; and (III) Implementation. We have made the language and approach more neutral and have provided additional examples in almost all the sections. We first have a discussion on qualitative versus quantitative research methods and have explained which type of research method is more appropriate for which type of research questions. Each chapter now deals with both types of research method. Part III provides concrete guidelines for designing and conducting quantitative and qualitative research, the two most commonly used research methods in our field. The last chapter gives section by section guidelines for report writing depending on the purpose of the report. Special attention has been given to international and cross-cultural business research as a new chapter on this topic has been added. Sections on ethical issues have been expanded. A number of examples have been added to make the text more accessible and easy to understand. A number of new features have been introduced. These include: (1) Boxes to provide illustrations and to strengthen the text. (2) At the end of each chapter a short list of 'further reading' has been provided. This can be particularly useful to teachers and students who want to probe deeper into a particular issue. These additional readings have been selected with great care to present a balanced and up-to-date view (classical as well as new perspectives) on different issues. (3) More questions are provided at the end of each chapter. They can be used to test the knowledge of the reader and can also be used as exam questions. (4) At the end of all chapters some exercises are provided to encourage discussion and debate in the class. We believe the fourth edition is more comprehensive, but still to the point and focused, and provides a set of guidelines for research methods in business studies. The data analysis chapters have been totally rewritten, and examples are provided to make the point and to make the book readable to students without a considerable background in statistics. Moreover, for those researchers who want to pursue their research using statistical/ qualitative methods, a list of further readings, in respective fields, is provided for deeper understanding.

We take this opportunity to thank our families who afford us time and stimulate us in these endeavours. Robert-Jan Bulter, Saad Ghauri and Naveed Elahi deserve our special thanks for helping us in preparing the manuscript and for typing and retyping several versions of the book. Finally we are grateful to Matthew Walker at Pearson Education, for his professional help and for sending us those 'nice' emails encouraging us to finish the manuscript on time.

Pervez N. Ghauri *Kjell Grønhaug*
London *Bergen*

Guided tour of the book

Exercises

using the same questionnaire. The equivalence and comparability of data in this case is highly questionable. Also, the method of data collection is important; for example, was the researcher present at the time of data collection or not? Later when data is sorted and prepared for analysis, through data reduction and categorization, it is important to obtain the real meaning. Dictionary translation is often not very helpful as this does not explain the intensity or the seriousness of the response. This has to be considered throughout the data analysis stage.

Further reading

Ghauri, P.N. and Firth, R. (2009) 'The formation of case research in international business', *Der Markt: Journal for Marketing*, 48: 29–40.
Grisar-Kassé, K. (2004) 'The role of negative personal experiences in cross-cultural case study research: failure or opportunity', in Marshan-Piekkari, R. and Welch, C. (eds) *A Handbook of Qualitative Research Methods for International Business*, Cheltenham: Edward Elgar, pp. 144–61.
Richards, T.J. and Richards, L. (2000) *Using N*VIVO in Qualitative Research*, 2nd edition, Bundoora: QSR International Pty.
Sinkovics, R., Penz, E. and Ghauri, P.N. (2008) 'Enhancing trustworthiness of qualitative research in international business', *Management International Review*, 48(6): 689–714.

Questions

1. Is cross-cultural research different from research in the same cultural setting? Discuss.
2. What is meant by the equivalence of the unit of analysis? Explain with examples.
3. Explain the two concepts emic and etic. How can we handle these issues in cross-cultural research?
4. How can a cross-cultural research project be most meaningful? What adjustments are necessary to accommodate cultural differences?

Exercises

1. A firm wants to go to a new market and is analysing Russia or India to enter. Do you think the firm can collect demographic data on the two markets and compare it to see which market is more suitable? Advise the company how it can enhance the comparability of the data collected in the two markets.

229

Further reading presents a balanced and up-to-date view – ideal if you want to delve deeper into a particular issue.

Questions and Exercises at the end of each chapter test your understanding of the issues discussed, and how well you can put the ideas into practice.

The test statistic is t distributed with $N - 1$ degrees of freedom and approaches the normal distribution as the number of observations increases.

Example

For a supermarket chain to add a new product, at least 100 units must be sold per week. The new product is tested in ten randomly selected stores for a limited time. A one-tailed test, that is a test when direction of findings is hypothesized, is appropriate, because it is only when the sales per store are at least 100 that the product will be introduced on a national scale. The null and the alternative hypotheses are:

$$H_0 : X \leq 100$$
$$H_A : X > 100$$

Assume the significance level to be $\alpha = 0.05$; that is, we reject the null hypothesis (H_0) when the probability for the null hypothesis is correct at 5 per cent ($\alpha = 0.05$). The significance level thus tells us at what probability we are likely to commit a wrong decision, that is, accepting the alternative hypothesis when in fact the null hypothesis is true.

By calculation we find that the mean $X = 109.4$ and the standard deviation $SD = 14.90$.
We also see that the standard error of the mean $SD_x = SD/\sqrt{N} = 14.90/\sqrt{10 - 1} = 4.55$.
Calculating t we find:

$$t = \frac{X - \mu}{SD_x} = \frac{109.4 - 100}{4.55} = 2.07$$

Critical t (i.e. the required t-value to reject the null hypothesis) as read from the t-table with one degree of freedom is 1.833 ($\alpha = 0.05$).
Here the t test is applied. The t test assumes normally distributed variables, but has been found to be rather robust. When N becomes large, i.e. $N > 30$, the t distribution approaches the normal distribution.

Box 11.1 Hypotheses

Hypotheses play a major role in research. They imply assumptions or beliefs, and are often stated as questions. Is A larger than B? Will the new product sell more than 100 units per week? Hypotheses can (in principle) be tested. In doing so we contrast the hypothesis, for example A is better than B, with the null hypothesis, there is no difference between A and B. To do so we need data on the performance of A and B. If sufficient difference exists we reject the null hypothesis and accept the alternative hypothesis. Thus, we gain insights, through falsification, that is we test our assumption or belief.

170

Examples and **boxed illustrations** from a wide range of sources help explain the ideas discussed.

Publisher's acknowledgements

We are grateful to the following for permission to reproduce copyright material:

Figures

Figure 2.3 adapted from *Social Research Methods*, Pearson Education, Inc. (Forcese, Dennis, P. and Richer, Stephen 1973) p. 22 © 1973. Reprinted by permission of Pearson Education, Inc., Upper Saddle River, NJ; Figure 8.1 adapted from *Business Research Projects for Students*, Thomson Learning (Jankowicz, A.D. 1991) p. 159; Figure 8.2 from *Mastering the Dynamics of Innovation*, Harvard Business School (Utterback, J.M. 1994) p. 41, based on data in E. Braun and S. MacDonald, Revolution in Miniature: The History and Impact of Semiconductor Electronics (Cambridge, England: Cambridge University Press, 1978); and J.E. Tilton, International Diffusion of Technology (Washington D.C.; The Brookings Institution, 1971), Reprinted by permission of Harvard Business School Press, Copyright © 1994 by the Harvard Business School Publishing Corporation; all rights reserved; Figure 8.3 adapted from Case research in marketing: opportunities, problems and a process, *Journal of Business Research*, 12, p. 205 (Bonoma, T.V. 1985); Figure 8.6 from *Research Methods for Managers*, Sage Publications Ltd. (Gill, J. and Johnson, P. 1991) pp. 76–77; Figure 9.1 adapted from *Marketing Research: Methodological Foundations*, 7th ed. (Churchill, G.A. 1995) p. 557, © 1999 South-Western, a part of Cengage Learning, Inc., Reproduced by permission. www.cengage.com/permissions; Figure 13.2 adapted from *How to Write a Research Paper*, 2nd ed., Pergamon Press (Berry, R. 1989), reprinted with permission of Ralph Berry; Figures 13.3, 13.4 from *International Marketing Research*, 2nd ed. (Craig, D.S. & Douglas, S.P. 2000) Copyright © John Wiley & Sons Limited. Reprinted with permission; Figure 13.5 from Data equivalence in cross-cultural research: a comparison of classical test theory and latent trait theory based approaches, *Australasian Marketing Journal*, 7(2), pp. 23–38. (Salzberger, T., Sinkovics, R. and Schlegelmich, B. 1999)

Screenshots

Screenshot 7.1 from MSU homepage, ciber.msu.edu, Michigan State University International Business Center

Tables

Table 7.2 adapted from *Business Research Methods*, Oxford University Press (Bryman, A. and Bell, E. 2003) pp. 215–16; Table 9.2 from *Applied Sampling*, Academic Press

(Sudman, S. 1976) p. 87, Copyright © 1976, with permission from Elsevier; Table 12.1 from Can computerised market models improve strategic decision making?, *Journal of Socio-Economics*, 32, pp. 503–20 (Fuglseth, A.M. and Grønhaug, K. 2003), Copyright © 2003, with permission from Elsevier; Table 13.1 from Enhancing the trustworthiness of qualitative research in international business, *Management International Review*, 48(6), pp. 696–98 (Sinkovics et al. 2008), with kind permission from Gabler Verlag and Dr Rudolf Sinkovics

Text

Epigraph on page 3 from *Older people and their Social World: The Subculture of the Aging*, F. A. Davis Company (Rose, A.M. and Peterson, W.A. 1965) p. 11, ISBN: 9780803676206; Epigraph on page 8 from Latent structure analysis (Lazarsfeld, P. 1959) *Psychology: A Study of a Science*, 3, p. 480 (Koch, S. (ed.) 1959), McGraw-Hill, reproduced with permission of The McGraw-Hill Companies; Epigraph on page 54 from The analysis of consumer actions (Kornhauser, A. and Lazarsfeld, P.F., 1955), *The Language of Social Research*, pp. 392–403 (Lazarsfeld, P. and Rosenberg, M. (eds)), Copyright © 1955 by the Free Press. Copyright renewed © 1983 by Patricia Kendall Lazarsfeld, all rights reserved, reprinted with the permission of The Free Press, a division of Simon & Schuster, Inc.; Box 6.1 from *Collective Market Orientation in Co-producing Networks*, doctoral dissertation, BI Norwegian School of Management (Silkoset, R. 2004); Epigraph on page 103 from Case research in marketing: opportunities, problems and a process, *Journal of Marketing Research*, 12, p. 199 (Bonoma, T.V. 1985), reprinted with permission by the American Marketing Association; Box 9.1 from *Business Research Methods*, Oxford University Press (Bryman, A. and Bell, E. 2003) p. 93; Box 12.1 from *The Management of Innovations* (Burns, T. and Stalker, G.M. 1961) pp. 120–21, by permission of Oxford University Press; Box 13.2 from International comparison of labour disputes, *Labour Market Trends*, pp. 195–201 (Davis, J. 2001), Source: UK Statistics Authority website www.statistics.gov.uk and Business Research Methods, Oxford University Press (Bryman, A. and Bell, E. 2003) p. 227 by permission of Oxford University Press. Crown Copyright material is reproduced with the permission of the controller, Office of Public Sector Information (OPSI).

In some instances we have been unable to trace the owners of copyright material, and we would appreciate any information that would enable us to do so.

PART I

Challenges and ambiguities of business research

Part I (Chapters 1 and 2) explains the purpose of the book and the challenges related to doing research in business studies. It sets the scene for the book and explains its perspective, target group and the purpose of doing research in general. It also takes up the ethical responsibilities of the researcher.

CHAPTER 1

Introduction

Facts do not simply lie around waiting to be picked up. Facts must be carved out of the continuous web of ongoing reality, must be observed within a specified frame of reference, must be measured with precision, must be observed where they can be related to other relevant facts. All of this involves methods.

(Rose and Peterson, 1965: 11)

1.1 Purpose of the book

The purpose of this book is to help students get rid of the myth that research is 'too scientific' or 'too abstract' and unnecessary in business studies. It is also intended to help them understand the language and approach of science and research. It will assist them in understanding how properly structured and argued reports can be more convincing and reliable than reports based on a random approach or on common sense. In our opinion, a scientific approach and common sense have much in common. The scientific approach, however, is a more systematic and controlled treatment of common sense. A layperson uses theories and concepts but in a loose manner. Often, people accept whatever sounds consistent with their beliefs and values: an increase in unemployment is because of immigrants or, in a business setting, the more money you spend on advertising the more you can sell, etc. A scientific approach, on the other hand, systematically examines assumptions and hypotheses before either believing or discarding them.

We have written this book to give practical guidelines for students and researchers. It is based on our own experience as researchers and as supervisors for numerous PhD and Master's theses, and that of many colleagues and students in business studies. The fourth edition has also been improved and expanded with help and assistance from our colleagues and students who have been using the first three editions. In this edition particular attention has been given to three important issues: the usage of case study research business studies, the impact of cross-cultural issues, and ethical issues in research. These issues are dealt with in each and every chapter and a new chapter has been added on case study research. Moreover, we have now highlighted examples throughout the book to make the text more accessible and easy to understand.

3

This book is designed to help students understand that a conscious (scientific) approach is the most appropriate for research and problem-solving projects. This means making students understand that, before beginning research on a project, they must be aware of what they are doing and what they are not doing. They have to clarify for themselves and for the reader the perspective they have chosen, and they must identify who should benefit from the study. In other words they must learn how to formulate a problem, how to choose a particular method and how to argue and motivate. They must also learn how to write a valid and reliable report, which is useful for the purpose of research and for managers or decision makers. We provide students and others involved in research in business studies with clear, hands-on guidelines for doing research. The book deals with the following:

- highlighting the importance of systematic research and problem solving;
- explaining how to cope with problems associated with doing research;
- explaining different types of research, the role of the researcher and the importance of methods and models;
- the practicalities of research, such as problem formulation, relating the research to previous studies, choosing a suitable methodology, presenting results and findings and drawing conclusions;
- a discussion of different methods of data collection and analysis, qualitative as well as quantitative, and their advantages and disadvantages; which type of method is suitable for which type of research problem and conditions;
- a special attention to case study research;
- the role of the researcher and ethical issues in doing research;
- how to test the assumptions necessary for the method and techniques being used, and whether these assumptions are valid: in other words, validation of methods and models and not only validation of hypotheses;
- the impact of cross-cultural (international) issues on the research process and how to handle these issues;
- the practical issues around research in business studies, providing some practical guidelines for questionnaire development, interviewing and data analysis;
- step-by-step guidelines for report writing, the format and writing of a report as a thesis and for publication purposes;
- concrete guidelines for oral presentation.

1.2 Readership

This book is primarily meant for MBA, Master of Science (MSc) and advanced undergraduate students in business studies. It is also meant for PhD students and other researchers at the earlier stages of their research endeavours. Most schools and universities require their graduate as well as undergraduate students to write a thesis or a research report at the final stage of their studies. These students are the primary target for this text. Students often find the books available in the market either too general or too narrow, dealing with only one aspect of research, such as surveys, interviews or case studies, or else at a higher philosophical level that is often irrelevant and difficult to comprehend. This book, on the other hand, has an integrative approach and is especially adapted to research in business studies. It will also be highly useful for consultants and business people working with research projects, problem solving and report writing. Considering the above-mentioned target groups, we have kept the language and discussion simple and accessible. A rather direct and to-the-point stance is taken and a number of examples are given to make the reader understand and comprehend the point under discussion. The book is organized in three parts: Part I (Chapters 1–2) dealing with the challenges of business research, Part II (Chapters 3–10) dealing with the research process, and Part III (Chapters 11–14) dealing with analysis, implementation and report writing.

In Chapter 2 we discuss the meaning of research with special reference to business studies. The focus here is to discuss the difference between research and practical problem solving or common sense, and the different research orientations and knowledge and skills required for research. The final part of the chapter deals with ethical issues and responsibilities. In Chapter 3 the role of theory in business research is discussed. Here the focus is on the research process and on the explanation of important concepts, such as theory, models and knowledge. Chapter 4 deals with the research problem. It is our observation that most students of business studies face difficulties in formulating the research problem, and in differentiating between a research problem and a research topic. In this chapter we also discuss the importance of models and systematic thinking in research and the role of reviewing past literature.

Chapter 5 deals with the research design and problems related to the choice of research design: how the research problem is, and should be, related to the design. Different types of research designs are presented and their usage discussed. Examples are used to illustrate the importance and relevance of research design. Problems related to validity and reliability are also dealt with in this chapter.

Chapter 6 handles the important problem of measurement and operationalization of research concepts and data. Measurement of empirical research is a difficult task as the quality of information depends to a large extent upon the measurement procedures used in gathering and analysing data. The chapter takes us through different types, levels and scales of measurement. Validity and reliability in measurement are particularly stressed. Some guidelines are provided to improve the measurement. A special section is devoted to measurements in qualitative research. Chapter 7 deals with different types of data resources and what is meant by the right kind of data. Sources of secondary as well as primary data collection and their advantages and disadvantages are discussed.

Chapter 8 thoroughly explains data collection methods. It starts with a discussion on qualitative versus quantitative methods and explains when to use which type of data collection method. It then explains main methods of data collection in business studies, such as surveys, interviews and focus groups. Chapter 9 discusses different types of sampling techniques and how we should go about drawing a sample. Some suggestions are also given for sampling in qualitative research. Chapter 10 takes up the difficult job of preparing and analysing data. It handles issues such as coding and editing and explains the role of statistics in data analysis and presentation. The chapter also thoroughly discusses the role of computers and how the use of computers can help improve our data analysis. The last section deals with data analysis in qualitative research.

Chapter 11 provides guidelines and a practical demonstration of how to actually conduct data analysis. A number of techniques are presented and discussed for conducting both quantitative and qualitative data analysis. The chapter explains and gives examples of the most commonly used statistical techniques in our field. Chapter 12 provides guidelines on designing and conducting a case study. It discusses when to use a case study, how to collect data through this method and how to analyse data collected through a case study.

Chapter 13 discusses the extra care needed in cases of cross-cultural research as research involving an unfamiliar environment may complicate the understanding of the research problem, data collection and data analysis. The chapter also provides guidelines to handle multi-country research projects. In these projects, comparability of the data and equivalence of the understanding both of the researcher and the respondents are of utmost importance. The researchers have to be extra careful in categorization and measurement of cross-cultural data. The chapter deals with each stage of the research project, how it is complicated because of the cross-cultural setting and how each stage can be handled to eliminate items and concepts that may cause cultural bias and thereby influence the findings of the study.

Finally, Chapter 14 provides guidelines for writing a report. The process of writing up the final report is tiresome work. The report has to be concise, consistent and convincing. The writing style of the report is also important in order to convince the reader that the report is valid and reliable. In this chapter the structure of reports is discussed section by section, with examples and illustrations. Guidelines for form and style, for usage of footnotes and a bibliography are also provided. Different types of reports are discussed, such as thesis, oral presentation and a report written for publication.

1.3 On the use of the book

When working with the book, it is recommended that the reader first scans the whole text and thoroughly reads Chapters 1–5 before starting to work on a business research project. A thorough understanding of the role of theory in practical research and the objective of the research is needed. When actually working on the research projects, researchers should read Chapters 6–10; this will enable them to decide which research design is the most suitable and which data collection method is most appropriate for their research problem. At this stage they can also get help on how they should go about sampling and collecting data and on which type of analysis will be the most appropriate. While conducting the actual data collection and analysis, the researcher is advised to read the respective chapter from Part III, whichever is relevant. Finally, before sitting down to write up the report and findings, the researcher should read Chapter 14 about writing the report. The chapter provides concrete guidelines for report writing for different purposes. An added feature in the fourth edition is that at the end of each chapter a list of further reading is provided. Researchers who want to look more deeply into a particular issue (e.g. on different opinions on the study of management, on ethical issues on secondary data or how to handle a particular problem caused by cross-cultural data collection) can quickly look up these readings to enhance their understanding.

CHAPTER 2

Research in business studies

If we have mentioned the actual results of investigation first, the reader could have labelled these obvious also. Obviously, something is wrong with the entire argument of obviousness. It should really be turned on its head. Since every kind of human reaction is conceivable, it's of great importance to know which reactions actually occur most frequently and under what conditions; only then will a more advanced social science develop.

(Lazarsfeld, 1959: 480, reproduced with permission of the McGraw-Hill Companies)

The purpose of this chapter is to explain what we mean by research in business studies and to discuss differences between systematic research and common sense or practical problem solving. Different research orientations are also discussed to illustrate the influence of researchers' backgrounds and basic beliefs surrounding the research methods and processes. We believe that research papers or theses at the Master's level, when successfully completed, should demonstrate that the candidate can systematically handle and analyse a problem, arriving at valid conclusions. In other words, it is a professional training process through which we can learn to think and work systematically. The advantage of systematic thinking is that it contributes to accuracy and a more orderly approach and is reliable in handling research as well as business problems.

Example

A business firm experiences declining sales and – of course – managers and employees feel frustrated. Through systematic observations and thinking it becomes clear that the declining sales are caused by a newly introduced substitute. This results in a systematic effort to develop and introduce a new and improved product offering.

The increasingly complex nature of business operations and decision making demands a systematic and thoughtful approach. The importance of research in business studies, in schools, and in businesses has therefore increased. Practical problem solving and decision making are (or at least should be) becoming more and more similar to research. Business and marketing research are common activities in medium-sized and larger companies. And most of the decision making in these companies is based on research. For example, whether a company is launching a new product or trying to enter a new market, it has first to undertake some research to decide which segment to target, whether there will be some demand for its product (sales forecast) and how to develop a marketing plan for the new product or new market. All this requires research that has to be undertaken by the company itself or by a marketing research company that sells its services.

2.1 Why we do research

The basic purpose of research in education is to teach students to work systematically and for them to learn critically to analyse issues/matters before believing in them or acting upon them. However, research is essential for understanding even basic everyday phenomena that need to be handled by individuals and organizations. If we want to buy a car, we do some research, finding out which car satisfies our needs/criteria and where it is available; we compare prices at different dealers, or among different cars that fit into our criteria, and so on. In the same manner a company has to do research while making important decisions, whether it is to reorganise its structure or to merge or take over another company. Businesses are these days doing systematic research to handle their day-to-day activities (Sekaran, 1992).

> Businesses are beginning to develop a strategic monitoring program to identify and understand competitors' strengths, weaknesses and overall business strategies. Any firm can establish a competitor-analysis system that provides management with essential information about a wide range of strategies that rivals are likely to pursue. The key is knowing where to gather relevant information and how to combine separate pieces of data into a coherent profile of each competing operation.
>
> (Svatko, 1989: 59)

We really cannot take decisions on important issues unless we investigate (research) more deeply the relevant information, gathering more information on the particular aspect we are interested in. Then we analyse all this information to make a judgement about the right solution to our problem or answer to our questions. In business studies we normally work with problems faced by managers and companies. For example: How to enter a particular market? What are the factors that influence performance in joint venture relationships? What are the factors that influence the successful launch of a new product? Is advertising necessary, or how much advertising is necessary to market a certain product? Would acquiring a particular company fulfil our strategic objectives? And so on.

Without research we cannot answer the above or similar questions. As well as learning systematic information collection and critical analysis, we need to learn how things work, through research done by others, and then perhaps use that knowledge to see whether it is applicable to our problems/situations. Sometimes we need to make/suggest changes to apply them to our own problems. When this process has been done by several researchers, the ideas/theories are tested. Once theories are properly tested we can even predict the future. We can say with confidence that in this type of situation/problem, this should be the solution/ answer. The research, therefore, makes our life easier, not only in business but in general. The research can thus be considered as a process of problem solving for a specific problem under specific conditions (Kuhn, 1970).

Example

Through systematic research it was found that serious stomach and digestion problems were caused by the salmonella bacteria. Research also showed that the salmonella bacteria did not survive at a temperature of 80°C or higher, resulting in the practice of heating food to that temperature when suspecting the bacteria.

2.2 Research versus common sense

There is a common belief that research is an academic activity undertaken by researchers who are not at all familiar with managerial culture and the nature of problems faced by business managers. At the same time, several studies have revealed that managers do not know how to use research findings and therefore cannot utilize the results and conclusions of research (Whitley, 1984; Gill and Johnson, 1991). In our opinion, research in business studies and managerial problem solving are not much different from each other. Managers need to have some knowledge and evaluation capabilities to understand the consequences of their decisions. In other words, managerial decision making or problem solving, if done systematically, should lead to better decisions and results than those decisions made exclusively through intuition or personal likes and dislikes. Managers must have the capability to analyse their situations and to use investigative approaches to decision making and problem solving. The systematic procedures and approaches of advancing knowledge, suggested by the research process, also serve as a disciplined and systematic procedure for managerial problem solving.

Example

In business life firms and their managers experience negative surprises, for example that customers become dissatisfied and frustrated. An ability to obtain systematic insights into what causes dissatisfaction and frustration is crucial to solve the problem and improve.

As a first step, actors in both management and research activities need to decide what they want to achieve. This is followed by collecting relevant information and facts that can help in achieving the first objective. The information collected needs to be analysed and put into a structure that helps to achieve a purpose or initiate different actions. This process, deciding what to do, collecting information, discarding irrelevant information, analysing the relevant information and arriving at a conclusion/decision in a systematic procedure, is useful for the cumulative knowledge as well as the personal development of the researcher and manager alike (Revans, 1971; Gill and Johnson, 2002). Although some scholars differentiate between academic research and research done by companies, for practical problem solving, we believe in 'trans-disciplinarity' in research, where boundaries of a single contributing discipline can be crossed. The production of knowledge is thus not restricted to academic research. It involves academics, policy makers and managers, and useful knowledge is developed and exploited more quickly than if a different type of knowledge was developed by different parties (Gibbons et al., 1994; Tranfield and Starkey, 1998; Bryman and Bell, 2003).

The purposes of doing research are manifold, such as to describe, explain, understand, foresee, criticize and/or analyse already existing knowledge or phenomena in social sciences. The job of a researcher is often that of an observer, and each observation is prone to error; therefore we go out and research to find a better 'truth' or answers to our questions.

Box 2.1   Why do firms (organizations) exist?

It is costly to perform transactions. In a classic article, 'The nature of the firm', R.H. Coase raised the 'obvious' question: Why do firms exist? Coase was trained as a neo-classical economist. In neo-classical economics firms do not exist in highly competitive markets. Rather, transactions are mediated through markets. Coase explained the existence of firms as due to 'frictions' – or transaction costs. This insight is useful to understand why firms in some cases use the market to perform transactions, whereas in other cases they (transactions) are conducted internally.

If the role of a researcher is that of an observer, then what is the difference between an observer who can draw conclusions with common sense and a researcher? The difference is that observations made by the researcher should be systematic, arguable and challengeable. The researcher explains to us how he or she collects information, argues for the results obtained and explains their limitations. In an ideal situation, if anybody else had made observations using the same methods they would come up with more or less the same results. The role of the researcher thus becomes very important. When we look and observe, we see differently depending upon our background and what we know and expect. Two different people observing the same object may see two different things. It is thus very important to discuss the object and the observer and biases. For this reason the observer has to explain and convince the reader of the purpose and methods of observation.

findings show that employees tend to see problems and solutions from sition and tasks they are involved in. For example, a marketing person see marketing problems, a person involved in production sees most problems as production problems. The main reason is that individual actors are constrained by their limited cognitive capacity, that is limited capacity to notice, make sense of, store, retrieve and make use of information (data).

The usefulness of research is often discussed, especially when it comes to things that seem self-explanatory and common sense. But the very same common sense and self-explanatory objects/beliefs have proven to be wrong through research. Common sense and beliefs, influenced by society and culture, provide us with a non-conscious ideology, and we believe in things without being aware of the reality. As Bem (1979: 89) said, 'Only a very unparochial and intellectual fish is aware that his environment is wet.' This is further illustrated by the following:

> A man and his son are involved in an automobile accident. The man is killed and the boy, seriously injured, is rushed to the hospital for surgery. The surgeon takes one look at him and says, 'I am sorry, but I cannot operate on this boy. He is my son.'
>
> (Selltiz et al., 1976: 4)

Whenever we tell this story to our students many of them do not understand the catch. We unconsciously believe that a surgeon is always a man and therefore do not even consider the thought that the surgeon can be the mother of that boy.

Scientific research often challenges these non-conscious ideologies and beliefs by scrutinizing them. Challenging old beliefs, turning things upside down and creating new beliefs is not always comfortable. For example, in a number of somewhat conservative states, it is not allowed to include Darwin's evolution theory in the school curriculum, as it challenges the belief promoted by religion about the creation of mankind. Research corrects our misbeliefs, generates new concepts and broadens our perspectives and perceptions. This is particularly true because research does all that which is often beyond common sense – while common sense considers most things as given. The fundamental difference here is, as mentioned earlier, that research involves systematic methods. The conclusions drawn from research lead to new theories and beliefs. The purpose, however, and we hope everybody can agree, is to improve social life. In business research, the purpose is to understand how and why things happen. The research corrects our misbeliefs and provides new perspectives. At times it can be uncomfortable, as illustrated by the following example:

> A well-known scientist (some say it was Bertrand Russell) once gave a public lecture on astronomy. He described how the earth orbits around the sun and how the sun, in turn, orbits around the center of a vast collection of stars called a galaxy. At the end of the lecture, a little old lady at the back of the room got up and said, 'What you have told us is rubbish. The world is really a flat plate supported on the

back of a giant tortoise.' The scientist gave a superior smile before replying, and asked 'What is the tortoise standing on?' 'You are very clever, young man, very clever,' said the lady, 'But it's turtles all the way down.'

(Hawkins, 1988: 1)

The above discussion makes it clear that the difference between a scientific observation and a layperson's observation is that scientific research is done systematically and is based on logic and not beliefs: therefore, we stress a logical relationship between cause and effect. Most students in business studies get confused by the terminology used in books on traditional research methods. Although the language and the scientific approach is somewhat different from common sense, it is not strange or difficult to comprehend. In fact, quite the contrary, as, when understood, it seems logical and natural. As Whitehead (1911: 10) stated, common sense is not the right start for research: 'Its sole criterion for judgement is that the new ideas shall look like the old ones.' It therefore prepares us for new realities.

According to one idea, science is a systematic and controlled extension of common sense, as common sense is a series of concepts and conceptual schemes satisfactory for the practical uses of mankind (Conant, 1951: 32–3). Others believe that these concepts and conceptual schemes can be misleading in modern times. For example, it was self-evident common sense for many in the last century to use punishment as a basic tool of pedagogy. It has however been proved that this old view of 'common sense' may be quite wrong as rewards seem more effective in aiding learning (Kerlinger, 1964: 4). According to this belief, science and common sense differ in several ways (ibid.):

1. The first difference is that laypersons use *'concepts'* and *'theories'* loosely. They often accept explanations that fit easily with their beliefs and values, for example that illness is due to sinfulness. Scientists, on the other hand, systematically build up theories and test them for internal as well as external consistency. Moreover, they believe that the concepts they are using are human-made terms that may or may not exhibit a close relation to reality.

2. Laypersons often select theories and *test hypotheses*, but their evidence comes from their own hypotheses. They believe in their evidence as it fits their assumptions. Scientists, on the other hand, test their assumptions and hypotheses systematically and tend to be more careful in their selection.

3. Laypersons do not bother to control their explanations of observed phenomena. They do not try to *control external influences*, and they accept those assumptions that are consistent with their preconceived biases. They do not try to relate different phenomena. Scientists, on the other hand, are constantly looking for relations among different phenomena. They systematically try to study and control these relations.

4. Finally, laypersons often believe in *'metaphysical explanations'*, such as 'some people are poor because God wants them to be poor'. Scientists, on the other hand, do not accept metaphysical explanations. They are concerned with

13

that can be observed and studied. In other words, research is concerned
udying things that can be observed and tested. If things can be tested,
n be falsified. For example, a person may believe that drinking coffee
night keeps one awake. This assumption (assertion) can be tested.
Assuming that people tend to be equally awake whether they drink coffee
during the night or not, the stated belief is wrong (cf. section 11.1).

2.3 Different research orientations

The research process and the research method used are influenced by the
researcher's background when it comes to research orientation. A particular
research orientation prescribes the relationship between methods, data, theories
and values of the researcher. Social knowledge builds one upon another.
Scientific observations provide new theories, correcting, modifying, extending,
clarifying the older and existing ones. Most methodology books describe 'originality' or 'original contribution to knowledge' as a basic condition for a scientific
study. Although the demand for originality is perhaps the most controversial,
its importance and meaning should not be misunderstood. Students normally
believe that topics used by others in their theses should not be studied, because
by doing so they would lose originality. We believe 'originality' describes studies
that create a new dimension to already existing knowledge. It implies that
there is some novel twist, fresh perspective, new hypothesis or assumption or
new and innovative methods of handling an existing topic/knowledge that
makes the study a distinctive contribution. In business studies, it is equally possible or perhaps more useful to direct research projects towards more sharply
delineated tasks.

The researchers do not preach or ask whether the social activity observed is
good or bad; they just analyse, present and explain it. In fact, that is the starting
point of research: that we have a number of assumptions/speculations, but we
should not accept or reject them unless we study these assumptions critically
and unless we find logical and reliable explanations to accept or reject them.
The researcher thus tries to be as objective as possible. It is however, not always
possible to be objective, as put forward by Burrell and Morgan (1979: 225):

> What passes for scientific knowledge can be shown to be founded upon a set of
> unstated conventions, beliefs and assumptions, just as every day common-sense
> knowledge is. The difference between them lies largely in the nature of rules and
> community which recognises and subscribes to them. The knowledge in both cases
> is not so much 'objective' as shared.

In our opinion, thus, researchers in business studies may have different
orientations, from objective generalizable problem solving to specific practical
problem solving for a particular company (Burrell and Morgan, 1979; Gill and
Johnson, 2002).

14

2.4 Induction and deduction

A researcher observes and faithfully records what is seen without any prejudice. Some of these statements of observation are established as true and serve as the basis for theories and laws. There are two ways of establishing what is true or false and to draw conclusions: induction and deduction. Induction is based on empirical evidence, while deduction is based on logic.

Through *induction* we draw general conclusions from our empirical observations. In this type of research the process goes from observations → findings → theory building, as findings are incorporated back into existing knowledge (literature/theories) to improve theories. In this research, thus, theory is the outcome of research (Bryman and Bell, 2003). This type of research is often associated with the qualitative type of research. This process goes from assumption to conclusions and is illustrated as follows:

Assumption: Psychiatrists have found that psychological problems in patients depend upon their experiences in childhood.

Conclusions: All psychological problems are based on experiences in childhood.

It is, however, important to note that we can never be 100 per cent sure about the above inductive conclusions, as these conclusions are based on some empirical observations. Sometimes conclusions based on hundreds of observations can also be wrong.

This can be explained by the prognosis of election results in a general election. Although the prognosis concludes that the Labour Party is going to win the election, we cannot be sure until we have seen the final results. In other words, we can arrive at more or less probable results, but not with 100 per cent certainty.

By *deduction* we mean that we draw conclusions through logical reasoning. In this case, it need not be true in reality, but it is logical. The researcher in this type of research builds/deduces hypotheses from the existing knowledge (literature), which can be subject to empirical scrutiny (testing) and thus can be accepted or rejected. The researcher's main job is not only to build hypotheses from existing knowledge but also to present them in operational terms (operationalization), to show how information can be collected to test these hypotheses and the concepts being used (Merton, 1967; Chalmers, 1982; Bryman and Bell, 2003). In this type of research, theory, and hypotheses built on it, come first and influence the rest of the research process. This type of research is often associated with the quantitative type of research. The process of deduction goes as follows:

Assumption: All metals expand when heated.

Assumption: Rail tracks are built of metal.

Conclusion: Rail tracks will expand when heated.

The above examples explain the difference between induction and deduction. The difference is that facts acquired through observations lead us to theories and hypotheses, while with deduction (logical reasoning) we accept or reject these theories and hypotheses. This acceptance and rejection then helps us to explain or predict.

In the process of research, methods begin with ideas and facts, that we have known so far, that lead us to propositions, theories and predictions. New theories and predictions lead us to new ideas and facts, and a new cycle begins, leading us to new theories. When we utilize observed facts in generating a theory that is consistent with these facts, we are doing induction. In other words, induction is the process of observing facts to generate a theory and is perhaps the first step in scientific methods. While doing research we formulate propositions after observing the relationship between different variables of our study. Most researchers in business studies go through this method, observing facts or earlier results, that lead them to propositions and later to theories.

On the other hand, in deduction we look at the consequences of a theory. There is an established school of thought which believes that the entire research process is initiated by theories. Deduction involves the gathering of facts to confirm or disprove hypothesized relationships among variables that have been deduced from existing knowledge.

As we can see, discussion on induction and deduction presents us with alternative ways or stages of building theories. Most researchers and scientists believe that they have been using both of these in their research. The processes of induction and deduction are not totally exclusive of each other and induction includes elements of deduction and vice versa. In both cases researchers need to know the nature of the existing knowledge. In both cases, however, a great deal of creativity and imagination is demanded from the researcher or investigator. Both induction and deduction demand that we go beyond statistical significance to systematic data collection, and that we are aware of the sensitive question of the relevance of data to theory or study. Moreover, both demand that the investigator keep up to date with theories and ideas and with scientific methods.

| Box 2.2 | Deductive and inductive reasoning |

Deductive reasoning – the logical process of deriving a conclusion from a known premise or something known as true.

Inductive reasoning – the systematic process of establishing a general proposition on the basis of observation or particular facts.

2.5 What comes first: theory or data?

It is often assumed that theory should precede data, that is, observations. This impression is easily supported by the way the 'research process' is illustrated (see Chapter 3), and research often takes place this way. For example, this is the case when a researcher carefully reviews relevant literature and 'sees' a research opportunity, that is a gap, a weakness or unanswered question in present insights. In this case the researcher often (but not always) has a clear research problem: for example, do variations in X explain variations in Y? Often, however, this is not the case. The researcher may observe something s/he does not understand, typically resulting in questions such as: 'Why?', or 'Why does this happen?' For example, the researcher may observe a specific practice, a way of doing things that is counterintuitive or in conflict with that which s/he has been exposed to previously. This is often the case in 'qualitative' research with a prime emphasis on gaining understanding. A key purpose in this latter case is to 'construct theory', that is to come up with an adequate explanation (see Figure 2.1).

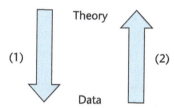

Figure 2.1 Theory or data as starting point

It should be emphasized that when doing research, interactions between theory and data take place. For example, a researcher conducting a structural survey to test a specific hypothesis gets an unexpected finding, triggering off speculations as to why this might be so: that is, the researcher tries to theorize to come up with an adequate explanation. The unexpected finding shows that the hypothesis (theory) can be wrong, and thus forces the researcher to rethink prior belief.

2.6 Knowledge skills and research

Basically we do research because we want to know more about ourselves and the world around us. A number of scholars have explained different ways of knowing (Cohen and Nagel, 1934; Buchler, 1955; Kerlinger, 1964: 6–9):

1. *Method of tenacity*, where we hold firmly to the truth or the truth we know to be true, as we have always known it to be true. We may find ways to

strengthen our belief even if the proposition or new developments may show otherwise. For example, the world is flat.

2. *Method of authority*, where it has been established that this is the case. For example, the Bible states that there is a God. In fact, even if such knowledge seems unsound in certain situations, we live our lives according to this authoritative knowledge.

3. *A priori method* or *method of intuition*, where knowing is based on propositions that are self-evident or 'agreeable to reason'. However, something that is self-evident to one person might not be self-evident to another. For example, is it self-evident that US education is inferior to European education – is this 'agreeable to reason' (Kerlinger, 1964)?

4. *Method of science*, where we find a way of knowing, where everybody's final conclusion is the same. In other words, there are things whose characters are entirely independent of our opinions about them (Buchler, 1955). Scientific approach to attaining knowledge has self-correction as one of the characteristics. We must, however, point out that this is a rather deterministic view of science. In our opinion, there can be several methods of acquiring knowledge that can be called scientific . . . but this is the most widely accepted view. Some scholars call it objectivity (Kerlinger, 1964). As Polanyi (1958: 4) states, scientists systematically and consciously use the self-corrective aspect of the scientific approach. Considering the above, as expressed by Braithwaite (1955: 1):

> The function of science . . . is to establish general laws covering the behaviours of the empirical events or objects with which the science in question is concerned, and thereby to enable us to connect together our knowledge of separately known events and to make reliable predictions of events as yet unknown.

2.7 Why research never stops

As mentioned in section 2.1, while solving problems we need to look at what is already known about this type of situation/problem. In some cases, for example in exploratory research, we make some observations to get better clarification of our research topic or field. What is known in the field and/or these observations help us to understand our problems better. They also help us to ask the right questions. Once we have better knowledge of our problem area we try to look at our field in a rather systematic manner. With the help of this clarified picture we then build hypotheses or assumptions. Hypothesis building or deriving assumptions leads us to the concepts and/or constructs we should study to get answers to our questions. These concepts, when put together, in relation to each other, lead us to our model.

Having a clear understanding of problems, assumptions and concepts, we start thinking how to go about finding answers to our questions. At this stage we have to come up with a research design. Also, how are we going to collect the information needed and what are we going to do with it? In other words, how are we going to analyse that information? Once we have the design we can proceed to actually collect and analyse data. The analysis will lead us to our interpretation, what we understand from the information we have collected and analysed.

Example

A PhD student advances the hypothesis, based on extensive reading, that degree of market orientation covaries positively with firms' performance in competitive markets. S/he develops measures for the key constructs market orientation and business performance. Furthermore, s/he selects a sample of firms operating in competitive markets varying in degree of market orientation. Assume s/he finds a correlation coefficient between degree of market orientation and performance $r = 0.45$. This finding is in the direction of the hypothesized. If the sample size is $n = 30$ this finding is statistically significant ($p < 0.05$).

Through this interpretation we draw our conclusions, thus improving existing knowledge or helping in practical problem solving. This also means that researchers coming after us, working on the same topic, will start where we left off. In other words, while classifying their problem they will review earlier knowledge, including our study. The never-ending research activity is illustrated in Figure 2.2.

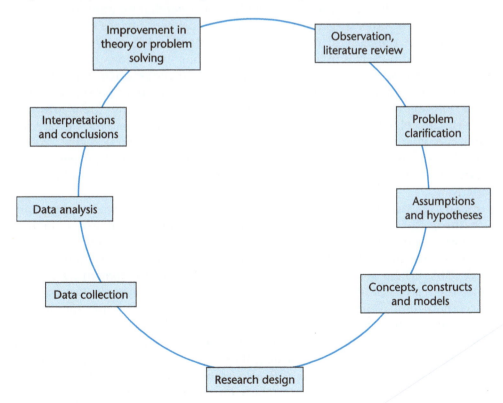

Figure 2.2 The wheel of research

2.8 Research and ethics

Ethics are moral principles and values that influence the way a researcher or a group of reseachers conduct their research activities. In fact, ethics apply to all situations and activities in which there can be actual or potential harm of any kind to anybody (Churchill, 1999).

Researchers have a moral responsibility to explain and find answers to their questions honestly and accurately. They have to point out the strengths of their methods and models but also have to inform us about the weaknesses and reliability of their results. The readers and users of our research reports are often less analytical and believe what we say. They might not understand underlying uncertainties and complexities. The reader should, therefore, be informed that the results or conclusions might be misleading. Also, if not properly clarified, our results and reports might be misunderstood in a way that creates more problems than solutions to existing problems (Ross and Harris, 1994).

Ethical responsibility of a researcher starts with problem formulation. For example, if we want to study the role of subsidies in the export performance of companies, it might not be a difficult issue to find data sources, do an analysis and come up with some conclusions. On the other hand, if we want to study the role of bribes or other illegal methods in the export performance of companies, we might face difficulty in finding data sources and doing analysis. Moreover, we might find ourselves in a moral dilemma if our study shows unexpected or drastic results. We would then have to ensure that the research did not cause embarrassment or any other disadvantage to people who have provided us with data (information). This leads to another important matter: the extent to which you should collect data from a research population that is unaware they are the subject of your research and have not given their consent (Saunders et al., 2000). This is a ticklish issue. One way of coping – in particular use in experimental research – is debriefing, that is the subjects are told about the study and purpose afterwards.

Many researchers have problems in deciding whether it is morally appropriate for them to continue doing research while ignoring ethical issues, mainly because it is difficult, time consuming or does not fit into their research plans. They believe, quite often, that if they are not doing anything illegal, it is morally acceptable. There are differences between whether or not something is legal and whether or not it is ethical. Many researchers do not even consider evaluating ethical dimensions of their research. In business studies, the importance of ethical issues and the responsibilities of researchers are growing, with increasing debate on social responsibility and consumer well-being, so that there is a danger that business research, if not aware of ethical issues, might lose respect or credibility. Companies are also becoming more aware of the impact of our research and can sue researchers for misleading results. For example, Beecham Products sued Yankelovich Clancy Shulman, a research company, which was fined for more than $24 million for negligent misrepresentation of research findings, because its market share forecasts were not upheld during the launch of Delicare, a detergent for fine fabrics (Churchill, 1999: 42). The usage of the Internet for data collection has also raised several ethical questions regarding invasion of privacy and using information on people without their consent.

2.8.1 The researcher and the respondent

The researcher–participant (subject) relationship is the most sensitive one in the process of research in business studies. Quite often a researcher struggles with the decision of whether to inform the participant about the real purpose of the research. They believe that telling the whole truth might result in the participant refusing or being reluctant to give full cooperation. Often our students, while doing internship in a company and working on their theses on a particular company's problem, want to do a competition analysis. Where information on competition is not available, they want to interview one or more of the competitors. In this case, they believe that if they expose the fact that they are doing internship in one of the competing companies, the others will not give them access. In our opinion, you have to be honest and open with the participants and convince them that their position will not be endangered. The violation of ethics is often associated with disguised observations and the use of deception while collecting data. One way is to consider whether the participant has a right to know the whole truth or not. Churchill (1999: 50) presents ethical concerns on eight areas of the researcher–participant relationship (see Table 2.1).

Table 2.1 Ethical issues in the researcher–participant relationship

1. Preserving participants' anonymity
2. Exposing participant to mental stress
3. Asking participants questions detrimental to their self-interest
4. Use of special equipment and techniques, e.g. tape recorder, video or health-hazardous equipment
5. Involving participants in research without their consent
6. Use of deception
7. Use of coercion to get information
8. Depriving participants of their rights, e.g. of self-determination

Ethical issues thus require attention at an early stage of the research process. Otherwise a researcher might waste a lot of time and resources, if he or she realizes halfway through or sometimes even at the final stage of the process that the project cannot be completed due to ethical problems. It is the responsibility of the researcher to assess carefully each and every point mentioned in

Table 2.1, and in case of doubt a researcher must take all reasonable/possible precautions to inform and safeguard the respondents. The issue of confidentiality is particularly important. If the researcher has promised anonymity and confidentiality, s/he has to take extra care that in no way can the identity of the participant/organization be detected. This may involve legal repercussions for the researcher. Deception is another difficult issue: this is when researchers intentionally present their research or its objectives as other than what they are. The best way to improve the researcher–participant relationship in this respect is to consider the following:

1. Plan and evaluate ethical issues right from the beginning of the research project, from the problem formulation stage.
2. If you suspect some problems, discuss these with your supervisor, fellow researchers and potential participants.
3. Provide a complete picture of your research project, its purpose, objectives, and the type of information and access needed for the project to the participants.
4. Assure the participants of anonymisty, confidentiality (if required) and that they will not suffer any harm.
5. Use appropriate and simple language while interacting with participants. They might not be aware of the terminology or detail of the topic of research, and they might be reluctant to ask.
6. You must facilitate the understanding and answering of questions.
7. You must establish a trustworthy and credible relationship with the participants.
8. Where there are any costs involved in answering your questions or providing you with information, you should be responsible for meeting these costs.
9. Assure the participants that they will be able to comment on the report before it is made public.
10. Assure the participants that they will get a copy of the final report when it is ready.

Ethical issues arise particularly at the data collection stage, where a participant cannot be forced or coerced to answer questions. Depending upon the method of data collection, a researcher has to convince the participant to answer. In surveys, researchers are happy if they get a 30–40 per cent response rate. In interviews, they may have to call/contact tens of potential participants before they get an interview.

Reporting your results objectively and honestly is the most important aspect of ethics. The results should be presented in such a way that they do not cause embarrassment, disadvantage or harm to any of the participants (Zikmund, 1997; Saunders et al., 2000). Moreover, they must not be distorted to fit your purpose, favour a particular participant/target group or be presented so that they do not reflect reality. Any misinterpretation of data will lead to misleading results and is ethically wrong.

2.8.2 The researcher's moral responsibility

The moral responsibility of the researcher deals with social guidelines and constraints upon research techniques and measurements. The researcher has to make a moral judgement about the appropriateness of research procedures. Although value judgement of the research depends on the researcher's own perception and interpretation of the findings, this evaluation is also influenced by the researcher's environment and time period. It has to do with whether or not to accept and reveal certain findings that conflict with one's beliefs, customs or religion. As no research findings are final, the researcher has to make a decision on whether the evidence is strong enough to draw certain conclusions out of these findings. Exactly how strong is strong enough can be an ethical issue, as results based on trivial information could be misleading (Forcese and Richer, 1973).

Research findings might lead to action that is against the principles of the researcher or the funding organization. They may suggest a certain treatment of a labour force or a certain method of decision making to achieve optimal efficiency which is against today's management ethics. The results might influence an important decision to be made by policy makers, for example regarding mergers and acquisitions, anti-trust measures or standards setting for a particular industry. Or, they might discourage subsequent research on the topic. In these cases the researcher has to be ethically correct in reporting his or her results and also the methods, techniques and instruments used, so that the readers can make a judgement about the reliability of the findings.

Figure 2.3 summarizes the factors that may influence conducting research and the acceptance, rejection, concealing or revealing of its results.

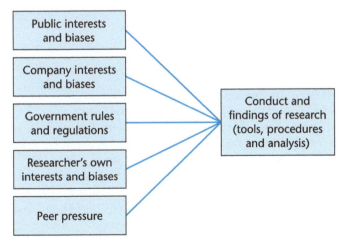

Figure 2.3 Factors influencing research

Source: Based on Forcese and Richer (1973: 22). © 1973. Reprinted by permission of Pearson Education, Inc., Upper Saddle River, NJ.

As we can see, public interest in a particular issue might encourage or discourage a researcher to reveal or conceal results. For example, a study on racial discrimination in recruitment or promotion policies of companies or public organizations might be a sensitive issue at a particular time, close to elections or at a time when there is a risk of riots. Studies on the labour/management relationship, where the results might be in favour or against the interest of the management might influence a researcher's conduct. A study might lead to findings that are against government rules and regulations, but are ethically and morally correct. In a similar way, most researchers have their own interests and biases. Some research is funded by industrial sectors, government institutions or companies. Researchers in many cases are dependent on continuous support from these organizations. If case findings are against the interest of these organizations, the researcher may be reluctant to reveal them for fear of losing funding. In some cases, the researcher is under peer pressure to use a certain method (e.g. quantitative methods) even if it is not suitable or reliable for a particular research problem. Peer pressure can also induce a researcher not to reveal the findings of his/her research, especially at a particular time. All these factors carry ethical implications for researchers and may influence procedures, methods and analysis. Researchers need to be aware of these and should take an ethical stand. A number of academic associations have drafted codes of ethical conduct in research. Some of these are listed below:

Academy of Management (AoM)
www.aomonline.org/aom.asp?ID=&page_ID=54
Market Research Society (MRS) www.mrs.org.uk/code.htm
Social Research Association (SRA) www.the-sra.org.uk/ethical.htm
American Sociological Association (ASA)
www.asanet.org/about/ethics.cfm

 ## Further reading

Alvesson, M. (1995) 'The meaning and meaninglessness of postmodernism: some ironic remarks', *Organization Studies*, 16(6), pp. 1047–75.

Maanen, J. van (1995) 'Style as a theory', *Organizational Science*, 7(4), pp. 641–52.

Malinowski, B. (1916/1948) *Magic, Science and Religion and other Essays*, New York: Natural History Press.

Pettigrew, A. (1985) 'Contextual research: a natural way to link theory and practice', in Lawler, E.E., Mohrman, A.M., Mohrman, S.A., Ledford, G.E., Cummings, T.G. and Associates (eds), *Doing Research that is useful for Theory and Practice*, San Francisco, CA: Jossey-Bass.

? Questions

1. A researcher is interested in sensitive information from a group of people. The individuals are unwilling to give this information. This information can, however, be obtained through others and/or by the use of specific techniques (projective techniques – i.e. individuals tend to project to others what are symptomatic for themselves). Do you think this raises ethical dilemmas?

2. How does research differ from practical problem solving?

3. What are the main differences between inductive and deductive types of research?

4. 'Research never stops . . .' Comment on this statement.

Exercises

1. As a marketing manager, you are asked to launch a product (pick a product) in China. Make a plan of how you would collect and analyse information that can help you make a decision for this launch.

2. You have been asked by a company to do a competition analysis for its product in a particular market. As there is no secondary information available you have also to collect information from competitors of your company. How would you handle ethical issues in this case? Draft a letter to send to competing companies asking for their assistance.

PART II

The research process

Part II (Chapters 3 to 10) covers important activities from identifying a research topic to framing and structuring the research problem, determining the research design, the strategy on collecting information in the most adequate way, development of adequate measurements and collecting and analysing data.

CHAPTER 3

The research process

This chapter deals with some conceptual (theoretical) foundations of research. Practical business research is often thought of as collecting data from various statistical publications, constructing questionnaires and analysing data by using computers. Research, however, also comprises a variety of important, non-empirical tasks, such as finding/'constructing' a precise problem, and developing perspectives or models to represent the problem under scrutiny. In fact, such aspects of research are often the most crucial and skill demanding. The quality of the work done at the conceptual (theoretical) level largely determines the quality of the final empirical research. This is also the case in practical business research. Important topics focused on in this chapter are the research process and the role of concepts and theory.

3.1 The process perspective

Research is often thought of as a *process*, that is a set of activities unfolding over time. A main reason for considering it so is that research takes time and consideration. Insights may be gained gradually, and may also be modified and/or changed over time. It is also useful to look at it as a process with distinct stages, as different stages entail different tasks. This can help researchers to perform these tasks systematically and to understand what is to be done at a particular stage. For example, we first have to clearly define our research problem and objectives before starting to collect information/data. Also, we first have to think and state which type of data is needed and how best it can be collected before actually doing it.

Figure 3.1 illustrates a prototypical research process or cycle. The illustrated process is a simplified one. In reality, however, the process is not so orderly and sequential and is rather messy (see e.g. Morgan, 1983; Pettigrew, 1985; Bryman, 1988; Watson, 1994). Researchers should therefore not be surprised/worried if their research process is not as systematic as presented in Figure 3.1, and if in practice they have to go back and forth in the process all the time. For example, at one stage, such as when doing observations, something unexpected may be discovered resulting in a return to an earlier stage, such as modifying the research problem. Thus feedback loops between the various stages are more common.

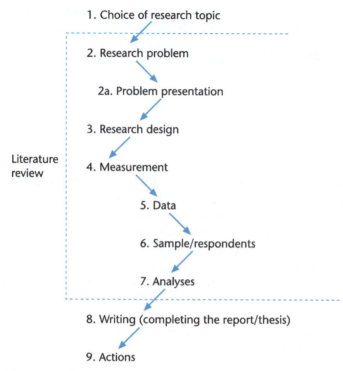

Figure 3.1 The research process

It should also be noted that the starting point could be some observation triggering off theorizing about the actual problem (see section 2.6). Research may also lead to new questions, which is why research seemingly never stops (see section 2.7).

The starting point in Figure 3.1 is the *research topic*, that is the phenomenon or theme to be studied (1). For example, you may be interested in how firms organize their activities, how business firms conduct R&D, or how firms enter foreign markets. Choice of research topic is important for several reasons. For example, is the topic worth pursuing, and is it practicable? A research topic is not a research problem. It is usually broader and more general than a (good) research problem, such as, what organization structure is most efficient.

When moving from the more general research topic to a research *problem* (2) a more specific question is addressed. For example, you may ask (after having reviewed the literature): Are firms organized in a bureaucratic way less innovative than firms organized in an 'organic' way?[1] The relationship between research topic and a research problem is illustrated in Figure 3.2.

From the above discussion we see that a research problem is a question. When we have really established what we want to know, and how this relates to present insights, we have a clear research problem. This is the point of departure for further research activities.

30

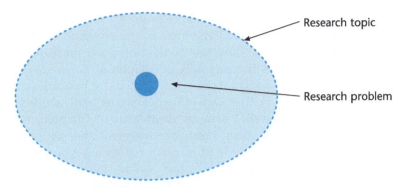

Figure 3.2 From research topic to research problem

Any problem must be captured or *represented*. This is done by a set of inter-related concepts, or a 'model', implicitly or explicitly (2a in Figure 3.1). The way the problem is captured influences how the problem is framed and understood. How the research problem is captured influences:

- choice of research design
- measurements
- data collection
- sample
- data analysis, and
- recommendations.

In Chapter 4 we discuss more fully how to define and capture research problems.

Research design relates to the choice of strategy to collect the data needed to 'answer' the stated research problem. As will be discussed later, research problems are multiple, and they come in many forms. In some cases the purpose is to understand a specific phenomenon. This will often be the case in 'qualitative' research. In other cases the purpose can be to determine the most adequate action, best mode of market entry and so on. Research designs are dealt with in Chapter 5.

Inspection of Figure 3.1 shows that after the choice of the overall strategy to cope with the research problem empirically, the choice of research design follows a series of activities. Data are carriers of information. A variety of data sources will often be available (Chapter 7). The various sources have both advantages and disadvantages. One can also use several data sources, that is 'triangulation'. More recently, modern information technology, for example the Internet, has become an important source for gathering the data needed (wanted). Choice of data and how to collect them, from whom, and in what way, are important. Such choices are dependent on type of problem, information needed and, not least, data possibilities.

Empirical measurements relate to theoretical, unobservable constructs (concepts). For example, 'power-game' is a concept. How can/should this be captured?

Another example is the concept of 'friend'. How do we recognize that a person is/has become a friend? Good measurements are a prerequisite for high-quality empirical research. It is a demanding task to develop good measures. Measurement problems will be dealt with more fully in Chapter 6.

Data must be handled, analysed and interpreted to become meaningful information (7 in Figure 3.1) that can influence subsequent actions. Various aspects and methods of analysing data are dealt with in Chapters 10 and 11. Also in qualitative research, data must be analysed and interpreted (see Chapter 12 for further discussion). Most research efforts are reported in written form (8), for example as research reports, but also as theses. Craftsmanship is needed to write a good research report (thesis). This is dealt with in Chapter 14. In business the outcome of research efforts often results in or influences actions (9). This, however, is beyond the scope of this book, and thus is not dealt with here.

3.2 Levels of research

Going back to Figure 3.1, a distinction can be drawn between activities at the theoretical (conceptual) level (2, 2a) and the measurement (empirical) level (4, 5, 6 and 7). Choice of research design may be seen as the 'bridge' between activities at the conceptual and empirical levels.

The following should be noted: *all* research – irrespective of discipline – requires activities at the conceptual level. So-called 'theoretical studies' deal only with this level. For example, studies in mathematics and pure (theoretical) economics primarily relate to specific problems without seeking empirical evidence. Also, in business studies important contributions have been made that are primarily 'theoretical' (even though inspired by empirical observations) such as the influential contributions by J.D. Thompson (1967) and J.G. March and H.A. Simon (1958), which have shaped very much the thinking of and research in business administration disciplines. Theoretical studies correspond to Circle 1 in Figure 3.3.

However, an empirical study – even a study for practical business purposes – requires efforts at the conceptual level. See Circle 2 in Figure 3.3. Surpassing such

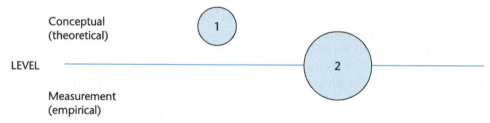

Figure 3.3 **Two levels of research**

activities and jumping to the 'raw empirical data' is seldom or ever very success-ful. The fact that this is often done in business does not mean that such research is good; rather it reflects lack of insight.

3.3 Research and knowledge

Even if it is not the prime purpose of doing particular research, the main purpose of research is to produce insights or knowledge. Knowledge implies that we 'know' something, and that what we know 'holds true', that is the produced knowledge is valid. Doing research also implies that we *add* to present knowledge that exists: that is, research is done to create new insights. For example, if a business firm conducts a study to examine what buyers emphasize, while buying a particular product, this is done to create new insights believed to be important to the firm, so that it can improve its marketing efforts. Knowledge can be classified in various ways (Naegel, 1961):

- theories/models
- concepts
- methods/techniques
- facts.

New insights can be acquired in any of the above categories. For example, the researcher may develop a new theory to describe and explain how buyers behave. New methods or techniques can be developed to assist business managers in their decision making, and new facts may be uncovered. For example, before entering a new market, the firm needs knowledge to assess the size of the market and the competitive situation in it; these are prerequisites to developing a marketing plan for the new market.

New insights may be acquired by demonstrating new practical implications of a theory as well: by testing hypotheses derived from theory, and by applying a method to a new problem. The important point is that any research should have an *intended contribution*, that is to bring or add something new.

3.4 What comes first: theory or research?

In the research literature, a distinction is often made between the following two strategies:

1. theory before research, and
2. research before theory.

In the first case, present knowledge allows for structuring the research prob-lem so that the researcher knows what to look for, what factors are relevant and what hypotheses should be tested empirically. From the above discussion it

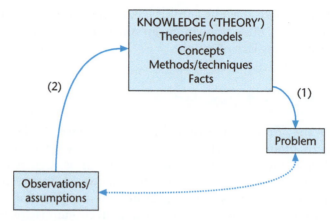

Figure 3.4 Production and use of theory

follows that, when wrestling with problems, the researcher also makes (or at least *should* make) use of available knowledge (earlier studies on the topic and its related areas).

Figure 3.4 illustrates the two research strategies. In the first case (1), important tasks are to identify relevant concepts, theories and so on, and to adjust the concepts (theory) to the problem under scrutiny (which also requires a clear understanding of the research problem). In the second case (2), the prime task is to identify relevant factors and construct explanations (theory). This relates to different contexts of research, that is the 'context of justification' (1) and the 'context of discovery' (2) (see Popper, 1961 for a lucid discussion). An interesting observation is that route 1 also corresponds to the use of 'theoretical' knowledge for practical problems. The user must select adequate theories and methods and adjust them to the actual problem, which is a demanding task.

Figure 3.4 shows a broken line between the two strategies, indicating that when applying present insights to specific problems, new observations and new questions may give rise to a search for new explanations, methods or techniques.

3.5 Some important issues

3.5.1 Concepts

Concepts are the building blocks of any theory or model (see also Chapter 4). A concept is an abstraction representing an object, a property of an object, or a certain phenomenon. 'Cost', 'income', 'market share' and 'business strategy' are all examples of common concepts in business administration disciplines.

Concepts are crucial in the researcher's tool bag. They serve a number of important functions:

- Concepts are the foundation of *communication*. Without a set of agreed concepts, meaningful communication is impossible.
- Concepts introduce a *perspective* – a way of looking at the empirical world.
- Concepts are means of *classification* and generalization.
- Concepts serve as *components* of theories (models) and thus of explanations and predictions.

Concepts are the most critical element in any theory, because they *direct what is captured*. For example the concepts 'cognitive' and 'dissonance' direct the theory of cognitive dissonance, and 'supply' and 'demand' are key concepts in economic theory. Even though many concepts used in everyday life are ambiguous (e.g. 'democracy' and 'influence'), they must be clear and agreed upon to be useful in research.

3.5.2 Definitions

Clarification and precision of concepts are achieved through *definitions*. Here we will distinguish between two types of definitions, *conceptual* and *operational*.

1. Definitions that describe concepts by using other concepts are conceptual definitions.

Examples

The concept of 'market' as defined in marketing literature, that is:

all the potential customers sharing a need or want who might be willing and able to engage in exchange to satisfy that need or want.

In this definition 'customers' and 'need/want' are among the concepts used to define the concept of market (Kotler, 1997).

Another example is the concept of 'industry' defined in strategy literature as:

the group of firms producing products that are close substitutes for each other.

Here 'firms', 'products' and 'substitutes' are key concepts to explain industry (Porter, 1980).

A useful definition is that concepts should:

- point out *unique* attributes or qualities of whatever is defined;
- *not be circular*, i.e. must not contain any part of the thing being defined; defining 'market exchange' as 'exchange taking place in the market' does not enhance communication;
- be stated *positively*, i.e. contain the properties of the concept defined;
- use *clear* terms.

2. An operational definition is a set of procedures that describe the activities to be performed to establish empirically the existence or degree of existence of what is described by a concept. Operational definitions are crucial in measurement. They tell what to do and what to observe in order to bring the phenomenon defined within the range of the researcher's experience.

Examples

'Market share' may be defined operationally as:

> A company's sales of products in category X in area A during time t/Total sales of product category X in area A during time t, which also requires specifications of 'sales', product category X, area and time period.

In accounting, 'sales' during a specific time interval is often defined operationally as:

Inventory at t_0	Sales
Purchases	Inventory at t_1

Or:

$$\text{Sales} = \text{Inventory at } t_0 + \text{Purchases during the period } (t_0 - t_1) - \text{Inventory at } t_1.$$

This definition gives sales as measured in cost (purchase) prices or in terms of volume (quantity). If measured in sales prices, profit will hopefully be present.

Note that the value defined differs depending on whether it is measured in volume or value and, if it is based on value, whether the cost or sales value is used for 'sales'. Operational definitions will be dealt with in more detail when discussing measurements (see Chapter 6).

When we move from the conceptual to the empirical level in research, concepts are converted into *variables* by mapping them into a set of values. For example, assigning numbers to objects involves the mapping of a set of objects into a set of numbers. A variable is a property that takes two or more values and is subject to change, while a constant has only one value.

Example

Construct (concept)	Variable
height	. . . 150, . . . , 180, . . . cm
gender	1 (= women), 0 (= men)

3.5.3 Theory

Theory may be viewed as a system for ordering concepts in a way that produces understanding or insights (Zaltman et al., 1977). A theory includes more than one concept and how these concepts are linked together. A theory is:

> a set of interrelated concepts, definitions and propositions that present a systematic view of specifying relations among variables with the purpose of explaining and predicting phenomena.

It is important to note the purposes of theory, that is to explain whether it is related to understanding or prediction. For example, a researcher holds a theory of how 'advertising works', and uses this theory to allocate the firm's advertising budget based on a prediction of an outcome resulting from the spending of the advertising money. Also note the notion of 'proposition', that is an assumed relationship between two concepts, such as between 'performance' and 'satisfaction'.

The above definition of theory also claims it should present a systematic view, to enhance explanation and prediction, meaning that the concepts and relationships involved should represent a coherent 'whole'.

It is important to notice that theories focus on specific aspects of the phenomena or problems studied. This is done to capture the actual problem, and (hopefully) understand (solve) it better. On the other hand, some aspects are left out. This is done because human beings have limited cognitive capacity, making it almost impossible to take everything into account at the same time.

3.5.4 Methods

Research methods are rules and procedures, and can be seen as 'tools or ways of proceeding to solve problems'. Research methods play several roles, such as:

- 'logic' or ways of reasoning to arrive at solutions;
- rules for communication, i.e. to explain how the findings have been achieved;
- rules of intersubjectivity, i.e. outsiders should be able to examine and evaluate research findings.

Figure 3.5 illustrates the role of methods for arriving at solutions. An important aspect is that there must be a valid reason (or 'theory') underlying the actual method so that it will result in the 'correct' solution.

Moreover, choice of methods requires understanding of the actual research problem. In addition, command over the methods and the ability to adequately choose among (and combine) methods are needed.

Problem/task   Solution/answer

Method

Figure 3.5 Use of methods

3.6 Concluding remarks

Research is often associated with constructing and designing questionnaires, measurements, statistical procedures and so on, which can be subsumed under the umbrella concept 'research methodology'. Research methodology can be conceived as a system of rules and procedures. Such rules and procedures are important in research for several purposes:

1. Research methodology can be conceived as rules for *reasoning*, i.e. a specific logic to acquire insights.
2. Research methodology is important for *intersubjectivity*, i.e. by reporting (in detail) how the researcher has obtained his or her finding, the researcher enables others to evaluate it.
3. Research methodology can also be considered as rules for *communication*. By reporting on the rules and procedures used, others may try to replicate, or they can criticize the approach chosen and the reported findings.

Qualifying research requires competence in logical reasoning and analysis. The researcher thus needs to have command over the research methodology to be used. Research methodology is thus an important tool in the researcher's tool box. Research, however, is also closely related to finding, selecting, structuring and solving problems. In order to grasp, represent and understand problems, concepts, theories and models are crucial. Theoretical knowledge, and the ability to think conceptually are important and a prerequisite for doing qualified research. Problems represent the point of departure in research. Perception and the structuring of problems influence subsequent research activities. Qualifying empirical research requires both conceptual and methodological insights. Skills related to topics dealt with in this chapter are crucial to making relevant use of other tools in research.

Note

1. Inspired by Burns and Stalker (1961).

Further reading

Douglas, S.P. and Craig, C.S. (1997) 'The changing dynamic of consumer behavior: implications for cross-cultural research, *International Journal of Research in Marketing*, 14(4), pp. 379–95.

Fox, D.J. (1969) *The Research Process in Education*, New York: Holt, Rinehart & Winston (Chapter 2).

Frankfort-Nachmias, F. and Nachmias, D. (1996) *Research Methods in the Social Sciences*, 5th edn, London: Edward Arnold.

Locke, L.F., Spirduso, W.W. and Stephen J. Silverman, S.J. (2000), *Proposals That Work: A Guide for Planning Dissertations and Grant Proposals*, 4th edn, Thousand Oaks, CA: Sage.

Rudestam, K.E. and Newton, R.R. (2001), *Surviving Your Dissertation: A Comprehensive Guide to Content and Process*. Thousand Oaks, CA: Sage.

? Questions

1. Why is research often considered as a process – and not only as an outcome? And, what is a research process?

2. What do you think are major sources of research problems?

3. Explain and point out the differences between 'concepts' and 'theories'.

4. How do theories differ from methods?

Exercises

1. A firm wonders whether to increase advertising expenditure for its core products. What do you consider the research problem that should be identified and answered before it does so?

2. A firm has designed a market test to assess the effect on sales of a particular discount scheme. What do you consider to be the decision problem?

CHAPTER 4

Research problems

Problems, that is 'questions', drive research. Without research questions there would hardly be any research at all. Research problems are not 'given'. They are detected and constructed. How research problems are captured and framed drives subsequent research activities. In normal research situations, we first select a topic and then construct a research problem within that topic. The process of constructing a research problem is not quite straightforward and often involves a lot of back and forth adjustments. In this chapter we particularly focus on how to cope with and adequately capture research problems.

4.1 Research ideas

The starting point of any research effort is some idea or observation that attracts attention and initiates speculation. The researcher might have a particular interest in a certain topic, such as consumer behaviour towards imported products, or understanding mergers and acquisitions. However, to make the topic researchable it must be turned into a research question. Because a key purpose of research is to create new insights, there must be something 'new', that is, something we do not already know. Even when replicating a previous study there is an aspect of novelty. Example: in a study conducted among large firms a specific budgeting procedure has been observed to be very effective. Is this procedure also effective in middle-sized and smaller firms? Or do companies perform better after merging with a competing firm?

An important source for research ideas is the past literature. Reading the past literature is often also necessary to determine whether the intended research will contain an element of novelty. Returning to Figure 3.1, it is seen that the literature is consulted throughout the whole research process. For example, the literature is consulted to identify a research problem, to plan sampling, formulate questions and choose statistical tests. In section 4.5 we will return to literature review to be included in the research report (thesis).

Example

A researcher is interested in a particular type of decision, captured by the so-called 'garbage-can models or decisions', characterized by situations where 'solutions are searching for problems'. This is similar to the situation where the researcher has a tool, for example linear programming, and is searching for a problem to apply the tool to. Review of the literature reveals that such decisions primarily have been studied and found in public organizations. The researcher raises the question: Do such decisions also take place in private firms (organizations)?

Once the researcher knows the topic it is a good idea to look at earlier theses and journal articles on that topic. Many of these present ideas for future research in the particular research topic. Reading the literature is not the only way to get good research ideas. Probably reading is not even the most important way in a very early stage. The newsletter for ACR (Association of Consumer Research) had an interesting piece (*ACR News*, 1995) suggesting, first, that good research ideas relate to creativity. To foster creativity one may brainstorm with other people interested in the topic. A common observation is also that one idea may generate new ones. So let ideas flow. The best ideas are not always the first ones.

Important sources for good research ideas are:

- The real world. Look at how people and organizations are working (or not working) to generate questions as to why things happen the way they do (e.g. go to a shopping mall and actively observe everything as if it was for the first time).
- Look for 'missing holes' in the literature: what has really been addressed, and what has been neglected (e.g. Do the studies on mergers and acquisitions deal with performance? Do they deal with mergers between two competing firms?).

To improve your research idea as input to your research problem, get *feedback*. Discuss your research idea with friends, colleagues, your supervisor – and other people who are interested in similar topics.

4.2 Wrestling with research problems

The first step in (practical) research is wrestling with problems. To answer (solve) a research problem, the researcher must be able to answer the following *two* questions:

1. What is the actual problem?
2. What is the best way to solve the problem?

Although some questions *seem* trivial in the beginning, the more we read and brainstorm, the more we realize that this is not, in fact, the case. Answering the first question implies that the researcher really *knows what s/he wants to know*. A common mistake is to go ahead with data collection and other 'practical' activities before knowing the specific research problem. Such an approach often ends up in a situation where 'a bunch of data is searching for a problem'; time runs out and money is wasted. To avoid misunderstanding, this does not mean that no

41

observations should be done prior to the research. Very often during some pre-liminary observation (a pilot study) it is very useful to explore, get acquainted with the phenomenon (problem) and arrive at the actual research question.

A useful strategy to get hold of the research problem is to ask *questions*. Good questions have the following characteristics:

- They express relationship(s) between two (or more) variables (e.g. Would an increase in marketing budget increase our profits?).
- They are clear, that is what is asked is understood (e.g. Is culture the main problem in the post-merger integration of two competing firms?).

The advantage of expressing relationships between variables is that they can be tested. For example, a marketing manager wonders whether the marketing effort should be directed towards large or small households, depending upon where the propensity to purchase the firm's product is the highest. A possible question is thus:

Is there a relationship between household size and propensity to pur-chase the particular product?

Or more specifically:

Are large households more likely to buy the particular product than smaller households?

Note that in the above case the following two concepts are included: house-hold size and propensity to purchase. The relationship between the two concepts is a *hypothesis*. As discussed in Chapter 3 we use operational definitions to meas-ure concepts (constructs). The actual measures, for example scores on scales, become *variables*.

Given available data, for example data gathered through test marketing in a specific area of household size and whether bought or not, the hypothesis can be tested. Assume that a test marketing programme followed up by a survey study based on a random sample of the households shows the following:[1]

Household size	No. of households	Purchase
Large	200	50
Small	300	30
Total	500	80

Here it is evident that the propensity to purchase, meaning purchase/number of households, is higher for large households, that is $50/200 = 0.25$ and $30/300 = 0.10$, respectively. This also allows for statistical testing.[2]

An important point is that by expressing relationships as in the above question (hypothesis) *falsification* is allowed (which is at the heart of hypothesis testing).[3]

An initial research problem is often rather vague and general. For example, a small business manager has difficulty in understanding what influences the firm's performance in 'good' and 'bad' times. How can this ambiguous problem be approached? From cost accounting we know the following:

$$\text{Profit} = (\text{Price} - \text{Variable costs}) \times \text{Quantity} - \text{Fixed costs}$$

Based on this simple equation (model), we may ask several questions, such as:

- Do the prices for the firm's product fluctuate?
- Does the firm use a specific raw material, which fluctuates highly in price?
- Does the demand for the firm's product fluctuate?

By asking such questions the problem can be narrowed down, and the effort concentrated on solving the real problem. But there is more to this, such as what initiates the questions? In the above examples the questions are all *theory driven*, that is, existing theory (cf. the above model) is used as the basis for the questions raised. In fact, a prime value of theory is to identify factors (variables) and relate them to each other and examine such relationships to provide explanations.

In the above examples questions were used to 'structure' the problems. By using existing knowledge the researcher will often be able to structure the problem, for example so that hypotheses may be derived and tested.

Problems may be more or less understood. A distinction is often made between 'structured' and 'unstructured' problems. It should be noted that it is not the problems per se, but the understanding of the problems that is more or less structured. The structuredness of the research problem has implications for choice of research design and research methods. Research practice is also influenced by the researcher's philosophy of science perspective (see Chapter 2), training and so on. In most cases a multi-method strategy is used while formulating a research problem, which varies from literature review, managerial practices and researcher's orientation (Brewer and Hunter, 1989). How understanding of the problem influences choice of research design is dealt with in Chapter 5. The notions of 'quantitative' and 'qualitative' methods relate partly to differences in problem structure, but also to differences in the philosophy of science perspective held by the researcher (Figure 4.1).

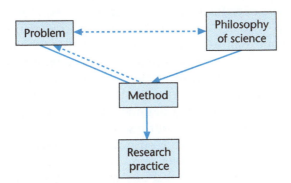

Figure 4.1 Problem, methods and research practice

For example, the research problem, that is what the researcher wants to know intuitively, will have an impact on the choice of research approach. For example, the researcher may be interested in how managers think about strategic issues, initiating the question: How can such insights be obtained? The researcher may have some 'favourite' methods (e.g. use of surveys) that may also influence their choice of approach. The researcher's beliefs about what constitute relevant insights and how such insights may be obtained will also influence the choice of research approach. Strauss and Corbin (1990: 34–6) suggest that there are several sources of researchable problems, such as: *assigned research problem*, as perhaps suggested by the supervisor/professor. This is often useful for students, as it will provide them with 'a do-able' and 'relevant' problem. Another source is *the technical literature*, which can point out a relatively unexplored area or a topic that needs further development. It may also suggest a new approach to solve an old problem. The reading of technical literature would also stimulate the researcher and enhance his/her curiosity. Finally, *personal and professional experiences* are often the source of a research problem. Professional experience often leads to the judgement that existing practice is not efficient, fair or equitable. Research into the issue would then correct this situation.

4.3 Research problem and research purpose

The first step towards finding answers is to discover a problem/question. In case you are not able to formulate a problem clearly, your answer cannot be correct. In other words, you need to find a problem in your reality (topic/field). Questions do not exist, they have to be asked. 'If we drop an apple, it falls to the ground. This is obvious for everybody – except for Newton.' (Wiedershein-Paul and Erikson, 1982: 38).

While research problem explains what you are going to investigate, the purpose explains why and how extensive the investigation will be. This also explains what you really want to find out and how your answer can be used. The purpose therefore cannot be explained in one sentence and has to be explained in a paragraph or two. This is important because the reader/supervisor/examiner will check from your result whether you have achieved the purpose. If it is not clear then it is difficult to make that judgement. The purpose can, however, be changed during the research process. If this happens, then it is the responsibility of the researcher to inform the reader. It should be clear whether the purpose of this research is to describe, explain, understand or predict, and for whom. In other words, who can make use of your results?

The researcher needs to revisit the purpose of the research while presenting results and/or drawing conclusions and explain whether the purpose was achieved as suggested in the earlier sections. In case the original purpose has not been achieved, then you need to explain why and how the original purpose was adjusted/modified during the research process, for example, due to problems in data collection, time constraints or costs involved.

One of the most frustrating things for business students is writing theses and research reports. Students often have problems understanding the importance of theory and methodology in writing good business reports and theses. This frustration is further aggravated by the absence of a suitable text that they can use as a guide to methodological issues in their project work. The message of this book is that scientific methods are a question of consciousness and awareness, and should not be seen as difficult, strange or unnecessary.

Research is a process of planning, executing and investigating in order to find answers to our specific questions. In order to get reliable answers to our questions, we need to do this investigation in a systematic manner, so that it is easier for others to understand the logic of and believe in our report.

Students need to understand the basic methodological approaches to management and business research. This understanding helps them in the initial stages of their thesis and project work, providing them with confidence and purpose. We do not intend to give students ready-made tools or advocate a particular approach. The idea is to let students understand that there is not one 'best' method for business research and that the choice of method depends upon the research problem, the research design and the purpose of the research. Moreover, it is also dependent on the capabilities and resources we have for the particular research. It is more important to first understand what you really want to know, than to look for a systematic and an easy/quick way to do it. Although there are several schools and opinions on management and on the study of management and other social sciences, our purpose is not to get involved in this discussion (see e.g. Whitley, 1984; Pfeffer, 1993, 1995; van Maanen, 1995; Holland, 1999). Instead, we want to synthesize and simplify this research to provide practical guidelines to students so that they can efficiently handle their research projects and write good dissertations and project reports.

4.4 Models in research

In our discussion above the research problems were – through questions – mapped by a limited set of factors (variables). When dealing with a research problem some *representation* of the problem is needed. This is also the case 'in real life'. For example, when the business manager instructs employees to smile, the following representation or *model* may be in his mind: 'When my employees smile, the customers feel comfortable and are more willing to buy.' The manager's model can be illustrated as follows:

Smiling employees → Customers feel well → Willingness to buy

We all hold such representations/models. Often, however, they are implicit and ambiguous.

Another example is the following. When firms (organizations) advertise for employees, they usually indicate the qualifications required, such as educational background, experience and so on. Firms seek employees to perform. The implicit assumptions or model underlying such ads are thus:

Criteria (qualifications) → Performance
e.g. education, experience

Models play a dominant role in research. They are closely related to the notion of theory, implying a systematic organization of, and relationships between, concepts. Key characteristics of a model are:

1. *Representation*, that is the object or phenomenon is represented by the model. The model is not the object or phenomenon itself.
2. *Simplification*: a model simplifies by reducing the number of factors included. This is done to make it manageable because taking everything into account often becomes impossible.
3. *Relationship(s)* exist(s) between the factors included. In research one is very often interested in relationships between factors (constructs), and, as will be discussed later, in *causal* relationships in particular, because when knowing cause–effect relationships, one may influence the outcome.

Example

Above we used the 'profit planning' model known to business students:

Profit = (Price – Variable cost) × Quantity – Fixed cost

First, this model is a general representation to capture economic aspects important to firms (and is definitely not the firm itself). Second, it is definitely a simplification, as a variety of other factors that may influence the firm and its performance are left out. Note how *few* concepts (variables) are used, that is 'costs' (variable and fixed), 'quantity', 'price' and 'profit'. Third, it is easily seen that the various factors are related. By changing, say, price, and keeping the other factors to the right of the equal sign constant, profit will change.

In research (and this is also the case in practical research), a prime task is to 'structure' the problem. This, to a substantial degree, relates to identifying relevant factors and relating them to each other to *map* and *frame* the problem under scrutiny.

As noted above, research problems may be more or less structured. This has implications for choice of research strategy. In the research literature, a distinction is often made between the following two strategies:

1. theory before research
2. research before theory.

In the first case, important tasks are to identify relevant concepts, theories and so on, and to adjust the concepts (theory) to the problem under scrutiny, which also requires a clear understanding of the research problem. When this is the case the researcher knows what to look for, what factors are relevant, and what hypotheses to test empirically.

The second strategy (research before theory) starts with observations/gathering of data. A couple of things before choosing such a strategy should, however, be noted:

1. There should be a *reason* for choosing such an approach. If relevant knowledge already exists, this easily ends up as 'reinventing the wheel' (see the above discussion of understanding the research problem).
2. This approach implies 'theory construction', which is different from 'theory testing'. The knowledge/skill requirements for doing such research are different but equally demanding, as doing structured theory testing includes use of statistical methods. Most students in business administration have almost *no* training in such research. If for some reason the student dislikes, say, statistics, this in *no* way guarantees that s/he can do a good 'theory-constructing' study, rather the opposite will be the case.

In the latter case, the prime task is to identify relevant factors and construct explanations (theory).[4] This, however, does not mean that inspecting the literature is irrelevant. Past insights will often allow for ideas or 'hunches' on what to look for and how to understand the research problem.

4.4.1 General concepts and specific use

It is also important to be aware that theories/methods and concepts are *general*, meaning that they allow for subsuming a variety of specific research problems, which of course is useful. On the other hand, when general, the various theories, concepts or models possess almost no content about the actual problem. The researcher's task is thus to give the concepts/theories/models some content.

The notion of the 'value chain' is known to any students who have had a course in business strategy. To become of any use for the firm, this general term must be adjusted to the specific firm in question. This may include the identification and classification of the actual firm's activities as well as linkages between the activities. In order to make use of the general concepts (theories) the researcher must be able to *select, adjust and apply* such tools to her or his specific problem. This is a demanding task, which requires insight and training. Misuse and non-use of relevant knowledge – as frequently observed – reflect lack of such skills, and not, as is often believed, 'practicality'.

4.4.2 Model purposes

Models may be used for a variety of purposes. At the general level we may distinguish between:

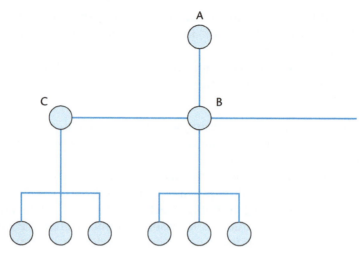

Figure 4.2 Organizational chart (a model)

1. description
2. explanation
3. prediction/forecasting
4. guidance of activities.

1. A *description* tells us how 'things are'. An example of a descriptive model is the organizational chart. Figure 4.2 represents a (naive) description of the *formal* organization. Note that this general model only contains *one* class of variables, that is positions (A, B and C). The direction of the lines indicates authority–responsibility relationships. A has formal authority over B, B is responsible to A, and B and C are at the same authority level.

Are such simple models useful in business research? Description of the formal authority in a firm may, for example, be combined with analysis and assessment of knowledge and skill requirements of the various positions, and can thus be used for identification of knowledge gaps to be filled; or description of the actual formal structure may be compared with some 'ideal' structure, which may be used for improving the organizational structure; or such descriptions conducted at different points in time may be used to study structural changes.[5]

Descriptions come in many forms. Assume that a researcher wants to describe the *informal* organization of a company. This requires a specified and detailed definition of the concept 'informal organization', including *what aspects* should be addressed. For example, the researcher may end up studying the communication flow in the company, that is who is interacting with whom; or s/he may study who influences decisions, to uncover potential deviations in communication flow or from power reflected in the formal organizational chart.

Another example is the researcher who wants to study the buying behaviour of a firm's business customers. Depending on the purpose of the study, it can be framed in several ways. For example, the study may focus on *what* the business firms are buying; or the study can focus on *how* the business firms buy. This may include mapping how buying processes are triggered, events taking place and how they are related in the buying processes.

2. Many studies are conducted to *explain* phenomena. The model of 'profit planning' used earlier may be used for explanation purposes. In this model, profit is explained by the difference between unit price and variable cost per unit multiplied by quantity sold minus fixed costs.

A researcher wants to explain why some firms succeed while others fail in an industry. This requires a definition of what is meant by success. Moreover it requires an identification of factors and processes that may produce success and failure.

Lave and March (1993) have proposed the following approach to map (model) problems:

- *Observe* some facts (e.g. success and/or failure of firms).
- Look at the facts as if they were the end results of some unknown *process* (model). Then speculate about processes that might have produced such a result.
- Then *deduce* other results (implications/consequences/predictions) from the model.
- Then ask yourself whether these other implications are true and produce new models if necessary.

The main advice from the recommended approach is:

- Think 'process'.
- Develop interesting implications.
- Look for generality.

When working with problems and models it is useful to keep them as *simple* as possible. More variables should only be included when it is useful, that is to improve the quality of the explanation. A good model – or, more correctly, its implications – should be *testable*. For example, a football team has just lost a game. The coach explains the loss as follows: 'I'm sorry. The problem was that our players didn't have enough fighting spirit, enough will to win.' The coach's (implicit) model can be depicted as follows:

$$\text{Outcome (win/loss)} = f \text{ (fighting spirit)}$$

This model is *circular* as it explains any outcome. The model can never be falsified as it cannot be tested.

3. Many business studies are preoccupied with *prediction/forecasting*, for example forecasting of sales, prices and so on. In its simplest form such predictions are based on extrapolation of past behaviour (development). For example, the following model has been developed to predict population size in a given area:

$$P_{t_i} = P_{t_0} \times 1.007^{(t_i - t_0)}$$

where:

P_{t_i} = population size at time t_i

P_{t_0} = population size at a specific point in time, e.g. 1 January 2005

Closer inspection of the model shows that it contains only one variable, i.e. time $(t_i - t_0)$. Both P_{t_0} and 1.007 are constants.

When calculating different values for $(t_i - t_0)$, 0, 1, 2, . . . , n, a smoothly growing curve emerges. Is this a good or bad model? It only maps a specific pattern (depending on the size of the constants), unable to catch the impact of sudden changes, for example unemployment due to emigration or people flocking to the area due to new business opportunities.

4. When models are used to *guide* business decisions, either a descriptive or an explanatory model must be complemented with a *rule of choice*. For example:

(a) Drop product if (price – variable cost) < amount k.
(b) Drop product if (price – variable cost) × quantity < contribution c.
(c) After describing market size – enter market if total sales greater than X.

Example

A study shows that students' satisfaction with a programme is influenced by: (1) the attention given by the instructor, (2) whether they feel the grading is fair, and (3) exam score. The study also reveals that the students have difficulties in understanding how their performance is evaluated. Here the research findings indicate that an important task is to clarify – make explicit the evaluation criteria used, and explain how these criteria are applied.

4.5 The role of reviewing past literature

When a business student is conducting a research project as a part of their degree, he or she is supposed to use 'relevant' theory', that is they must demonstrate that they can apply *relevant* parts of the knowledge that they were exposed to in the actual programme. There is nothing 'unpractical' in this, as all qualified research builds on prior knowledge. To most business students, nagging questions are: What to include? and How should the literature be reviewed? In order to answer such questions, it should be noted that above we have emphasized the word 'relevant'. This means that what is included should be of *importance* for the study. For researchers using quantitative methods, existing literature has a more specific use as they can discover the gaps in understanding. It also helps them to develop theoretical and conceptual frameworks and models and to identify important variables and test the relationships between them. For qualitative studies, quite often the researcher wants to discover relevant variables and relationships between them and to put together these variables in a new way. In this case you need to develop the theoretical framework that evolves during the research itself. As your research evolves, you have to incorporate relevant elements from previous studies (Strauss and Corbin, 1990: 51). Moreover, the following should be taken into account:

1. The prime *purposes* of the literature review are to:

   (a) *frame* the problem under scrutiny;
   (b) *identify* relevant concepts, methods/techniques and facts; and
   (c) *position* the study. (Any study should add something 'new'.)

   Wrestling with a research problem is the search for structure and identification of the 'real' problem; that is trying to answer questions such as: What do I want to know? and How do I want to map the problem? (Cf. the above discussion of problems and models.) As emphasized, such questions are important in research. A useful strategy at the initial stage of the project is to expose yourself to a variety of sources dealing with the topic, for example by reading journal articles and textbooks, and having discussions with 'experts' (such as a supervisor or people from the industry). It should be noted that broad exposure to information and 'incubation' are considered important in most creative techniques.

   Hint: To get quick insights, start with recent 'state-of-the-art reviews' or up-to-date reviews done by others, which are available in most disciplines.

   Then, after this exposure to information, start active questioning to frame the problem. The more precise the problem statement, the better direction for the research activities to follow. This will also help clarify what the *intended contribution* of the study is supposed to be.

2. Based on the activities in (1) above the researcher should be able to state the *criteria* for inclusion in the written literature review.

3. Based on (2), a *systematic* search for relevant contributions, e.g. by using computerized library services, can be undertaken, and the various sources gathered to supplement the initial search (1).

4. In writing up the literature review, conscious considerations on what to emphasize should be made. If the focus is on mapping the problem, the emphasis may be on prior conceptualizations. If, however, the main focus is on how the variables should be measured, the emphasis should be mainly on measurement procedures used in prior studies. (This implies that literature inspected need *not* necessarily be included in the written literature review. What to include should be determined by the problem and the criteria used.)

Example

A researcher has observed that the propensity to invest in foreign markets varies across industries. Many theories and perspectives have been applied in the study of foreign direct investments. In this study s/he is particularly interested in whether conditions to perform transactions may vary across

51

industries when they are operating internationally. This gives directions for reviewing theory of transaction cost economics, and empirical studies of transaction costs (and influencing factors) in various industries.

5. A literature review should also include *evaluation* and *critique* of the literature reviewed. To evaluate and critique, some criteria are needed. Such criteria can be thought of as 'ideals' with which to compare past research, and they must be found or constructed. For example, a researcher is interested in studying entry modes in foreign markets. The researcher observes that the great majority of past studies have been conducted in Western countries, thus identifying the criterion 'global' or 'all countries'. Based on such evaluation and critique the researcher's own choice of conceptualization and later research design should be argued for.

NB: The search for and review of literature takes time, not least because it is demanding and time consuming to get hold of the research problem. Therefore, try to get a head start! Reading *and* thinking often produce fruitful results. Here are some good sources to help you find relevant literature:

1. state-of-the-art articles/reviews
2. databases (the Internet)
3. conference proceedings/journals
4. conference participation/network(ing)
5. 'experts'.

Notes

1. Survey studies are dealt with in Chapter 11.
2. For statistical testing of hypotheses see Chapter 10.
3. A key assumption is that researchers advance knowledge not by verifying, but by *falsifying*, i.e. by letting the assumed hypotheses be tested so that they can be rejected.
4. This relates to different contexts of research, i.e. the 'context of justification' and 'context of discovery' respectively. See Popper (1961) for a lucid discussion.
5. Comparisons of structural description(s) at different points in time (t), S_{t_1}, S_{t_2}, . . . , can be seen as a special case of comparative static analysis as frequently used in economics. Changes are inferred by comparing the static descriptions from different points in time.

Further reading

Churchill, G.A. and Iacobucci, D. (2002) *Marketing Research: Methodological Foundations*, 8th edn, Mason, OH: Thomson Learning (Chapter 3).

Lilien, G.L., Kotler, P. and Moorthy, K.S. (1992) *Marketing Models*, Englewood Cliffs, NJ: Prentice-Hall.

McCaslin, M.L. and Scott, K.W. (2003) 'The five question method for framing qualitative research study', *The Qualitative Report*, 8(3), pp. 447–61.

Strauss, A. and Corbin, J. (1994) 'Grounded theory methodology: an overview', in Denzin, N.K. and Lincoln, Y.S. (eds), *Handbook of Qualitative Research*, Thousand Oaks, CA: Sage, pp. 273–85.

? Questions

1. What are the roles of ideas and speculation in research?

2. What are the key characteristics of models?

3. Explain the differences between descriptive and explanatory models.

4. Are decisions in business based on models? Give an example.

5. Why do researchers review existing literature when conducting research?

Exercises

1. You are in charge of a financial institution offering credit. Naturally, you are interested in limiting losses for your institution. Develop a model that can guide your decisions as to whether or not applicants should be allowed credit.

2. You are employed by a firm selling your product directly to private households. It is costly to visit private homes. You have also observed that some households buy at the first visit, some at the second one, and that some households never buy in spite of several visits to their homes. Suggest a model to determine number of visits. Also, specify your assumptions.

CHAPTER 5

Research design

> **Research designs are master techniques . . .**
> (Kornhauser and Lazarsfeld, 1955: 396, reprinted with permission of The Free Press)

The research design is the overall plan for relating the conceptual research problem to relevant and practicable empirical research. In other words, the research design provides a plan or a framework for data collection and its analysis. It reveals the type of research (e.g. exploratory, descriptive or causal) and the priorities of the researcher. The research methods, on the other hand, refer to the techniques used to collect data. The type and quality of empirical research are greatly influenced by the underlying research design, as emphasized in the above quote. This chapter focuses on important problems to be handled by the researcher in selecting an adequate research design for her or his empirical study.

5.1 The design problem

Empirical research is conducted to answer or elucidate research questions. Poorly formulated research questions will lead to misguided research design. Some advocate an open approach, with no research questions. This is however a very risky approach (Hammersley and Atkinson, 1995; Bryman and Bell, 2003). Strategic choice of *research design* should come up with an approach that allows for solving the research problem in the best possible way – within the given constraints. In other words, a research design should be *effective* in producing the wanted information within the *constraints* put on the researcher, for example time, budgetary and skill constraints. This last point is important, even though too frequently overlooked. In business, research results must often be produced within strict time constraints, limiting the number of possible research options. What is more, the business student usually has a limited amount of time to produce a research report for her or his degree. In most cases the amount of money available for doing the research is also limited, and the student's research competence and experience (usually) have their limitations as well.

Choice of research design can be conceived as the overall strategy to get the information wanted. This choice influences the subsequent research activities, for example what data to collect and how they should be collected. The respected

54

social scientists Kornhauser and Lazarsfeld once claimed that research designs played the role of 'master techniques', while statistical analysis of the data collected was termed 'servant techniques' (Kornhauser and Lazarsfeld, 1955).

Design errors occur too often, often through neglect of the design problem. The typical approach: 'Let's prepare a questionnaire and get some data' easily ends up with 'a bunch of data', which – after time has run out and the money has been used – leaves the researcher (student) with 'a bunch of data searching for a problem' and a research design.

Other common mistakes are making wrong and/or irrelevant design choices, for example by examining a badly understood problem with a very structured design or, as seems even more common as 'qualitative methods' have become increasingly more popular, by examining structured, well-understood problems by 'unstructured' methods, making it difficult to solve the research problem adequately. The importance of the problem–research design relationship is discussed below.

Example

Firms are often interested to know what consumers think about their product/service offerings. The research challenge is to design a study allowing access to such information. One way to proceed is to ask consumers directly. However, the consumers may not hold explicit thoughts of a firm's products. Thus a study that gradually uncovers whether the consumers know the products at all, or whether they have even given the products a thought, will probably be preferable.

5.2 Problem structure and research design

Research problems are infinite, and they come in many forms. Consider the following examples:

1. A political party wants to conduct a poll to examine its share of voters. This is a structured problem. The political party knows what information is wanted, that is, the fraction (or percentage) of voters.
2. An advertising company has produced two sets of copy and wants to know which is the most effective in an advertising campaign. Again, the research problem is structured. The company wants to know which (if either) advertisement copy (A and B) is the better, that is whether A > B, B > A, or A = B. Moreover, in this case the advertisement is seen as a 'cause' that may produce some effect (e.g. awareness, interest or sales).
3. Company X's sales have dropped in the last three months. The management does not know why. In this case the management has made an observation, that the sales are dropping. The management does not know what has caused the decline in sales. This is a more unstructured problem.

The above examples show (among other things) that problems may vary in structure. Based on problem structure, we may distinguish between the three main classes of research design:

Research design	Problem structure
Exploratory	Unstructured
Descriptive	Structured
Causal	Structured

5.2.1 Exploratory research

When the research problem is badly understood, a (more or less) exploratory research design is adequate. An example will illustrate this. Consider your favourite Friday night detective TV series. Most such stories start with a phone call leading the detective to a dead person, apparently murdered. The problem the detective is confronted with is: Who did it, who is the guilty person (if any)? How should the detective proceed? He (or she) collects data and tries to find a lead. As new information comes up, the picture becomes clearer, and at the end the detective has found the answers.

A key characteristic of the detective's approach to solving the problem is its *flexibility*. As new pieces of information are available the search for the solution may change direction. But there is more to this:

- Research problems may be more or less understood. There is *no* reason not to use available a priori information. As the detective does, so too may the researcher have 'suspects'. This is often the case in medical research, where potential causes are examined in a laboratory experimental setting. (This indicates that even experiments can be used in exploratory research: see section 5.4.)
- As with other types of research, exploratory research should be conducted in the best possible way.
- Exploratory research requires skills, as do all types of research, but the skill requirements differ. Key skill requirements in exploratory research are often the ability to observe, collect information, and construct explanation, that is theorizing.

5.2.2 Descriptive research

In descriptive research the problem is structured and well understood. Examine the case where a firm wants to look at the 'size of market M'. The problem as such, is clear. What is needed is first a classification of what is meant by 'market'. Is it the number of people – the actual and potential buyers of a specific product group within a specific area, within a specified time period? (Cf. the discussion of concepts and definitions in Chapter 3.) Assume agreement on the latter interpretation, that is actual and potential buyers of a specific product group (e.g. X) within a specified time period (say one year). The researcher's task now is to produce this information. What would be the best research strategy?

Assume that relevant secondary data is not available. The researcher plans to collect the data by a survey using personal interviews. A detailed plan must be made with regard to how many and who to interview, that is a sampling plan. The researcher must also construct questions, that is measurements, to get information about purchase (or use) of the product. Good measurements are crucial in research (see Chapter 6 for detailed discussion). Then procedures must be made on how the interviews should be conducted, questions reported, and so on. All interviews should be conducted in the same way, meaning that the variation in the data collection should be as small as possible. Thus key characteristics of descriptive research are *structure, precise rules* and *procedures*. A good example is the procedure used by medical doctors when examining a person's height. The person has to take his shoes off, stretch his legs, and look straight ahead. The same procedure is used for *all* persons measured.

Descriptive studies may include more than one variable. For example, for some reason the researcher wants to describe smokers by social class. Again the researcher is confronted with conceptual and definitional problems. When solved, procedures on how to collect the data must be determined to produce the data needed to answer the research question. In this case the task can be conceived as completing the cross-table in Table 5.1. (Preparation and analysis of cross-tables are dealt with in Section 10.4.)

Table 5.1 **Cross-table**

		Social class				
		I	II	III	IV	Total
Smoke	Yes					
	No					
	Total	100%	100%	100%	100%	100%
	$n =$	( )	( )	( )	( )	( )

5.2.3 Causal research

In causal research, the problems under scrutiny are structured as well. However, in contrast to descriptive research, the researcher is also confronted with 'cause-and-effect' problems, as illustrated in the advertising example earlier. The main tasks in such research are to isolate the cause(s), and tell whether and to what extent the 'cause(s)' result(s) in effect(s). Examples of questions in causal research are:

- Is the medical drug effective?
- What dose is the most effective?
- Does the advertising help in achieving greater market share?

Such problems are discussed more fully in the following sections.

Box 5.1 Weight loss programme

A sample of middle-aged people is randomly assigned to four weight reducing programmes: (1) diet, (2) exercise, (3) education about nutrition; or to (4) control group (the group not following any of the programmes). The people were weighed on 1 February 2004 and again five months later. The findings show:

	Groups			
	Diet	Exercise	Education	Control
Weight loss:	−5.2 kg	−4.1 kg	−6.1 kg	−1.5 kg
	(2.3)	(1.5)	(3.5)	(1.2)
$n =$	(30)	(30)	(30)	(30)

The data report average weight losses, standard deviations, and number of participants in each group.

The data show that all groups – on average – have lost weight, but the diet, exercise and education groups lost more than the control group. Here diet, exercise and education are seen as potential causes of weight loss.

5.3 The problem of 'cause'

The problem of 'cause' and 'effect' is an old one that has intrigued scientists for hundreds of years. It is beyond the scope of this chapter to review various perspectives on this problem.[1] The main objective is to focus on some key characteristics of the problem.

Cause

Examine the following examples:

- A dealer has reduced the price of TV sets by 10 per cent, and sales increased by 20 per cent. Is the price reduction a (the) cause of the increased sales?
- Managers are often preoccupied with 'success factors'. For example, in the well-known book *In Search of Excellence*, the authors Peters and Waterman (1982) claimed that 'being close to the customers' is an important factor in explaining success. Is closeness to customers a cause of success?

1. In order to be a cause, *concomitant variation* is needed: that is, there should be a covariation between the cause and the effect. For example there should be covariation between price reduction and change in sales. Examples of such covariations are shown in Table 5.2.

Table 5.2 Covariation

		Price reduction					Close to customers	
		Yes (10%)	No				Yes	No
Sales increase	Yes	20%	–	Success	Yes		30%	–
	No	80%	100%		No		70%	100%
		100%	100%				100%	100%

In both the above examples 'effect' (i.e. sales increase and success respectively) is present only when 'cause' is present (i.e. price reduction and closeness to customers). A closer look at Table 5.2 also shows that 'effect' is not always present when cause is present. For example, in 80 per cent of cases with price reductions, no increase in sales occurs. This indicates that *if* price reduction can be considered a cause, the cause–effect relationship is – at best – *probabilistic*, that is it is more likely that sales will increase when price reductions are present compared with when this is not the case.

2. The cause should *precede* the effect. Did the price change take place before the sales increase? If closeness to customers is a cause it should be established that it occurred *before* the firm's success. Thus the *time order* of occurrence of variables is important.

3. Other possible causal factors should be eliminated. Did the sales increase occur immediately after an announcement of a price decrease of TV sets? Or were the sales increases observed the week before a big sporting event, such as the Olympics? Thus a key problem is to *rule out alternative causes*. For example, can a firm's success be explained by excellent products, superior cost control, market or power?

The problem of ruling out other factors is also present, even when not confronted with causal problems. Researchers often observe covariation, for example as measured by correlation coefficient.[2] An important question is often whether an observed correlation coefficient, such as between advertising spend and sales, is a 'true' one, or whether the covariation changes or disappears when controlling for other factors, for example size of market or type of product.

5.3.1 The importance of theory

The question of cause–effect also calls for a priori theory in research. The need for theory can be illustrated in the following way. Assume two variables, X and Y. For these two variables the following relationships are possible:

1. $X \rightarrow Y$ (X causes Y)
2. $Y \leftarrow X$ (Y causes X)
3. $X \rightleftarrows Y$ (mutual causation)
4. $X \neq Y$ (no relationship).

For two variables there are thus four possible relationships. Assume a study involving six variables. With six variables there are:

$$\binom{6}{2} = 15 \text{ two-variable combinations}$$

which amount to:

$$4^{15} > 1073 \text{ million potential relationships.}$$

Without a priori theory, that is knowledge of what to look for, it will be almost impossible to muddle through.

As mentioned earlier, there are many roles for theory in research, including the following:

- identifying research problems
- raising questions
- identifying relevant factors (concepts/variables) and relationships
- interpreting (understanding) observations (data)
- advancing explanations.

Box 5.2   Uses of theory

The famous theory of search developed by March and Simon (1958) roughly states that when confronted with a problematic situation people tend to start their search in the immediate surroundings and stop their search when a satisfactory alternative is found.

This theory may help to:

1. Identify that when firms have made successful moves they tend to make similar moves, e.g. continue to introduce similar products.
2. Ask the question: Are firms experiencing success more likely to repeat past behaviours than firms not experiencing success?
3. Identify closeness to past problems/behaviours as an important explanatory factor.
4. Explain why firms seldom introduce major innovations, but rather tend to introduce variations.

5.4   The classic experiment

Possible research designs are multiple. Reported below is the 'classic' experiment in its simplest form. Even though many (most) business studies are not experimental, as we cannot control organizational behaviour, the classic experimental research design is useful for understanding all other designs (see Figure 5.1).

	Experimental group	Control group
	R	R
Pre-test	O_1	O_3
	X	X
Post-test	O_2	O_4
Difference	$(O_2 - O_1)$	$(O_4 - O_3)$

Figure 5.1 **The classic experiment**

In Figure 5.1, O_1, O_2 ... denote observations. X is the experimental stimulus. Observations are made both before (pre-test) and after manipulation of the experimental stimulus (post-test). Two groups are included, the experimental group, that is the group which the experimental stimulus is assigned to, and a control group not exposed to the experimental stimulus. R indicates randomization, meaning that the subjects are randomly assigned to the two groups.

The *independent* variable is the experimental stimulus. In the present case the experimental variable (the 'treatment') takes two values only, the experimental stimulus can be present (1) or absent (0) respectively. The dependent variable is some effect measured. If the experimental stimulus has an effect, then $(O_2 - O_1) > (O_4 - O_3)$.

In the experiment, the researcher has control over the independent variable(s), meaning that the researcher can *manipulate* the various experimental conditions. As will be discussed below, outside factors may also influence the observed effect. The impact of outside influences is assumed to be 'levelled out' through randomization.

Why use a control group(s)? If a group is given some treatment, for example a medical drug for a headache, it is impossible to evaluate whether the drug has any effect at all, as most people recover from headaches without using a medical drug.

Example

Assume that 100 people diagnosed with influenza were randomly assigned to two groups, a test group that was given an effective drug, and a control group which was given an ineffective one (a placebo).[3] The subjects were instructed to come back in one week, and then asked: Do you feel better?

Inspection of the results in Table 5.3 shows that a higher fraction of the test group reports 'better' than is the case for the control group. The difference in reported improvement is statistically significant ($p < 0.001$), that is the probability of wrongly rejecting the null-hypothesis (no effect is less than .001), meaning that it is very likely the drug has had an effect.

61

Table 5.3 **Reported improvement in the test and control groups**

		Group		
		Test	Control	Total
Feel better	Yes	80%	20%	50%
	No	20%	80%	50%
	Total	100%	100%	100%
	$n =$	(50)	(50)	(100)

The treatment is considered a 'cause' in the present case. Because of control, that is the ability to manipulate the treatment and randomization, one may be fairly confident that the effective medical drug really can be seen as a cause of improvement.

Table 5.3 shows the experiment in its simplest form. Here the dependent variable is whether or not the person is feeling better (yes, no). The independent variable is whether or not the person received a treatment (test, control). Inspection of Table 5.3 shows that more people receiving the treatment felt better than those who did not.

The independent variable (the treatment) can definitely take more than two values. For example, assume a company is interested in knowing which one of the following selling strategies is the most effective: S_1 (phone call), S_2 (advertisement), S_3 (personal selling), S_4 (personal + advertisement).

More than one independent variable (treatment) may also be included. Assume one variable (treatment) is selling message using either (1) one-sided or (2) two-sided arguments, and another variable is gender, that is whether the salesperson is (1) a woman or (2) a man. In this case it is possible to capture the effects of:

1. type of message
2. gender and
3. interaction effect (if any).

Interaction: Assume that an experiment has been conducted. Table 5.4(a) shows the result. It can be seen that the effectiveness scores (e.g. sales) are the highest for two-sided messages both for women (60 – 50) = 10 and for men (50 – 40) = 10. It is also seen that the reported effects are larger for women for both one-sided (50 – 40) = 10 and two-sided (60 – 50) = 10 messages. Futhermore the differences between one- and two-sided messages are the same for both women and men. This indicates that *no* interaction effect is present.

Moving on to part (b) of Table 5.4 it can be seen that the difference between two- and one-sided messages is higher for women (70 – 50) = 20 than is the difference for men (50 – 40) = 10. This indicates that an interaction effect between gender and message is present.

Table 5.4 **The effects of message and gender**

		(a) Message			(b) Message	
		One-sided	Two-sided		One-sided	Two-sided
Gender	Women	50	60	Women	50	70
	Men	40	50	Men	40	50

When going back to Tables 5.3 and 5.4 it is evident that the dependent variables are feeling better and effectiveness respectively. The independent variables are gender and message in Table 5.4 and treatment in Table 5.3. In both cases one wants to explain something, variations in the dependent variables. Also, in these situations experiments are appropriate.

5.5 Validity threats

A key purpose of the experimental design is to isolate and estimate the effect(s) of potential cause(s) (see section 5.3). The experiment is a 'strong' design as it allows for manipulation of treatment (cause) before and after measurements and thus for identification of covariation between treatment (cause) and effect, determines time order (cause precedes effect), and offers some confidence in ruling out the effect of other explanations (randomization). The idea of experimental design is useful in many studies. Some examples are pre-test of alternative advertisement copy, studying the effectiveness of various selling strategies, and field tests of marketing programmes.

The researcher wants to obtain *valid* knowledge (see section 4.2), that is, wants results that are 'true'. For example, if a study shows that advertisement A is more effective than advertisement B, the researcher should be confident that this is the case. There are many types of validity.[4] In the above advertisement case, the question of validity refers to *internal* validity, the question of whether the results obtained *within* the study are true. In other words, for internal validity we have to be confident that causal variation among variables our study is suggesting is true, that x is really causing the variations in y, at least as one of the influencing factors (Bryman and Bell, 2003). On the other hand, *external* validity, refers to the question of whether the findings can be *generalized*, for example to other populations, settings or periods, beyond the study at hand. This becomes extremely important in quantitative research. The sampling procedures in this type of research thus become very important, so that the researcher has a representative sample (for a good sample see e.g. Scase and Goffee, 1989); as only in the case of a representative sample can one claim the generalizability of the results.

There are several *threats* to validity (for further discussions see Campbell, 1975 and Cook and Campbell, 1979).

63

1. *History*, specific events external to the study (experiment) that occur at the same time and which may affect the response (criterion variable).

Example

Consider a TV store that reduces prices by 10 per cent and observes a sales increase of 20 per cent. A potential external threat is the announcement of a price increase for TV sets next month. Note that the experiment (see Figure 5.1), by including one (or more) control group(s), allows for controlling the impact of such effects.

2. *Maturation*, processes which are operating within the test units in the study as a function of the passage of time per se, for example the patient has received a medical drug and recovers. Often patients recover without such treatment. Thus what is the cause of the patient's recovery, the medical drug or their immune system? Maturation is a serious threat to validity in many studies.

Example

A company recognizes the need for reorganization to enhance performance and survive, and succeeds in doing this. Is the success due to the reorganization per se, or might it be explained by the fact that the reorganization has made the employees aware of the serious situation and motivated them to perform better in order to keep their jobs?

3. *Test effect* indicates the experiment/test itself may affect the observed response.

Example

A group of employees is chosen for a specific programme, and obtains superior results after the programme period. Is their performance caused by the programme, or by the fact that they are the chosen ones and thus motivated to perform (see Box 5.3)?[5]

4. *Selection bias* (self-selection) is a serious threat to validity when the subjects are not (or cannot be) assigned randomly.

Example

In assessing advertisement effects, the following procedure has frequently been applied (Colley, 1961). Assume the producer of the cigarette 'Z' wants to know whether its advertising campaign has been effective. A random sample of people are asked the following questions:

Q1. 'Have you seen any advertisements for cigarettes during . . . ?'
    'For what cigarettes?'
Q2. 'Have you bought cigarettes during . . . ?'
    If yes, 'What brands?'

Box 5.3	The experiment effect: the Hawthorne case

During the 1920s and 1930s a number of investigations were carried out in the Hawthorne factory of Western Electric Company in the USA. Some of the workers doing manual tasks were taken away and asked to work in a separate room. A number of changes were introduced (e.g. in heating, lighting, etc.) to see whether these would influence workers' productivity.

As the lighting was increased day by day the workers were asked whether they liked it or not. The workers said that they did. Then the investigators changed the lights, but put back the same size bulbs, thus in reality not changing the lighting. The workers perceived that the lighting had been improved and replied favourably. After some days the investigators started to decrease the light day by day, letting the workers know about the change and asking for their comments. After some days the investigators repeated the earlier experience of changing the bulbs but not changing the intensity of light/illumination. Again the workers complained that they did not like the lesser light.

As the experiment went on it was realized that productivity did increase, but irrespective of the changes introduced. It was eventually recognized that the workers were reacting positively to the attention and special treatment awarded to them. The investigators thus concluded that the changes in productivity were not due to changing working condition (increase or decrease in light) but due to favourable circumstances/perceptions created by the experiment itself. These findings contributed to 'stimulating the human relation' approach and emphasized how important it is to provide 'psycho-socio' support at the workplace.

Source: Based on Roethlisberger and Dickson (1939: 17); Van Maanen and Kolb (1985: 6)

From the results shown in Table 5.5 it could be argued that 20 per cent of those who have seen the advertisement bought, while only 5 per cent of those who did not see the advertisement bought. Thus the advertisement has 'contributed' (20 − 5) = 15 per cent.

Is the observed finding valid? It may be, but the result may equally well be explained by other factors, such as selective perception, that is persons who smoke and regularly buy brand 'Z' are more inclined to see the advertisement for 'Z'.

Table 5.5 Reading of advertisement and purchase

		Seen advertisement for 'Z'		
		Yes (%)	No (%)	Total (%)
Bought 'Z'	Yes	20	5	25
	No	80	95	175
	Total	100	100	200

5.6 Other research designs

In real life it is often difficult or impossible to conduct a true experiment. For example, randomization becomes impossible, and it may also be impossible to manipulate treatment. This is particularly true for research in business studies. Experiments are most appropriate when studying *stimulus–response* relationships, that is situations where the 'treatment' can be manipulated, or varies in a natural setting (natural experiments). Often the researcher is preoccupied with studying the relationships between *properties* and corresponding *dispositions*.

Example

The researcher wants to study relationships such as organizational size and innovativeness, or gender and career paths. Intuitively the researcher cannot manipulate the size of organization or gender. Moreover, when studying property–disposition relationships there can be several constraints:

1. The *time interval* can be rather long, often covering years or decades, making an experiment impractical. The relationship between gender and career is a good example.
2. The effects of properties are often *general*, lacking the specificity of the experimental stimulus, and thus make it difficult to establish the relationship between cause and effect. Organizational size and innovativeness is a good example here.
3. Establishment of identical groups to *compare* through randomization may also be difficult or impossible. For example, in gender research a number of factors have to be identical, such as qualification, age, commitment to a certain career, etc.
4. The *time order* of events is often difficult to determine when studying property–disposition relationships. For example, acquired properties such as education can both determine and be determined by other factors.

Thus the research designs applied often deviate from the 'true' experiment. This, however, does not mean that the logic underlying them is useless. In fact the ideas underlying the experiment to make (valid) causal inferences can be applied to evaluate – and improve – the research even when the experimental design cannot be directly applied.

5.6.1 Cross-sectional designs

The study reported in Table 5.5 deviates from the classical experiment in several ways. There is no control group, and there is no randomization. The 'cause' (advertisement reading) and effect (purchase) variables are also measured at the *same time*. This is what is termed a *cross-sectional* or *correlational* research design.

Table 5.6 Innovativeness by organizational size

| | | Organizational size | | |
		Small	Large	Total
Innovativeness	High	20%	80%	50%
	Low	80%	20%	50%
	Total	100%	100%	100%
	n =	(50)	(50)	(100)

When looking closer at Table 5.5 the researcher is confronted with several tasks in order to 'prove' that advertising may 'cause' purchase. First, s/he must control for the potential effect of other factors. What is termed 'control-for-a-third-variable' (which in fact may also involve control for fourth, fifth or sixth and so on) exactly pinpoints this problem. This can be done in several ways. Table 5.6 shows a cross-table between organizational size and innovativeness. A closer look reveals that innovativeness is apparently substantially higher in large rather than smaller organizations. The researcher wonders whether 'industry' may be an explanatory factor. In the present case (Table 5.6), the sample of organizations (firms) is from two industries I(1) and I(2). By controlling for industry the picture in Table 5.7 emerges and now shows that organizational size has *no* effect. The variation in innovativeness is now explained by industry.

Note that Table 5.7 is a simple, illustrative example only. More than two categories of each variable can be included, as can control for more than one variable. The control for other variables can be done in several ways. In a correlation analysis, control can be done by using *partial* correlation analysis.[6]

To be a cause, the change in the causal factor should precede the effect. In cross-sectional research, data on independent and dependent variables are gathered at the same point in time (cf. Table 5.5). Often the researcher has some a priori knowledge to assume the time order of variables. For example, it may seem reasonable to assume that gender precedes choice of occupation. A priori knowledge is often used to establish 'weak' causal ordering as in so-called path analysis and 'causal' modelling or SEM (structural equation modelling).[7]

Table 5.7 Control for 'third' variable

| | | Industry | | | | |
| | | I(1) Org. size | | I(2) Org. size | | |
		Small	Large	Small	Large	Total
Innovativeness	High	80%	80%	20%	20%	50%
	Low	20%	20%	80%	80%	50%
	Total	100%	100%	100%	100%	100%
	n =	(25)	(25)	(25)	(25)	(100)

5.6.2 Time series

The researcher often acquires observations of a given phenomenon over time. A typical time design can be depicted as follows:

$$O_1 \, O_2 \, O_3 \, x \, O_4 \, O_5 \, O_6 \ldots$$

The problem confronting the researcher is to determine whether the independent variable (x) has had any effect. To what extent this is possible will partly depend on the problem, the number of observations, and the observed pattern.

Example

US president John Kennedy's assassination occurred on 22 November 1963, and the Dow Jones Index of Industrial Stock Prices in the US fell 21 points on that day. Is the assassination a potential cause of the decline in the Dow Jones Index? If variations of 21 points (or more) are common, it does not seem very likely. If, however, the index had been steadily increasing for some time, and it was registered that the index value fell immediately after the announcement was made (as well as being controlled so that no other factors could explain the decline), it seems more likely to conclude that the assassination was a possible cause of the decline in the Dow Jones Index.

5.6.3 The one-shot case study

This design consists of observing a single group or event at a single point in time, usually after some phenomenon that may have produced change (Eisenhardt, 1989; Yin, 1994). Such a design may be depicted as part (a) in Figure 5.2.

In its pure form, the one-shot case study, part (a), is an extremely weak design as it does not allow for any *comparisons*,[8] neither before the treatment (X) nor with other unexposed groups. The design can be improved by trying to 'reconstruct'

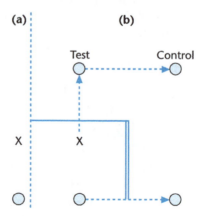

Figure 5.2 The one-shot case study

the past, that is before X occurred, and by trying to make comparisons with some unexposed units during the period, indicated by broken arrows in part (b) of Figure 5.2. An example of the extreme case of this design is exposure of an advertisement for a given product and measurement of, for example, brand recognition without prior measurement of this variable (brand recognition).

Usually case studies include many observations to be analysed. In other words the 'case' may be more the *unit of observation* than the *unit of analysis*. For example, a researcher studies one firm intensively, with the purpose of getting insights on how decisions are made. S/he maps several decisions in detail, which are analysed. If well planned, the case study secures *variations* along the variable included, allowing for comparisons of critical factors (see Campbell, 1975; Ghauri, 2004).

Example

A researcher is interested in whether trust has any impact on commitment in relationships. S/he studies the relationship between a firm and its main supplier over a lengthy period. Assume the researcher has adequate measures of the two variables 'trust' and 'commitment'. Over time trust and commitment may vary, also allowing for examining whether there is any covariation between the two variables. Also assume that s/he observes that a rise in trust always precedes a rise in commitment. This may – very cautiously – be interpreted as trust influencing commitment.

5.7 Requirements in research design

When moving from the research problem at the conceptual level to empirical research, questions arise such as: how to proceed? and how to do it? As noted at the outset of this chapter, the research design represents the overall strategy on gathering the information needed to answer the research problem under scrutiny.

After thinking through what the research problem is, and if possible how it should be represented (see section 5.2), and the potential hypotheses derived (if any), the first question to answer is: What *requirements* should the actual research design satisfy? A few examples will illustrate this point.

Examples

A study was conducted to explore whether firms (managers) within the same industry perceive and interpret their surrounding environments differently and, if so, whether this might influence organizational actions and performance (Grønhaug and Haukedal, 1989). A case study was chosen for the research purpose. The following criteria were, however, established for the selection of the cases, that firms should:

- belong to the same industry, and be embedded in similar environments;
- be of approximately the same size;

- be in an industry where it was possible to identify major environmental change(s);
- at the outset have approximately the same economic resources; and
- have demonstrated different response(s) to the environmental change(s).

The above requirements also demonstrate that even in 'qualitative' (case) research a priori theorizing can be useful in structuring the research problem (see Chapter 4).

Assume a study involving a set of hypotheses, for example:

H_1: The higher the consumer's knowledge about her/his rights the more likely it is that s/he will complain.

Inspection of the above hypothesis shows that two constructs (variables) are included: (1) knowledge about rights and (2) propensity to complain. The first requirement to test this hypothesis is information on these two variables. Moreover, *variation* in knowledge and propensity is needed. Reading the hypothesis also shows that nothing is said about causation; only covariation between the two constructs (variables) is indicated. Thus a cross-sectional (correlational) design is appropriate.

Consider the following hypothesis:

H_2: An increase in advertising expenditure will lead to an increase in the probability of getting more orders.

Again, two variables are present: (1) advertising expenditure and (2) probability of getting orders. Information on these two variables is needed. The hypothesis also expresses a causal relationship, 'will increase'. In order to demonstrate causality, a design taking the time order between change (increase) in advertising expenditure and change in probability of getting orders is needed.

5.7.1 Research and choices

Research involves *choices*, problematic choices. When the design requirements have been specified, decisions must be made on how the requirements should be met, and how the information needed should be collected. Important decisions in this respect are (McGrath, 1982):

- How should the concepts (variables) be measured (operationalized)?
- What type of data is needed? Secondary or primary?
- If secondary: What secondary data sources are available?
- If primary: How should the data be gathered? Through observation or interviewing?
- If interviewing: Personal interviews, by phone or through questionnaires?
- If interviewing: How should the questions be formulated; structured or unstructured?

● Who should be interviewed? How should they be selected (sampling plan)? How many should be included (sample size)?

This list of questions is in no way complete, but clearly indicates that research involves choices. Quality research implies conscious, reasonable choices, and the needed skills in performing the activities involved. Several of these questions will be dealt with in the following chapters.

Notes

1. For an excellent overview, see Cook and Campbell (1979), Chapter 2.
2. A (Pearson) correlation (r) is a measure of covariation between two variables, x and y, which can vary between −1 and +1. A correlation coefficient $r_{xy} = 1$ shows that the two variables covary perfectly.
3. This is done because giving a 'treatment' per se may have some effect on the subjects, whether or not it is effective in the way intended.
4. See Chapter 6 for a more detailed discussion, and Cook and Campbell (1979) for thorough treatment. Validity requirements and criteria in qualitative research are discussed as well.
5. Test effects have been found to be a serious threat to validity, for example in the recognized 'Hawthorn studies', aimed at explaining the impact of various work conditions.
6. The key purpose of partial correlational analysis is to control for the effect of one or more other variables. See section 11.2.2 for more detailed explanation.
7. Several statistical program packages are available for such analyses, such as LISREL, AMOS and EQS.
8. This is an important point as all research involves some sort of *comparison*, e.g. before and after; exposed versus non-exposed; observed versus expected.

Further reading

Altheide, D.L. and Johnson, J.M. (1998), 'Criteria for assessing interpretive validity in qualitative research, in Denzin, N. and Lincoln, Y.S. (eds), *Collecting and Interpreting Qualitative Materials*, London: Sage, pp. 283–312.
Ghauri, P.N. and Firth, R. (2009) The formalization of case study research in international business, *Der Markt*, 48(1), pp. 29–40.

Questions

1. Describe the key elements of the classical experimental design.

2. What do you consider to be the basic uses of exploratory research?

3. Explain what is meant by: (1) dependent and (2) independent variables.

4. What is meant by: (1) validity and (2) validity threat?

5. How would you decide whether a factor can be considered to be a 'cause' of something?

Exercises

1. An advertising agency has developed two advertisements to be used in a magazine. It wants to select the most effective before the ad is printed. Design a study allowing the agency to select the most effective one.

2. An Internet bank is concerned with improving its services. In particular the bank wants to know if its customers are dissatisfied with current services and the nature of this dissatisfaction. How would you design a study allowing the bank the desired insight?

3. A researcher has observed that some firms in the furniture industry outsource activities such as transportation services while others do not. S/he wants to study: (1) why firms outsource/do not outsource and (2) whether outsourcing influences firms' performance. Suggest a study to enquire into these research questions.

CHAPTER 6

Measurements

The GIGO principle: Garbage in, garbage out.

Business is 'context bound', related to specific markets, customer groups and competitive situations. Often the prime purpose of business studies is to gather information about this context to improve business decisions. For example, a firm may want to know the size of a given market, useful ways to segment the market, who the most likely purchasers are and what their priorities are. Or the firm wants to know how decisions are made by industrial companies, and who is involved. The purpose of business studies may also be more general, such as to examine the effectiveness of various advertising media. Problems to be studied in business research are almost endless. Often studies are empirical, implying the gathering and use of data.

Empirical research always implies *measurements*. The reason for gathering data is to obtain information of importance for the research problem under scrutiny. The quality of the information is highly dependent on the measurement procedures used in the gathering of data. In this chapter the concept of measurement is explained, levels (or scales) of measurement discussed, and the importance of validity and reliability emphasized. The chapter also offers advice for improving the quality of measurements in business research.

6.1 Defining measurement

We all make use of 'measurements' in everyday life, even though our measurements are often implicit or not considered as measurements at all. For example, a beauty contest can be conceived as some sort of measurement, as can be picking the best advertisement, or assessing the strength of competitors. These examples involve a key element in all types of measurement, the *mapping* of some properties. For example, selected advertisements may be evaluated according to use of colour, content, and so on. By use of some (usually implicit) rule a 'score' is obtained. Based on the 'scores', a rank order of the advertisements is established, and the best one is chosen. A common observation is that people often disagree in such judgements.

Measurement can be defined as *rules for assigning numbers (or other numerals) to empirical properties*. A *numeral* is a symbol of the form I, II, III, . . . , or 1, 2, 3, . . . and has no qualitative meaning unless one gives such a meaning to it. Numerals that are given meaning become numbers enabling the use of mathematical and statistical techniques for descriptive, explanatory and predictive purposes. Thus, numbers are amenable to quantitative analyses, which may reveal new information about the items studied.

Example

In an international study a research team examined whether people of different race varied in their attitudes towards work. Race was coded as: White = 1, Black = 2, Hispanic = 3, Other = 4. A multi-item scale was also developed. The scale could measure the attitude of people of different race. In the data analysis race was turned into a 'dummy' variable (see Chapter 11) allowing the researchers to assess the effect of race on work attitudes.

In the above definition, the term *assignment* means mapping. Numbers (or numerals) are mapped on to objects or events. Figure 6.1 illustrates the idea of mapping and is to be read as follows. The domain is what is to be mapped or measured. In the present case it consists of five persons, P_1, . . . P_5. Based on the characteristic gender they are mapped into 1 (= women) and 0 (= men).

The third concept used to define measurement is that of *rules*. A rule specifies the procedure according to which numbers (or numerals) are to be assigned to objects. Rules are the most significant component of the measurement procedure because they determine the quality of measurement. Poor rules make measurement meaningless. The function of rules is to tie the measurement procedure to some aspect of 'reality'. Meaningful measurement is achieved only when it has an empirical correspondence with what is intended to be measured.

Figure 6.1 Mapping (assignment)

Figure 6.2 Measurement – the link between the conceptual and empirical levels

Assume that we are going to measure some aspect of 'reality', for example 'competitiveness', 'organizational climate' or 'consumer satisfaction'. The task ahead can be illustrated as shown in Figure 6.2.

First, we need a good *conceptual definition* of the aspect to be measured, *X* (as discussed in Chapter 3). Next, we need a *rule specifying* how to assign numbers to specific empirical properties. Thus, by measurements we map some aspects of the empirical world. From this it is also seen that measurement is closely tied to the idea of operational definitions discussed above (section 3.5 gave a few examples of operational definitions). To obtain measurements, some rules (operational definitions) are followed.

Why do people often disagree in their judgements? There might be several reasons. First, it is often not clarified what aspects should be emphasized, that is, clear conceptual definitions are lacking (see section 3.5). Next, often the rules according to which the scores are assigned are implicit, and the rules followed may even vary across observers. Going back to the example above, a major reason for the researchers' disagreements is that the concepts 'attitude' and 'work' were not defined clearly. Such evaluations, to be useful, require clearly defined concepts: that is, the precise meaning of what to subsume under the concept must be clarified.

6.1.1 Objects, properties and indicators

From the above discussion it also follows that we are not measuring objects or phenomena as such; rather we measure specific properties of the objects or phenomena. For example, when studying human beings, a medical doctor might be interested in measuring properties such as height, weight or blood pressure. A cognitive psychologist might be interested in properties such as cognitive style and creativity, while a marketer might focus on preferences and propensity to purchase among consumers in a specific market. To map such properties we use *indicators*, that is the scores obtained by using our operational definitions, for example responses to a questionnaire (see Figure 6.3).

The phenomenon/object may for example be an individual, the specific property of interest – blood pressure, and the measures obtained in a medical test – indicators.

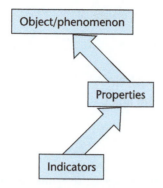

Figure 6.3 Object/phenomenon, properties and indicators

What do you think are relevant indicators to capture the concept of 'quality' for hotels?

6.2 Levels (scales) of measurement

In empirical research distinctions are often made between different levels of measurement (also termed scales of measurement). This relates to specific properties of the obtained measurements, which determines the permissible mathematical and statistical operations.

6.2.1 Nominal level (scale)

The lowest level of measurement is the *nominal* level. At this level numbers (or other symbols) are used to *classify* objects or observations. Objects that are alike are assigned the same number (or symbol). For example, by using symbols 1 and 0, it is possible to classify a population into females and males, 1 representing females and 0 males. The same population can be classified according to religion, place of living, and so on. The inhabitants in a city can be classified according to where they live, for example 1 = city centre, 2 = south, 3 = north, 4 = east, and 5 = west.

6.2.2 Ordinal level (scale)

Many variables studied in business research are not only classifiable, but also exhibit some kind of relation, allowing for rank order. For example, we know that grade A is better than grade B, and B is better than C, but we do not know the exact distance between A and B, or between B and C. However, we do know that A > B > C ('>' greater, better than), or C < B < A ('<' less than). When objects/

persons can be ranked, they can of course also be ranked as equal, e.g. B = B. Another example is consumers completing an evaluation of what extent they are satisfied with a product. Assume the following:

In this case C is more satisfied than B, and B is more satisfied than A. If degree of satisfaction/dissatisfaction is considered to be an ordinal scaled phenomenon, we can only say that C is more satisfied than B and A, but not how much more satisfied.

6.2.3 Interval level (scale)

When we know the exact distance between each of the observations and this distance is constant, then an *interval* level of measurement has been achieved. This means that the differences can be compared. The difference between '1' and '2' is equal to the difference between '2' and '3'.

Example

Assume that the temperature over a period rises from: (1) 8°C to (2) 10°C to (3) 12°C. The increase from period 1 to 2 is 2°C, which is the same increase as from period 2 to 3. The temperature scale is a classic example of an interval scale. But is 20°C twice as warm as 10°C? The answer is *no*. An example can demonstrate why this is so. John is 180 cm and Ann is 165 cm tall. The difference is 15 cm. Let us assume that we cut the scale so that 150 cm = 0. On this new scale John is (180 – 150) = 30, and Ann (165 – 150) = 15. Obviously John is not 30/15 = 2, that is, twice as tall as Ann. The reason is that the scale no longer has a natural zero. By changing the scales, it is very easy to be misled.[1]

6.2.4 Ratio scale

The ratio scale differs from an interval scale in that it possesses a natural or an absolute zero, for which the location is universally agreed on. Height and weight are obvious examples. With a ratio scale, the comparison of absolute magnitude of numbers is legitimate. Thus, a person weighing 200 pounds is said to be twice as heavy as one weighing 100 pounds.

Note that the more powerful scales *include* the properties possessed by the less powerful ones. This means that with a ratio scale we can compare intervals, rank objects according to magnitude, or use numbers to identify the objects.

The properties of the measurement scales (see Table 6.1) have implications for choice of statistical techniques to be used in the analysis of the data. For

77

Table 6.1 **Scales of measurement**

Scale	Basic empirical operations	Typical use	Measures of averages
Nominal	Determination of equality and difference	Classification: – Male–Female – Occupations – Social class	Mode*
Ordinal	Determination of greater or less	Rankings: – Preference data – Attitude measures	Median*
Interval	Determination of equality of intervals	Index numbers: – Temperature scales	Mean*
Ratio	Determination of equality of ratios	Sales Units produced Number of customers	Mean*

* For definitions of these terms see pp. 76–77.

example race is a nominal scaled variable. Assume we have a group of 5 White, 10 Black and 20 Hispanic. In this case it is appropriate to say that 14 per cent are White, but not that a person is 14 per cent White. The mode in this case is Hispanic, because this race occurs most often. This will be dealt with in Chapters 10 and 11.

6.3 Validity and reliability in measurements[2]

When we measure something we want *valid* measures, that is measures capturing what they are supposed to capture. However, measurements often contain *errors*. The *observed* measurement score may (more or less) reflect the *true* score, but may reflect other factors as well, such as:

1. *Stable characteristics*. For example, it is known that people vary in *response set*, that is the way they respond, some people tend to use the extreme ends of response scales, while others tend to centre their answers around the mid-points. Thus two respondents, A and B, holding the same opinion (e.g. that a given product is good), may answer by circling their response alternatives on a seven-point scale:

$$\begin{array}{ccccccc} & & & & & B & A \\ -3 & -2 & -1 & 0 & 1 & 2 & 3 \end{array}$$

2. The response may also be influenced by *transient* personal factors, such as mood.
3. Other factors that may influence the responses are *situational* factors, for example time pressure, variations in administration of the measurement, and *mechanical* factors, such as a mark in a wrong box or incorrectly coded responses.

6.3.1 Validity and reliability

In order to clarify the notions of validity and reliability in measurement, we will introduce the following equation:

$$X_0 = X_T + X_S + X_R$$

where:

X_0 = observed score
X_T = true score
X_S = systematic bias
X_R = random error

In a valid measure the observed score should be equal to or close to the true score, that is $X_0 \approx X_T$. It should be noted that often this is not the case. An important point is that validity is an 'ideal', where more valid measures are preferable to less valid measures. Also note that valid measures presume reliability and that random error is modest.

Reliability refers to the stability of the measure. Let us assume that John's true height is 180 cm. The scale used, however, has been cut, and repeated measurements show that John is 170 cm. This for one thing indicates that the measure is reliable, but not valid, that is the observed score, $X_0 = X_T + X_S$. This tells us that a valid measure also is reliable, but a reliable measure does not need to be valid.

Let us assume that John is measured by using a rubber band. The obtained scores vary between 140 cm and 210 cm, with the mean 180 cm, which is his true height. In this case the random component, X_R, is high, and the measure is neither valid nor reliable.

In business studies we are often interested in studying relationships between variables. An example (see Figure 6.4) may illustrate how random measurement errors may influence the findings.

In the present case the true, unobserved correlation coefficient between the two variables X (e.g. organizational climate) and Y (e.g. profitability) is $r = 0.8$. However, in both cases, the correlation coefficients between the concept and

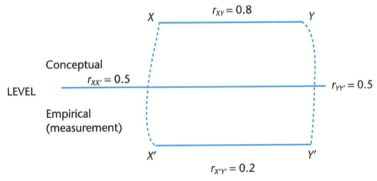

Figure 6.4 Random errors

79

obtained measure for the two variables are $r = 0.5$. The *observed* relationship (correlation) is thus:

$$r_{X'Y'} = r_{XY} \cdot r_{XX'} \cdot r_{YY'} = 0.8 \times 0.5 \times 0.5 = 0.2$$

which is considerably lower than the true relationship. (This simple example assumes that the observed $r_{X'Y'} = 0.2$ is only influenced by factors reported in Figure 6.4.)

6.3.2 Multiple indicators

In business studies *multiple* indicators are often used to capture a given construct. For example, attitudes are often measured by multiple items combined into a scale. Why so? An example will clarify this. Assume that somebody is going to determine your mathematical skills. You get only one problem to solve. The outcome can be classified as 'correct' or 'false'. Probably you will not be happy with the test. At best it can only reflect a modest fraction of your mathematical skills. Thus the main reason for using multiple indicators is to create a measurement that covers the domain of the construct that it purports to measure. Measures based on multiple indicators are also more robust, that is the random error in measurement is reduced.

Box 6.1   **Multiple indicators to measure investments in customer adaptation**

Activity investments in adapting:

1. opening times
2. season start and end
3. personnel
4. types of activity
5. marketing
6. training of employees
7. purchasing

Physical investments in adapting:

8. products
9. service
10. accountancy
11. computer systems
12. equipment and tools
13. infrastructure
14. other types of adaptation

Source: Silkoset, R. (2004)

In the research literature, the so-called Crohnbach's α is often reported. This measure can be conceived as a measure of the intercorrelations between the various indicators used to capture the underlying construct. The assumption is that the various indicators should correlate positively, but they should not be perfectly correlated. (If all the indicators were perfectly correlated they would all capture exactly the same thing.) The underlying assumption is that one indicator alone is inadequate to capture the construct. This way of reasoning refers to what is termed '*reflective*' measurements: that is, the various indicators are reflections of the underlying concept. This is in contrast to so-called '*formative*' measurement, that is elements supposed to map the underlying construct. An example is 'school performance' measured as summing up the grades obtained in the various subjects covered. In this case, there is no specific reason why the scores for the various subjects should correlate.

6.3.3 Construct validity

So far we have dealt with one aspect of validity, or more precisely, one aspect of *construct validity*. Construct validity is crucial and can be defined as 'the extent to which an operationalization measures the concept which it purports to measure' (Zaltman et al., 1977: 44). Construct validity is necessary for meaningful and interpretable research findings and can be assessed in various ways.

Example

In a study the researcher was interested to know whether 'trust' affects 'commitment'. To do so requires that the research has/develops clear definitions and adequate measures for the two constructs, and not that the measures for the two concepts are the same, or they capture something different, for example 'influence'.

1. *Face validity* tells us to what extent the measure used seems to be a reasonable measure for what it purports to measure. A simple test for face validity is to ask for the opinion of others acquainted with the actual topic.
2. *Convergent validity* tells us to what extent multiple measures of and/or multiple methods for measuring the same construct yield similar (comparable) results. Correlational techniques are often used to assess convergent validity. Temperature can be measured by different scales, such as Celsius and Fahrenheit. We know the interval 0–100°C corresponds to 32–212°F. By a simple linear transformation the score on one scale may be transformed to a score on the other scales. Assume that we measured the temperature over a period of time with these two scales; the correlation between the two sets of scores should be $r = 1.0$.
3. *Divergent validity* tells us to what extent a construct is distinguishable from another construct. If a researcher measures, say, 'innovativeness', he or she should be confident of not measuring another construct, say 'organizational resources'. If, for example, we measure a person's height and weight we should

81

Table 6.2 Two methods, two constructs

		M_1		M_2	
		X	Y	X	Y
M_1	X	1	0.35	0.82	0.27
	Y		1	0.30	0.79
M_2	X			1	0.29
	Y				1

be sure when we measure these two properties respectively. In this case there will be little doubt because there is common agreement on what is meant by weight and height, as well-developed measures exist. In other cases this may be more difficult and ambiguous, because of ambiguous concepts, such as 'influence' and 'power'.

To assess convergent and divergent validity, the so-called multi-trait multi-method approach is often used (in addition to other methods such as factor analysis). A very simple example is shown in Table 6.2 (which in no way demonstrates all aspects of the approach).

Table 6.2 is to be read as follows: research has measured two constructs, X and Y, by two methods, M_1 and M_2. The table reports the correlation coefficients between the different measures. The correlation coefficients for X and Y obtained by the two methods are $r = 0.82$ and $r = 0.79$, respectively. It is also seen that these correlation coefficients are substantially higher than any correlation coefficient between the X and Y measures. As correlation coefficients for the same construct measured by different methods are high, and substantially higher than any between-construct correlation coefficients, it is reasonable to assume convergent validity. Because the correlation coefficients between the constructs are modest and substantially lower than the correlation coefficients for the same construct measured by different methods, we may conclude that convergent validity is present. Construct validity can also be assessed in other ways, for example by the use of factor analysis, which will be explained in Chapter 11.

Going back to Table 6.2, it is also evident that by using only one indicator or method for each construct, neither convergent nor discriminant validity can be assessed.

In a business study the following question was asked to assess a firm's competitiveness:

How competitive is your firm?

Not competitive at all   −3   −2   −1   0   1   2   3   Very competitive

Do you think this is a valid way of measuring competitiveness? Why/why not?

6.3.4 Other forms of validity

Internal validity

As emphasized in Chapter 5, researchers are often preoccupied with cause–effect relationships. Internal validity refers to the extent to which we can infer that a causal relationship exists between two (or more) variables.

A correlation between two variables does not necessarily indicate that there is a causal relationship, as the correlation coefficient does not tell us anything about direction, or whether the relationship is influenced by other factors (see section 5.3). However, even in correlational research we might be interested in knowing whether a correlation coefficient between two variables is 'true' without being concerned whether a causal relationship is present. Then, we need to control for and rule out the impact of other possible factors.

Example

In a study a positive correlation is found between consumption of coffee and cancer, $r = 0.25$. However, this covariation may be due to some other factor(s), such as smoking. By taking the effect of smoking into account, the correlation may be reduced to $r = 0.02$. To take the effect of other factors into account we may calculate the partial correlation, which is the correlation between two variables when the effect of other factors is taken out (see Chapter 12).

Statistical conclusion validity

In order to prove a causal relationship (or a covariation) the results must also be statistically significant. Thus, statistical conclusion validity is a prerequisite for making inferences about causal relationships (and covariance). To prove statistical conclusion validity, the study must be sufficiently *sensitive*. Statistical conclusion validity also relates to the question of '*effect size*' and sample size needed.

'Effect size': an example

The impact of 'effect size' on statistical conclusion validity can be illustrated as follows. Assume that a researcher is willing to reject the null hypothesis (i.e. there is no effect – see section 10.5) and thus accept the alternative hypotheses if the findings are significant at the 5 per cent level or better.[3] In the present case the researcher has hypothesized a positive relationship between income (X) and propensity to buy (Y). Based on previous findings it is believed that the correlation coefficient between the two variables is close to $r_{XY} = 0.5$. For the sake of simplicity, the researcher sets the critical value for rejecting the null hypothesis at the 5 per cent level ($\alpha = 0.5$) to $t = 2$. (Inspection of the t-distribution will show that the critical value is influenced by the number of observations. As the number of observations increases, the t-distribution approaches the normal distribution (see Chapter 11)). The standard deviation of a correlation coefficient

83

is $1/\sqrt{(N-1)}$, where N = number of observations. Solving the problem yields the result that approximately 17 observations are needed.

If, however, the assumed correlation between the two variables was $r = 0.10$, the number of observations needed would be approximately 400! In the present case, the correlation coefficient between the two variables captures the notion of 'effect size'. From the above example it is clear that the weaker the assumed relationship, the more observations are needed to demonstrate statistical conclusion validity.

A variety of factors may violate statistical conclusion validity, such as the assumptions underlying the statistical test(s) used, and 'fishing', that is searching for statistically significant findings (correlations). By chance 'significant' findings may occur. For example, by *chance* 5 out of 100 correlation coefficients are expected to be significant at the 5 per cent level! Measurement errors may also be a threat to statistical conclusion validity (see Figure 6.4).

External validity

External validity relates to what extent the findings can be generalized *to* particular persons, settings and times, as well as *across* types of persons, settings and times. For example, when conducting an election poll, external validity is usually used as a basis for generalizing the population of voters. Whether a research finding possesses external validity can be assessed in several ways, such as by taking random (probability) samples as is done in political polls. This is, however, not always possible. Assume that a medical team has developed a new treatment that worked in the study. If the same treatment works when replicated in other settings we may – with care – claim that it has external validity.

It should also be noted that if the study lacks construct validity the findings are *meaningless*, also destroying the internal and external validity of the findings!

Validity comes in many forms. The types of validity discussed above are commonly accepted in 'traditional' research. Somewhat different validity forms and criteria are applied in 'qualitative' research, which will be covered later (see section 6.5 and Chapter 12).

6.4 Improving your measurements[4]

In structured (that is descriptive and causal) research, and also in exploratory research, when one wants to examine potential relationships between variables (see section 5.2), one should proceed as follows.

1. Start by elaborating the *conceptual definitions* and specifying the domain of constructs to be used. When dealing with practical problems the point of departure should be the actual problem, and how the problem can (should) be represented (modelled) (cf. section 3.5). When the problem is represented, the

constructs used to map the problem should be conceptually defined as a basis for subsequent operationalization.

2. Next, adequate *operational definitions* (measures) should be developed. The researcher should inspect prior operationalizations/measurements used to capture the same constructs. In this phase the researcher should also assess the face validity of the measurements, for example by experts critically examining the proposed measures.

Example

Assume a firm is interested to know the market share for its product 'X'. To do so they conduct a consumer survey of 200 customers, asking the following questions:

'Have you bought . . . ?'

___ Yes   ___ No →

↓

'What brand?'

Assume that 170 had bought the product among these consumers, and 40 bought 'X'.

$$\text{Market share} = \frac{40}{170} \times 100 \approx 23.5 \text{ per cent}$$

Inspection of this operationalization of market share shows that neither amount bought nor frequency of buying are taken into account.

3. The measures should be *corrected* and *refined*. Often multiple measurements are appropriate. Assume that questionnaire items are developed to capture a construct. The construct is assumed unidimensional. This implies that the various indicators should correlate positively. Computing the intercorrelation between the various indicators shows that this is not the case for some of the indicators.

4. The measures should be *pre-tested* and their reliability and construct (convergent and discriminant) validity should be evaluated. When the measures are developed they should be applied to a sample from the target population, to see whether the subjects understand the questions, and whether the measures possess construct validity as discussed above.

5. The final measurement instrument is used in the study.

From the above discussion it also follows that questionnaire design is closely related to measurement. The starting point is *what* information is needed. The information requirements in structured research should be related to specific constructs, such as 'market size', 'competitive position', and so on. These constructs must, as noted above, be adequately defined. Then the questions are designed to generate the needed information.

85

Example

Market share for a producer of product 'X' may be operationalized by the following sequence of questions among a random sample of potential buyers (which must be defined):

1. 'Do you use (product category) . . . ?'
   ___ Yes ___ No
   If *Yes*,

2. 'Do you remember the brand name of the product you use (last bought)?'
   ___ Yes ___ No
   If *Yes*,

3. 'What brand?' . . . (brand mentioned)

One measure of market share (MS) is:

$$MS = \frac{\text{No. mentioning 'X'} \times 100}{\text{No. using the product category}}$$

Careful examination of this measure (operational definition) will show that the measured 'market share' rather reflects 'user share'. It should also be noted that this measure does not take into account variations in the quantity used.

In the same way, if data are generated through observations, the procedures for obtaining the observations must be specified in detail. The specified procedures for making observations correspond to operational definitions as emphasized above.

6.5 Measurements in 'qualitative' research

The research literature deals with measurement problems when it comes to exploratory/'qualitative' research only to a modest degree. But is the question of measurement irrelevant in such research? The answer is probably *no*.

1. In Chapter 5, a key characteristic of exploratory research is that the problem under scrutiny is only partly understood. If the problem is only modestly understood, a prime purpose is to obtain an understanding. Various approaches can be used (see Chapter 12 for more detailed discussion). Assume that the researcher approaches the problem by using semi-structured questions, based on an interview guide (developed by surveying previous studies and so on). As noted above, a key purpose of measurement is to map 'reality'. When the researcher asks her or his questions s/he gets responses (see Figure 6.5). A detailed example is given in Chapter 12 reporting the study by Burns and Stalker (1961) to capture characteristics of innovative and non-innovative organizations, which they termed 'organic' and 'mechanic' respectively.

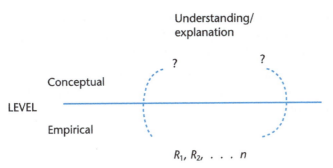

Figure 6.5 Responses and sense-making

The responses, R_1, R_2, ... are empirical manifestations that the researcher tries to understand. In this process the researcher will try to relate them to her or his knowledge base, and hopefully produce a reasonable explanation. This may partly be seen as 'data-driven' problem solving. However, without use of concepts and theory, an explanation (theory) will never emerge. Thus a mapping between empirical observations and concepts/theory is taking place. Besides noting that such research requires considerable conceptual skills, which is often overlooked, it should also be noted that the researcher should be able to demonstrate the validity of the findings. In order to handle such validity claims the researcher must supply evidence.[5] He or she should report the questions, responses, inferences made, and what supports these inferences. Thus, the *mapping*, *inferences* and *validity claims* have much in common with measurements as discussed above.

Example

Assume a medical doctor is examining a patient with symptoms $s_1, \ldots s_n$. During the examination s/he arrives at a specific diagnosis and decides on treatment. Has the doctor made some sort of measurement? S/he has observed the symptoms and related them to her or his knowledge base, and thus conducted mapping between the observable symptoms and theory (diagnosis). An expert observer who seldom makes diagnostic mistakes constructs *valid* mapping between empirical observations (symptoms) and theory (relevant diagnosis), which corresponds to excellent construct validity.

2. In business studies the researcher often makes use of secondary data. Such data are gathered by means of specific procedures, where specific measurements have been used as well. This indicates, when using secondary data, one should *always* inspect and evaluate data gathering and measurement procedures used.

3. Analysis of written texts, such as annual reports and business magazines, and taped and transcribed interviews, is often used in business research. Even here measurement problems are present. If the study is exploratory, the arguments

87

put forward at the outset of this section apply. If the research is structured (descriptive or causal), conceptual definitions must be developed, and specific procedures (operational definitions) specified.

The above discussion indicates that measurements are important and must be properly dealt with in research, where measurement problems have usually been given less attention.

Notes

1. For an excellent and entertaining demonstration, see Huff (1954).
2. For a detailed discussion, see Cook and Campbell (1979).
3. Hypothesis testing and the notion of significance will be discussed in Chapters 10 and 11.
4. For a more detailed overview, see Churchill (1979).
5. For an excellent discussion, see Kirk and Miller (1986).

Further reading

Althiede, D.L. and Johnson, J.M. (1994) 'Criteria for assessing interpretive validity in qualitative research', in Denzin, N.K. and Lincoln, Y.S. (eds), *Handbook of Qualitative Research*, Thousand Oaks, CA: Sage, pp. 485–99.
Churchill, G.A. (1991) *Marketing Research: Methodological Foundations*, 5th edn, Chicago, IL: Dryden Press (Chapter 9).
Kvale, S. (ed) (1989) *Issues of Validity in Qualitative Research*, Lund: Student Litteratur.
Yin, R.K. (2003) *Case Study Research*, 3rd edn, London: Sage.

Questions

1. Why are valid measures important in empirical research?

2. What is the difference between a conceptual and an operational definition?

3. Why might a researcher wish to utilize more than one question to measure satisfaction with a job?

4. You are supposed to measure the strategy followed by a competing firm in an industry of your choice. What do you think would be the relevant indicators to capture the firm's strategies?

5. How can you improve measurements in your research? Give examples.

Exercises

1. Determine whether each of the following measures is a nominal, ordinal, internal or ratio scale:
   (a) prices on the stock market
   (b) marital status, classified as married, never married
   (c) whether or not a respondent has ever been employed.

2. Define each of the following concepts, and develop operational definitions (measures) for the defined concepts:
   (a) a 'workaholic'
   (b) costs
   (c) power
   (d) market share.

CHAPTER 7

Data sources

According to Oriental folklore, a man called Nasiruddin was searching for something on the ground. A friend stopped and asked, 'What have you lost, Nasiruddin?' 'My key' replied Nasiruddin. The friend went down on his knees, trying to help, and they both looked for the key. After searching in vain for some time, the friend asked, 'Where exactly did you drop it?' 'In my house' answered Nasiruddin. 'Then why are you looking here, Nasiruddin?' 'There is more light here than in my house' replied Nasiruddin.

The purpose of this chapter is to look at: (1) what we mean by data collection, (2) what the sources of data collection are and (3) where to find the right data. Data sources are the carriers of data (information). A first distinction can be made between secondary and primary data sources. Secondary data are information collected by others for purposes that can be different from ours. Primary data are original data collected by us for the research problem at hand. These two types of data sources are discussed in some detail.

7.1 Secondary data

Secondary data are useful not only to find information to solve our research problem, but also to better understand and explain our research problem. In most research we need to begin with a literature review: earlier studies on and around our topic of research. They include books, journal articles, online data sources such as websites of firms, governments, semi-government organizations and catalogues. The first step is to locate these sources and then to evaluate the usefulness of the contents of each. Some research questions can be answered only through secondary data sources, where no further data collection is needed.

You must realize that a secondary data source provides the information that may have been collected for a different *purpose*. For example catalogues and websites of many companies are prepared to impress and convince the customer. This means that information is either exaggerated or biased. By contrast, information collected by other organizations, such as bureaux of statistics offer more neutral information and include not only the positive information but also the negative. In the same manner, the *scope* of the information can be different. For example, you need to be observant on the time period. Does the information represent the current year, or an average of some years, or a particularly good/bad year? Does the information refer to regional or national comparison? You also need to question the *reliability* of the information. Are the sources mentioned, and if yes, can you check the authenticity of the information? Once you use secondary data in your report, the reliability of the information becomes your responsibility (Cooper and Schindler, 2001).

This leads us to the point that you need to interpret and check the reliability of the information in the best possible way. You have to make a judgement that even if the information has been collected for a different purpose, can it be used for your study? Also, how could the purpose of the study (for example marketing material) have influenced its contents? For example, if a company's website claims that they are the market leaders for a particular market, can you verify that?

If we collect data from US Chamber of Commerce publications on the number of cars per thousand people in India and on characteristics of car owners to determine the size of the car market for different car sizes, we are collecting secondary data. They have been collected by the US Chamber of Commerce but we can use them to find answers to our questions.

There are more relevant data available than most researchers would believe. In this respect, researchers need to look at several sources for data availability on the topic/area of study in question. Once these sources have been located they need to look for data on their specific research problem and make a judgement on whether the information available can be used or not. Many research students underestimate the amount of data available from secondary sources. We should, therefore, start looking for secondary sources relevant to our research problem *before* going out to collect our own data. Secondary data can help researchers in the following manner:

- answering research questions or solving some or all of the research problems;
- helping in problem formulation and/or devising more concrete and focused research questions;
- deciding on the appropriateness of a certain research method or suggesting better research methods for a particular problem;
- providing benchmarking measures and other findings that can be compared later on with the results of the study at hand.

A number of government offices regularly collect information on different aspects of society. The census of population available in each country can provide us with an enormous amount of information on potential customers and segments in a society. Central bureaux of statistics and branch organizations collect information on different companies, their size and market shares, as well as their imports and exports. The following secondary sources can be important for our research:

- Websites of different companies and organizations (e.g. www.info.com/companies).
- Central and local government studies and reports, state budgets, rules on international trade regarding imports and exports, and policies on foreign direct investment (e.g. www.statistics.gov.uk, US Chamber of Commerce, National Trade Development Bureau (NTDB) and export councils).
- Studies and reports of institutions and departments such as universities, telecommunication departments, marketing and other research institutes, chambers of commerce and foreign missions such as embassies, trade centres and consulates.
- Census reports on demographics, income levels and consumption patterns.
- Academic as well as professional journals and newsletters relevant to the problem area.
- In many countries, different branch organizations publish journals on statistics regarding their own industry, market shares, revenues and imports and exports. For example, local chambers of commerce, small business associations and associations of retailers.
- Historical studies regarding the development of a particular discipline or problem area. For example there are 'handbooks' available on different topics, such as a Handbook on International Business or a Handbook on Qualitative Research Methods.
- Textbooks and other published material directly or indirectly related to the problem area.
- Commercial research companies selling data, such as AC Nielsen (www.acnielsen.com) and Synovate (www.synovate.com).
- International trade websites, United Nations, International Trade Statistics and the World Bank (www.worldbank.org), as well as World Investment report by UNCTAD (United Nations Conference on Trade and Development).
- And, last but not least, theses and reports written by other students in your own university and in other schools and universities. Many schools keep an up-to-date record of all the theses written in different disciplines. This is perhaps the most important secondary source at the earlier stages of your research process. They provide us with insight not only into our problem area, but also into the data sources mentioned above.

The websites listed as the number one sources above have become most important data sources, and are freely available. It is becoming increasingly easier to find relevant websites as there are scores of directories that can assist you to find information. Yahoo and Google are two of these web directories. You could also go to *Encyclopedia Britannica* (www.britannica.com) or Wikipedia (www.wikipedia.org). All these search services have a 'Help' option that can assist you to understand how the particular directory works. The *Financial Times* (www.ft.com) maintains a number of good data banks and can serve as an excellent data source. Some governments keep up-to-date sources of data relating

Table 7.1 Government and other data sources

Source	Website	Type of information
Business Week	www.businessweek.com	Information on companies, e.g. top 500 firms
Business Monitor	www.businessmonitor.com	Business-related information on emerging markets
Center for International Business Education and Research (MSU-CIBER). A centre at Michigan State University, USA	www.ciber.msu.edu	A website presenting different market information in the world
Corporate Watch	www.corporatewatch.org	Company profiles
Department of Business Enterprise and Regulatory Reform	www.berr.gov.uk	Information on UK companies and trade
Eurostat	epp.eurostat.ec.europa.eu	Statistics at European level that enable comparisons between countries and regions
European Union	europa.eu	Statistical information on member countries
Europe Direct	www.ec.europa.eu/europedirect	Information on the EU
Euromonitor International	www.euromonitor.com	Information on the EU and other countries, and companies
Financial Times	www.ft.com	Several data banks, e.g. on mergers and acquisitions
International Trade Administration, USA	www.ita.doc.gov	ITA helps US firms to compete in foreign markets
OECD	www.oecd.org	Statistics, economic indicators and other information on member countries
US Department of Commerce	www.doc.gov	Commercial data on countries
US Chamber of Commerce	www.uschamber.com	Information on US and other countries
US Patent and Trademark Office	www.uspto.gov	Information on patents applied for and registered
US Small Business Administration	www.sbaonline.sba.gov	Data on smaller firms in the US
US Census Bureau	www.census.gov	Data on US demographics
World Bank	www.worldbank.org	Economic, social and national/regional information on more than 200 countries

to industries, companies and countries, including detailed economic, social and consumer information, as well as data on rules and regulations and policy documents. Some of these sources are listed in Table 7.1.

Governments also keep statistics on demographics (e.g. census reports) that can help business researchers in their segmentation and location decisions. An historical analysis of companies' internal information can also help you to find patterns of different development and, thereby, forecast future trends. This is also called 'data mining' and is often used in marketing and financial issues (see e.g. Data Mining, 1997; and KDNuggets (www.kdnuggets.com)).

7.1.1 Advantages of secondary data

The first and foremost advantage of using secondary data is obviously the enormous savings in time and money. The researcher only needs go to the library, locate and utilize the sources. This not only helps the researcher to better formulate and understand the research problem, but also broadens the base from which scientific conclusions can be drawn. In other words, the verification process is more rapid and the reliability of the information and conclusions is greatly enhanced.

Most of the data collected by international organizations and governments are of high quality and reliable as they are collected and compiled by experts using rigorous methods. Some examples of this data are provided in Table 7.2. Moreover, in case you need to do a longitudinal study, secondary sources provide excellent historical data (e.g. from any of the sources listed in Table 7.2). The secondary sources can also be helpful in segmentation and sampling of your target group (see e.g. Household Panel Survey (BHPS) listed in Table 7.2.). Large data sets can be easily categorized or grouped in sub-groups (Addison and Belfield 2000, Bryman and Bell 2003).

Secondary sources also facilitate cross-cultural/international research, as it is easier to compare similar data from two or more countries. A number of international surveys, for example the World Bank and Euromonitor, provide comparable cross-country data (Coutrot, 1998) that can be used as a sole data source or in combination with some primary data collection.

Another advantage of consulting secondary data is that they can suggest suitable methods or data to handle a particular research problem. Moreover, they provide a comparison instrument with which we can easily interpret and understand our primary data. Quite often some research questions can best be answered by combining information from secondary and primary data. In most research questions it is necessary to consult some secondary data sources as this saves time and facilitates handling of our research questions.

Considering all these advantages, many scholars recommend that all research should, in fact, start with secondary data sources. As Churchill (1999: 215) put it, 'Do not bypass secondary data. Begin with secondary data, and only when the secondary data are exhausted or show diminishing returns, proceed to primary data.' Sometimes secondary data provides enough information to answer the research questions. In such cases there is no need to collect primary data. Figure 7.1 presents some guidelines to getting started with a search for secondary data.

Table 7.2 Large UK and European data sets suitable for secondary analysis

Title	Data set details	Topics covered
Annual Employment Survey; formerly Census of Employment	Since 1971, Census of Employment conducted the survey every two years. Provides a picture of the level and distribution of employment in Great Britain covering 1.25 million businesses. Since 1995, the Census of Employment has been replaced by the Annual Employment Survey (AES). www.statistics.gov.uk	Data are collected on the number of jobs by geographical location, detailed industrial activity (SIC code), and whether full or part time
British Household Panel Survey (BHPS)	Begun in 1991 and conducted annually by interview and questionnaire with a national representative sample of some 5500 households and 10,300 individuals. www.iser.essex.ac.uk/survey/bhps	Household organization; labour market behaviour; income and wealth; housing; health; and socio-economic values
Company-level Industrial Relations Survey	Conducted in 1985 and 1992. Sample comprises large UK organizations – with 1000+ employees in two or more cities. Sponsored by the Economic and Social Research Council (ESRC) and the Department of Trade and Industry (DTI)	The main differences between this survey and AES is the level of analysis; instead of focusing on the workplace as the principal unit of analysis, this survey concentrates on obtaining company-level data
European Community Studies and Eurobarometer	Since the early 1970s, public opinion surveys conducted on behalf of the European Commission at least twice a year in all member states of the European Union	Cross-national comparison of a wide range of social and political issues, including European integration; life satisfaction; social goals; currency issues; working conditions; and travel
General Household Survey (GHS)	Annual interviews since 1971 with members aged 16+ in over 8000 randomly sampled households	Covers standard issues such as education and health, about which questions are asked each year, plus additional items that vary annually
International Social Survey Programme (ISSP)	Annual programme, since 1983, of cross-national collaboration covering survey topics important for social science research. Brings together pre-existing projects, thereby adding a cross-cultural perspective to the individual national studies. Coordinated by the University of Cologne, accessible via UK Data Archive	Attitudes towards legal systems and the economy. Covers special topics including work orientations; the environment; and national identity
Office for National Statistics (ONS) Omnibus Survey	Survey carried out eight times a year since 1990 using face-to-face structured interviews on a sample of just under 2000 interviewees. Uses short, simple sets of questions to gain an impression of public attitudes concerning topics that change frequently. Accessible via UK Data Archive	Covers core demographic questions about respondents plus questions that change from month to month on topics that change frequently – e.g. food safety; eating behaviour; personal finance; sports participation; Internet access; human rights; Aids awareness

Source: adapted from Bryman and Bell (2003: 215–16)

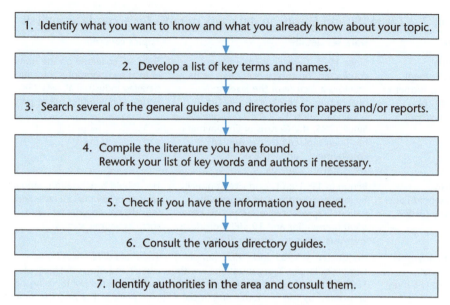

1. Identify what you want to know and what you already know about your topic.

2. Develop a list of key terms and names.

3. Search several of the general guides and directories for papers and/or reports.

4. Compile the literature you have found.
   Rework your list of key words and authors if necessary.

5. Check if you have the information you need.

6. Consult the various directory guides.

7. Identify authorities in the area and consult them.

Figure 7.1 How to get started when searching published secondary sources

Doing research in a company/organization will be facilitated by the fact that other departments/sections of the organization might have the information needed to answer the question at hand. Some types of studies, such as comparative and longitudinal, require some historical data, available only through secondary sources.

Secondary data are not only inexpensive but are relatively easy to access. As mentioned above, increasing use of electronic sources has enhanced availability of these sources. Secondary data help us understand the situation/research field and identify areas of potential concerns that merit in-depth investigation based on primary research (Craig and Douglas, 2000).

Begin with secondary data and only when they are exhausted proceed with primary data.

7.1.2 Disadvantages of secondary data

There are some serious drawbacks in working with secondary data. We should be careful in using data just because they are easily available and save us time and money. One of the main problems is that these data are collected for another study with different objectives and they may not completely fit 'our' problem. It is therefore of the utmost importance to identify what we are studying, what we already know about the topic, and what we want to have further information on. Here we should make a list of the terms and concepts on which we need to collect information. The idea is to take our research problem as the starting point for secondary data we need, and not the other way around. If the secondary data do not 'fit' with your specific problem, they should not be used. It is better to answer your question partially or not at all than to provide an answer based on wrong information.

One problem with accuracy is that we have to understand the purpose of data collection for the source we are using. For example, it is quite common for companies to utilize wishful thinking in their annual reports rather than facts, when they describe their market position. They may mention that they are market leaders or have a certain percentage of market share. However, if we are studying the competitive position of a company, we should make certain checks to see whether it *is* the market leader or has the market share it claims. Macro-economics and industry data collected by different countries and organizations vary considerably in their accuracy and equivalence. This is particularly problematic in developing countries where different sources report different values/data, for example variations may be observed in data on the number of TV sets or auto-mobiles per hundreds of the population. In some countries income of nationals working in foreign countries may be included in GDP.

7.1.3 Types of secondary data

As mentioned earlier (and illustrated in Figure 7.2), several types of secondary data are available, from government reports to companies' annual reports, that are always more upbeat than the reality. In business research, while doing work for a company, a lot of information is available from *internal sources*, including information on customers, suppliers, employees, marketing plans and efforts

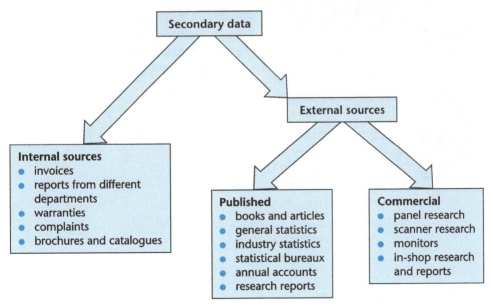

Figure 7.2 **Types of secondary data**

and, sometimes, even on competitors. The researcher cannot accept this information at its face value, although it is free and readily available. *External sources* include published books and journal articles, academic as well as professional and popular. And then there are data that have been collected by commercial organizations or companies for the purpose of selling them. In the business research field a lot of such data are available, on market structure, consumers, demographics, advertising results, and on different products and markets (see Tables 7.1 and 7.2 for some sources).

For published external sources, the best policy is to do a 'systematic search' in the library. You need to develop a list of main concepts and key words for your research problem. Search through the library by using these key words in different combinations. For example, if your research problem is to study export difficulties faced by small and medium-sized companies, you can use the following combinations: SMEs; small and medium-sized companies and export; export behaviour; export behaviour of SMEs; export problems; export subsidies, etc.

For this purpose you should also make use of search engines on the Internet and the various websites and data banks available. There are also export promotion bureaux and export credit banks. Some universities also maintain useful data banks (see e.g. Screenshot 7.1). Also, consult your adviser and reference lists from the publications you have found.

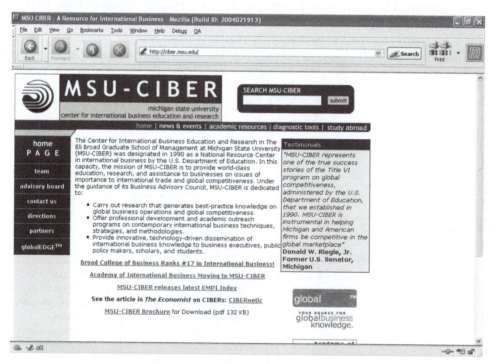

Screenshot 7.1 **MSU-CIBER**

Source: MSU homepage ciber.msu.edu

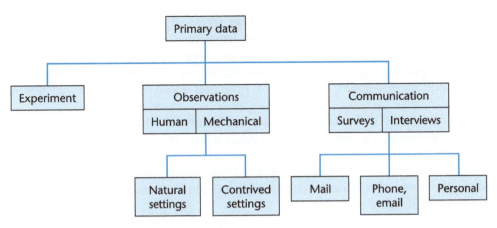

Figure 7.3 Advantages of primary data

7.2 Primary data

When secondary data are not available or cannot answer our research questions, we must collect the data that are relevant ourselves. Such data are called primary data. What we should look for, ask about and collect depends upon our research problem and research design. We have several options for collecting primary data. Normally this includes observations, experiments, surveys (questionnaires) and interviews, as illustrated by Figure 7.3. There are both advantages and disadvantages of primary data, as illustrated in Table 7.3.

7.2.1 Advantages of primary data

The main *advantage* of primary data is that they are collected for the particular project at hand. This means that they are more consistent with our research questions and research objectives. For business studies, for example, we may need specific demographic information about consumers such as education, income, lifestyle, personality and interests. This information might not be

Table 7.3 Advantages and disadvantages of primary data collection

	Communication	Observation
Scope	+	−
Cost	+	−
Objectivity	−	+
Precision/accuracy	−	+
Speed	+	−

99

available in a census report (or any other secondary source). Moreover, if we want to know about people's attitudes, intentions and buying behaviour for a particular product, only primary data can help us answer these questions. Through primary data we could also know the reasons behind consumer behaviour, management decisions or problems faced in internationalization efforts.

We can hardly learn about opinions and behaviour without asking questions directly to the people involved. Data/information on past events or experience can only be gathered by asking people who have been involved or have observed and can remember the particular event. Alternatively, if we are collecting data through survey or telephone interviews, we could cover a large geographic area with relatively little cost.

7.2.2 Disadvantages of primary data

The main *disadvantage* is that collecting primary data can take a long time and can cost a lot to collect. Moreover, it is difficult to get access: to find consumers, companies or other target groups who are willing to cooperate and answer our questions. This is particularly difficult if we are dealing with sensitive issues or research questions that can turn out to be an impossible mission. Another disadvantage/problem is that the researcher needs to be careful in using proper tools, procedures and methods of analysis, as otherwise s/he will jeopardize the reliability and applicability of the study. An important disadvantage is thus that the researcher has less degree of control in data collection. As a result, unexpected factors may influence and interfere with efficient data collection.

One major weakness in the quality and scope of information gathered through primary sources is that the researcher is fully dependent on the willingness and ability of respondents. There may be many reasons why people are reluctant or refuse to cooperate. These include lack of time, or lack of incentive; they may consider it a waste of their valuable time; there may be fear of any negative consequences if they are honest in their answers and fear of embarrassment in case of sensitive issues.

7.2.3 Types of primary data

Status and state of affairs data

These data are typical of a demographic or socio-economic nature, for example on age, education levels, profession, marital status, gender, income or social class. These types of data are used for cross-classification of information. For example, is purchase/usage of a particular product related to a certain age group? This type of data/information is used, for example, for segmentation and positioning in marketing.

Psychological and lifestyle data

This category refers to personality and behaviour data, that is information which can influence individual behaviour. These are measured with standard methods, explaining personal activities and interests, for example different types of buyers/consumers, proactive vs. reactive shoppers and traditional vs. innovative shoppers.

Attitude and opinion data

These reveal an individual's attitude and opinion about a certain idea, product, object or issue. This category also refers to cognitive behaviour such as assumptions or opinion on a certain matter/object and effects such as evaluation or judgement on a particular issue/object. Moreover, they reveal attitudes about the future, for example usage of a particular project.

Awareness and knowledge data

These describe what is known about a particular product, object or business activity. For example, this type of data is important in order to learn about the effects of a particular advertising campaign – whether the respondents recall the advertisement(s), with or without some help. Such data are needed if we want to find out what respondents know about a particular product and its characteristics, where it can be bought, its price level, who produces it and where, how it should be used, the functions it can perform, etc.

Data on intentions

This type of data can reveal, for example, whether or not the respondent's intention is to buy a particular product in the near future. Typically, this will explain the buying behaviour of customers. Moreover, this type of information will help in relating intentions to actual behaviour, for example how many buyers intended to buy and how many have actually bought the product.

Data on motivations

This information can help us understand what motives/stimuli can influence buyers' or managers' behaviour, for example factors such as needs, wishes, driving forces, or other motives that can influence behaviour towards a particular product, matter or issue. This also helps us to understand why people behave the way they do so that we can understand their past and predict future behaviour better. Motives are more stable than the behaviour itself and thus reveal valuable information.

Data on behaviour

Finally, this type of data helps us to understand what respondents have done or will be doing. For business studies, this type of information is very important.

📖 Further reading

Adler, P.A. and Adler, P. (1994) 'Observational techniques', in Denzin, N.K. and Lincoln, Y.S. (eds), *Handbook of Qualitative Research*, Thousand Oaks, CA: Sage, pp. 377–92.

Churchill, G.A. (1991) *Marketing Research: Methodological Foundations*, 5th edn, Chicago, IL: Dryden Press (Chapters 6 and 7).

Ghauri, P.N. (2004) 'Designing and conducting case studies in international business research', in Marshan-Piekkari and Welch, C. (eds), *A Handbook of Qualitative Research Methods for International Business*, Cheltenham: Edward Elgan, pp. 109–24.

❓ Questions

1. Explain the difference between secondary and primary data.

2. What are the advantages and disadvantages of secondary data?

3. Is all secondary data on a particular topic suitable for a research project on that topic?

4. 'First explore secondary data, only when secondary data sources are exhausted, then you can plan to collect primary data.' Comment.

Exercises

1. Select a product category. Estimate the total demand of that product in your home country. Also calculate the market share for the largest producer.

2. A company in the . . . industry (select industry) wants to learn about the market opportunities in . . . (select country). Visit websites listed in Table 7.1 to provide this information.

CHAPTER 8

Data collection

Since Hippocrates first presented 14 classic case studies of disease some 2300 years ago, science has proceeded along two divergent knowledge paths. One involves formulating a tentative theory of a phenomenon 'writ large', deducing implied empirical consequences, and controlling situational events in order to observe the validity of empirical deductions. The second path, less frequently used but equally valid, is to reason from individual and naturally occurring but largely uncontrollable observations towards generalizable inductive principles.

(Bonoma, 1985: 199, reprinted with permission by the American Marketing Association)

In business studies the majority of researchers need to collect some primary data to answer their research question. Once the researcher has decided to collect information/data through primary sources, s/he has to decide what kind of data collection method to use. As discussed earlier, s/he could do an observation, experiment, interview or survey. However, the choice of data collection will depend upon an overall judgement on which type of data is needed for a particular research problem. One important aspect is to identify/know the unit of analysis. Even in one-country research where data are compared and contrasted we need to be sure that firms which are consulted are comparable. This is also important for segmentation, new product development, demand forecast or country analysis for entry strategy studies.

While defining the unit of study, several dimensions are important. One is the *scope*: whether one study will cover a region (e.g. the EU), a country, or a particular area in a city or a country (e.g. north-west England or central London). Also, we need to define the *characteristics* of the unit. When we are studying firms, we should have clear criteria, such as: age, size, revenue and the industrial sector. Say we want to study 'Export behaviour of SMEs', should we study all firms in that category or only manufacturing firms? Should we study all firms or only those that have been in business for at least five years? Moreover, the type of answers we are looking for will determine which type of analysis we need. At the outset, a researcher has to decide whether s/he wants to use a qualitative or quantitative data collection and analysis method.

8.1 Qualitative versus quantitative methods

Alternatives to the standard approach, like unstructured interviewing, tend to be viewed as faulted variants . . . I am arguing, instead, that the standard survey interview is itself essentially faulted and that it therefore cannot serve as the ideal ideological model against which to assess other approaches.

(Mishler, 1986: 29)

In the literature on research methods there is some discussion on which methods or techniques are more suitable or 'scientific'. It is sometimes stated that structured and quantitative methods are more 'scientific' and thereby better. But in our opinion, methods or techniques are not 'better' or 'scientific' only because they are quantitative. As mentioned earlier, which methods and techniques are most suitable for which research (project) depends on the research problem and its purpose (Jankowicz, 1991).

Research methods refer to systematic, focused and orderly collection of data for the purpose of obtaining information from them, to solve/answer a particular research problem or question. The methods are different from techniques of data collection. By methods we mean data collection through historical review and analysis, surveys, field experiments and case studies, while by techniques we mean a step-by-step procedure that we follow in order to gather data and analyse them to find the answers to our research questions. These are concerned more with how to do things than what to do or why to do it. In business studies, we normally use techniques such as structured, semi-structured or unstructured interviews, surveys and observations (Bennett, 1986; Jankowicz, 1991).

The main difference between qualitative and quantitative research is not of 'quality' but of procedure. In qualitative research, findings are not arrived at by statistical methods or other procedures of quantification. Normally, the basic distinction between quantitative and qualitative research is that quantitative researchers employ measurement and qualitative researchers do not (Layder, 1993; Bryman and Bell, 2003). The difference between quantitative and qualitative methods and approach is not just a question of quantification, but also a reflection of different perspectives on knowledge and research objectives. We can do research on behaviour, events, organizational functioning, social environments, interaction and relationships. In some of these studies data may be quantified, but the analysis itself is qualitative, such as with census reports. It is quite common for researchers to collect their data through observations and interviews, which are the methods normally related to qualitative research. But the researcher may code the data collected in such a manner that would allow statistical analysis. In other words, it is quite possible to quantify qualitative data. Qualitative and quantitative methods are therefore not mutually exclusive. The difference is in the overall form and in the emphasis and objectives of the study. The differences in the emphasis between qualitative and quantitative methods are illustrated in Table 8.1.

Table 8.1 The difference in emphasis in qualitative versus quantitative methods

Qualitative methods	Quantitative methods
● Emphasis on understanding	● Emphasis on testing and verification
● Focus on understanding from respondent's/informant's point of view	● Focus on facts and/or reasons for social events
● Interpretation and rational approach	● Logical and critical approach
● Observations and measurements in natural settings	● Controlled measurement
● Subjective 'insider view' and closeness to data	● Objective 'outsider view' distant from data
● Explorative orientation	● Hypothetical-deductive; focus on hypothesis testing
● Process oriented	● Result oriented
● Holistic perspective	● Particularistic and analytical
● Generalization by comparison of properties and contexts of individual organism	● Generalization by population membership

Source: Based on Reichardt and Cook (1979)

Qualitative research is a mixture of the rational, explorative and intuitive, where the skills and experience of the researcher play an important role in the analysis of data. It is often focused on social process and not on social structures, which is frequently the focus in quantitative research. The skills needed to do qualitative research are thinking abstractly, stepping back and analysing situations, recognizing and avoiding biases, obtaining valid and reliable information, having theoretical and social sensitivity being able to keep analytical distance while utilizing past experience, and having a shrewd sense of observation and interaction (van Maanen, 1983; Strauss and Corbin, 1990). Although most researchers emphasize one or the other, qualitative and quantitative methods can be combined and used in the same study.

8.2 When to use qualitative methods

As mentioned earlier, the main reasons for doing qualitative research and using qualitative methods are the objective of the research project and depend on the background and previous experience of the researcher. Some disciplines, such as anthropology, or philosophical orientations, such as phenomenology, particularly advocate qualitative methods for data collection and data analysis. For our purpose, however, the main reason should be the research problem and the focus and purpose of the study.

Research problems focusing on uncovering a person's experience or behaviour, or when we want to uncover and understand a phenomenon about which little is known, are typical examples of qualitative research (Ghauri, 2004;

Marshan-Piekkari and Welch, 2004). Moreover, when an event or social process is difficult to study with quantitative methods, qualitative methods are most suitable and can provide intricate details and understanding. Qualitative research is thus common in social and behavioural sciences and among practitioners who want to understand human behaviour and functions. It is quite suitable for studying organizations, groups and individuals (Strauss and Corbin, 1990).

There are three major components of qualitative research (Becker, 1970; Strauss and Corbin, 1990; Miles and Huberman, 1994):

1. *Data*: often collected through interviews and observations.
2. *Interpretative or analytical procedure*: the techniques to conceptualize and analyse the data to arrive at findings or theories.
3. *Report*: written or verbal. In the case of students, the report is written in the form of a thesis or project.

One argument for using quantitative data is that quite often we collect individual data and aggregate it to analyse organizations. To separate predetermined elements we use predetermined instruments and analyse the results quantitatively. In this manner we can only get a limited reality because predetermined instruments may not suit the particular situation, and also because these methods cut reality into discrete pieces that are then combined into statistical clusters (for more details see, e.g., Glaser and Strauss, 1967; Weiss, 1968; Light, 1979; van Maanen, 1983; Eisenhardt, 1989). In spite of claims that relatively few studies use qualitative methods, it is not difficult to find support for the use of qualitative data:

> Qualitative data are attractive for many reasons: They are rich, full, earthly, holistic, real; their face validity seems unimpeachable, they preserve chronological flow where that is important, and suffer minimally from retrospective distortion; and they, in principle, offer a far more precise way to assess causality in organizational affairs than arcane efforts like cross-lagged correlations.
>
> (Miles, 1979: 117)

It is generally accepted that, for inductive and exploratory research, qualitative methods are most useful, as they can lead us to hypothesis building and explanations. According to this view, qualitative and quantitative methods are suitable at different stages or levels of research. At the first level, the problem is of an unstructured nature and qualitative methods are suitable. At the second level, quantitative methods are most useful, as we want to test different hypotheses that were arrived at through level 1. Quantitative methods allow us to accept or reject these hypotheses in a logical and consistent manner. At the third level, both qualitative and quantitative methods can be used. Often a combination of the two methods is used at this level.

Qualitative methods, as defined earlier in this section, are flexible and unstructured. When compared with quantitative methods, they employ a limited number of observations and try to explain different aspects of our problem area.

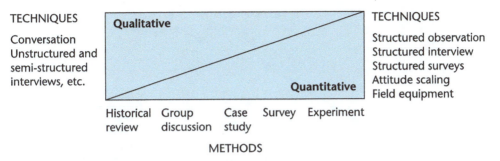

Figure 8.1 **Quantitative and qualitative methods and techniques**
Source: Adapted from *Business Research Projects for Students*, Thomson Learning (Jankowics, A.D. 1991) p. 159

Although the number of observations is low, several aspects of the problem area can be analysed. Low numbers are also justified because we often want to do in-depth studies or provide 'thick description', which is not possible in cases of numerous observations. Qualitative methods are, therefore, most suitable when the objectives of the study demand in-depth insight into a phenomenon.

Different qualitative methods are suitable for different types of studies. We have already stated that quite often we can combine qualitative and quantitative methods. Many scholars claim that the two approaches are complementary and cannot be used in isolation from each other (For this type of discussion see Jones, 1988; Martin, 1988; Jankowicz, 1991.) According to this view, no *method* is entirely qualitative or quantitative. However, the *techniques* can be either quantitative or qualitative. Figure 8.1 illustrates this point further.

As we can see in Figure 8.1, the methods from left to right become more quantitative and use more quantitative techniques. Historical review, group discussions and case studies are mostly qualitative research methods. These qualitative methods use relatively more qualitative techniques, such as conversations and in-depth, unstructured or semi-structured interviews.

8.2.1 Historical review

In cases of historical reviews, our job is to describe what happened in the past so that we can understand the present or plan for the future. Here we go through existing records and reports and talk to different people to get as true a picture as possible. The archives are reviewed in an interrogative manner with a particular research question/problem in mind. The main problem in using such a method is that we have to trust human memory, which records selective parts of reality. It is quite possible that two different people, while going through a certain situation or experience, will record or remember different things; sometimes they make mistakes or misunderstand things. It is therefore important that, while using such a method, we should cross-check one written source with another, or a written source with an interview, or two interviews with each other. In other words, we have to be critical and compare different explanations for the situation

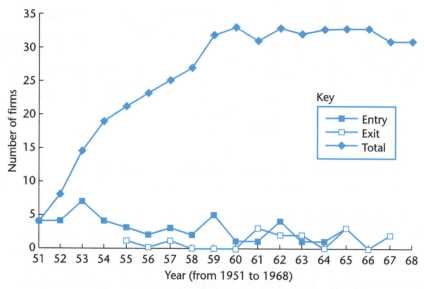

Figure 8.2 Number of firms in the US transistor industry

Source: Utterback, J.M. (1994: 41). Reprinted by permission of Harvard Business School Publishing. Copyright © 2004 by the Harvard Business School Publishing Corporation; all rights reserved. Based on data in E. Braun and S. MacDonald, *Revolution in Miniature: The History and Impact of Semiconductor Electronics* (Cambridge, England: Cambridge University Press, 1978) and J.E. Tilton, *International Diffusion of Technology* (Washington DC: The Brookings Institute, 1971)

or event. For further insight into historical reviews as a research method, we recommend Orbell (1987). Figure 8.2 presents an example of historical review in a particular industry.

8.2.2 Focus groups

The second qualitative method mentioned above is group discussion (also called focus groups). In this type of research method the researcher can get together with several respondents at the same time and initiate a discussion on a certain topic. The opinions of respondents are considered as information and analysed later. This method differs from other methods such as in-depth interviews in the sense that here the interaction is not only between the interviewer and the respondent, but also among the respondents. It is also considered a relatively cheap and convenient way of gathering information from several respondents in a short time.

Here we should be aware of the influence the group itself will have on the discussion and information that is exchanged. The discussion is influenced by the size of the group, its composition, the personalities of people involved, the roles they are asked to play, the physical and geographical arrangement of the meeting, and the 'chemistry' between the interviewer and the group or individuals. It is thus apparent that information gathered by this method will be different from information gathered through historical review and case studies. However, this method is widely used in some research cultures: for example, in the UK it is so widely used that it is regarded as synonymous with qualitative research (Kent, 1989).

8.2.3 Case studies

What is a case study?

The case study approach is often associated with descriptive or exploratory research, without being restricted to these areas (Ghauri, 1983; Bonoma, 1985; Yin, 1994). In business studies, case study research is particularly useful when the phenomenon under investigation is difficult to study outside its natural setting and also when the concepts and variables under study are difficult to quantify. Often this is because there are too many variables to be considered, which makes experiment or survey methods inappropriate (Bonoma, 1985; Yin, 1994).

As mentioned earlier, research in business studies emphasizes the role of deduction where the validity of all findings depends solely on the quality of logic employed in the study and precise measurement. However, the trade-off between precision and reduced generalizability is not a useful one in many situations. Many phenomena cannot be understood if removed from their social context. In these cases inductive, qualitative approaches are alternative methods to scientific investigation.

Case research, in our case, refers to qualitative and field-based construction and analysis of case studies. It is based on a process model as suggested by Bonoma (1985). Case study is a description of a management situation. A case study often involves data collection through sources such as verbal reports, personal interviews and observation as primary data sources. In addition, case methods involve data collection through sources such as financial reports, archives, as well as budget and operating statements, including market and competition reports. The case method is not suitable for all types of research. It is the research problem and the objective that decide whether the case method is suitable or not. With the above proviso, the case method is useful for theory development and testing. The main feature is the intensity of the study of the object, individual, group, organization, culture, incident or situation. We need to have sufficient information to characterize, to explain the unique features of the case, as well as to point out the characteristics that are common in several cases. Finally, this approach relies on integrative powers of research: the ability to study an object with many dimensions and then to draw an integrative interpretation (Selltiz et al., 1976).

When to use a case study

This is a preferred approach when 'how' or 'why' questions are to be answered, when the researcher has little control over events and when the focus is on a current phenomenon in a real-life context (Yin, 1994). Case studies are often of an explanatory, exploratory or descriptive nature. According to Eisenhardt, case studies are:

> particularly well-suited to new research areas or research areas for which existing theory seems inadequate. This type of work is highly complementary to incremental theory building from normal science research. The former is useful in early stages of research on a topic or when a fresh perspective is needed, while the latter is useful in later stages of knowledge.
>
> (Eisenhardt, 1989: 548–9)

When to use which research approach depends upon:

- the type of research questions
- the control of the researcher on behavioural events
- the focus on a current as opposed to a historical phenomenon
- what information is needed
- how this can be obtained.

When research questions concern only 'what', for example, 'What are the ways in which an effective firm is operated?', an exploratory study is justified. Here the objective is to develop hypotheses or propositions, which can later be studied. For an exploratory study, any of the five research strategies can be used. If the questions relate to How many? or How much?, survey or archival strategies are favoured. But when 'how' and 'why' questions are asked, a case study method as a research strategy is favoured.

Quite often it is stated that the case study method is used when we want to study a single organization and we want to identify factors involved in some aspects or behaviour of an organization or smaller unit, such as a marketing or finance department. However, it is equally possible to study a number of organizations with regard to a set of variables we have already identified or assumed. Such case studies are called *comparative case studies*. In this type of study we ask or study the same questions in a number of organizations and compare them with each other to draw conclusions.

The purpose of data collection in the comparative case study method is to compare (replicate) the phenomenon (e.g. strategy formation) studied in different cases in a systematic way, to explore different dimensions of our research issues or to examine different levels of research variables. In a survey, on the other hand, we are more concerned with the sampling of different organizations as we want to generalize our findings to all other organizations of the same type (Jankowicz, 1991). Yin (1994) compares the case study method with experiments and suggests three situations where case study is the preferred method:

1. If we want to follow a theory that specifies a particular set of outcomes in some particular situation, and if we find a firm which finds itself in that particular situation, we can use the case study method for a critical test of theory and its applicability to the organization.

2. If we want to study some specific characteristics of a rare or extreme situation in which an organization finds itself, we can use the case study method to compare and contrast.
3. If we want to study a situation or an organization which has rarely been studied and is unique in its nature, we can use the case study method. In this case, we hope to learn something new and important.

As most case studies are done through a review of existing historical material and records plus interviews, the case study method is quite similar to historical review, but it is different in the sense that here we have a possibility of direct observation and interaction. As mentioned earlier, we would like to make it explicit that the case study method is not synonymous with qualitative research or methods. A case study may very well involve quantitative methods or even be entirely quantitative.

In many cases, especially in business studies, students first decide which method to use – for example, case study or survey – and then formulate their problem. We have been advocating that it is the research problem and the research objectives that dictate the type of method we should use. Here lies a dilemma: should we decide the method first, or should our problem lead us to the method? Of course, the latter should be the case, as most problems and research objectives clearly suggest one form of data collection over another.

Preparing for a case study

When preparing to undertake the case study method for research, a theory/data/theory revision cycle, as suggested by Bonoma (1985: 204–6), is quite useful (see Figure 8.3). This revision process goes through four stages: 'drift', 'design', 'prediction' and 'disconfirmation'.

At the beginning of a research project the researcher is in a 'drift' stage and is trying to learn the area of research, concepts and terminology in the field. This drifting leads him/her to a priori notions about the phenomenon and how it operates. This stage widens the perspective of the researcher and often leads to modification in the basic research questions (van Maanen, 1983). In fact, most research methods involve this 'drift' phase in the early stages of the research project.

A researcher moves to 'design': choice of strategy to collect data needed to answer/elucidate the research question plus the stage when s/he starts developing tentative explanations of the observations so far. At this stage the researcher assesses and refines major areas of the research project as suggested by the drift stage. This facilitates the conceptualization of the research problem. At some time s/he has to go back to the drift stage, to get a better understanding.

'Prediction' occurs in the middle-to-late stage of the project. By this stage the researcher has a good understanding of the factors on which case information may be grouped and can proceed with further case construction and analysis. The researcher proceeds confidently, compiling more cases with the purpose

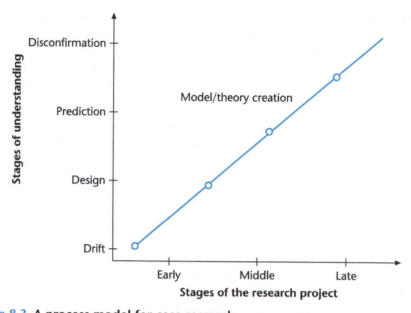

Figure 8.3 A process model for case research

Source: Based on Bonoma (1985: 205). Copyright © 1985, with permission from Elsevier

of drawing conclusions. As a result they can even develop some tentative explanations. Similarly they may realize that some generalizations are not very general and are valid only in particular circumstances, settings, industries or firms.

The final stage, 'disconfirmation', refers to further testing/analysis of the results suggested by the prediction stage. This can be done by applying the results to other or broader sets of cases. The idea is to apply the concepts to totally different cases or situations to test the generalizability of the results. As we can gather, these four stages do not really form some rigid/fixed hierarchy but rather an iterative evolution towards understanding (Bonoma, 1985: 205).

Coming to more practical details, once our research problem suggests case study as the preferred approach, we should deal with questions such as: What are the skills needed? What types of a priori assumptions do we have? How do we select the cases? How many cases shall we include in our study? How shall we conduct the case study?

As far as the *skills* required are concerned, this is not one of the easiest types of research to do, as it demands special skills from the researcher. Some training for specific cases is necessary, especially if the researcher has no previous experience of conducting case studies, or a research assistant is used when there are several cases. Unlike in surveys, where data collection is more routinized, in case studies the researcher has to be skilled in the dynamics of a case and should be able to take advantage of opportunities offered during the data collection.

While collecting data through semi-structured interviews a researcher must be able to control the situation, ask the right questions, adapt to new or unexpected situations and develop trust. All these skills can be learnt if the researcher is aware of them beforehand. Yin (1994: 67) recommends case study training as a seminar experience, especially when many cases and several researchers are involved. Moreover, he recommends a protocol to arrive at the final version. One purpose of these seminars and protocols should be to discuss potential problems and how to handle them. Such training may also reveal weaknesses in the research problem, in the study design and even in the capabilities of the researchers. All these can be improved if detected. It is also recommended that before the data collection is started a pilot study should be conducted. This serves as a rehearsal for the data collection procedure, indicating the time it takes and any problems it can cause or that may arise.

How to select the cases

As in other methods of data collection, it is important to decide the target population that is to be used for the investigation. It includes those firms, individuals, groups or elements that will be represented in the study. The next stage is to assess the accessible population, the population to which we can get access (Cooper, 1984). Out of this accessible population we have to select one or a few cases, objects or firms for the study. The time available for the study, financial resources for travelling and other practical issues are of great importance. For example, depending upon how much time we have to study, the type of organization or company we select for our study would be different. If we have very little time available, we should perhaps study a smaller firm, as in these firms the communication lines are smaller and faster, they are more flexible and it is easier to get overall or in-depth information.

On the other hand, if we are studying a specific and complex issue, we should perhaps study a bigger firm, because these firms experience complex problems and have expertise in-house that can provide us with in-depth information on the particular issue (van der Meer-Kooistra, 1993). The cases should also correspond to our theoretical framework and the variables we are studying. For example, if we are studying behaviour of industrial buyers, we have to select firms that are dealing with industrial marketing and purchasing. Once we have selected a firm, we should select a manager who is involved in the process of marketing and purchasing. An interview with the firm's public relations manager or an accountant would not provide us with the information we are looking for.

In bigger organizations it is very important to select the right department, section or individual. It is not a question of interviewing the most important individuals, but of interviewing the *right person* from an organization: right from the point of view of our research questions and study variables. Finding the right person is sometimes a long process. However, when we are able to establish contact with a key, or highly placed, manager, our goal should be to take his or her help in identifying the right person.

Students often ask how many cases they should include in their study. The answer to this question is very difficult as there is no upper or lower limit to the

113

number. Often one case is enough. As Mintzberg says, 'What, for example, is wrong with a sample size of one? Why should researchers have to apologize for them? Should Piaget apologize for studying his own children, a physicist for splitting only one atom?' (1979: 583). It is the research problem and the research objectives that influence the number and choice of cases to be studied. Moreover, what is meant by 'a case'? For example, if we are trying to understand the process of decision making in a firm, we may study several decisions on different issues, important/unimportant, novel/routine decisions, etc., in the *same* organization. This will provide variability among important factors (see, e.g., Campbell, 1975, who argues for the richness of detail within a single case by looking for many implications of the ideas under study).

> **There is no upper or lower limit with regard to the number of cases to be included in a study.**

Different types of case study design

Yin (1994) provides four types of case study design and presents a 2 × 2 matrix (see Figure 8.4), suggesting that single and multiple case studies reflect different design considerations.

The four types of research design are as follows:

1. single case design, holistic
2. single case design, embedded
3. multiple case design, holistic
4. multiple case design, embedded.

As we can see, the primary distinction is between single and multiple case designs. We should therefore decide, at an early stage, whether we are going to use single or multiple case design. *Single case* is appropriate when a particular case is critical and we want to use it for testing an established theory. It is a critical case because it meets all the conditions necessary to confirm, challenge or extend the theory. Another situation is when a single case is an extreme or a unique case. Finally, a single case design is appropriate when a case is revelatory. This means

	Single case design	Multiple case designs
Holistic (single unit of analysis)	Type 1	Type 3
Embedded (multiple units of analysis)	Type 2	Type 4

Figure 8.4 Basic design for case studies

Source: Yin (1994: 46). Copyright © 1994 by Sage Publications. Reprinted by permission of Sage Publications, Inc.

that we can observe and study a phenomenon that was previously not accessible and which can provide useful insight. We can also use single case design in other situations, such as a pilot study or an exploratory study that serves as a first step to a later, more comprehensive study (Yin, 2003).

Multiple case study design is considered more appropriate for studies which do not involve rare, critical or revelatory cases. In this approach we should be clear that every case has to serve a particular purpose in the study. In other words, we have to justify the selection of each case. However, as pointed out earlier, case study design is often flexible and can be changed, modified or revised with proper justification.

The use of a particular case study method depends also upon the type of study we are doing, whether it is inductive or deductive, and also upon whether we are looking for specific or general explanations. In the case of an inductive approach and specific explanation, we may use the single case. On the other hand, if we are doing a study with a deductive approach we can use the case study at an early stage to develop our hypotheses or propositions. If we are doing a study with an inductive approach but are looking for general explanations, then we should use a multiple case method. However, if we are doing a study with a deductive approach and are looking for generalizations, then the case study is a less recommended method. We suggest that students using this method should consult Yin (2003) for further guidance.

8.3 Observations

Observation as a data collection tool entails listening and watching other people's behaviour in a way that allows some type of learning and analytical interpretation. The main *advantage* is that we can collect first-hand information in a natural setting. Moreover, we can interpret and understand the observed behaviour, attitude and situation more accurately, and capture the dynamics of social behaviour in a way that is not possible through questionnaires and interviews.

The main *disadvantage* is that most observations are made by individuals who systematically observe and record a phenomenon, and it is difficult to translate the events or happenings into scientifically useful information. This is particularly important when the purpose is to generalize from these observations. Here questions about validity and reliability become very important and need to be answered satisfactorily. When we collect data through observations we have to make a number of choices regarding, for example, participatory versus non-participatory, laboratory versus field settings, etc. This is further illustrated by Figure 8.5.

In participant or *field observation*, the observer is a natural part of the situation or event. The researcher is a part of a company or organization and decides to study the same organization in one way or another. Sometimes a researcher

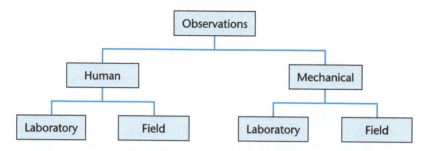

Figure 8.5 Choices for collecting primary data through observations

specifically joins an organization to be able to observe it as a participant. In other words, in this case the observation is not hidden or disguised: people who are being observed know that they are being observed and by whom. In business studies, participant observation can enable researchers to have access to what people actually do instead of what they might claim they do. One danger of participatory observation is that the observers can be so influenced by the event, situation, culture or everyday lives of the subjects that they become unable to take a neutral view of events and situations. On the other hand, observers can be so ethnocentric that they are not able to observe or analyse the situation because they believe the subjects have an inferior culture or that the observer knows best (Douglas, 1976).

A *contrived setting* refers to a method where reactions are observed in a controlled setting in a laboratory or in other virtual reality. In this method, the researcher is able to better control the observation without any disturbances. Moreover, it could be more efficient and less time consuming.

In *non-participant observations*, the observer or researcher observes a natural setting but is not part of the situation her/himself. It has been reported in several studies that the behaviour of people is influenced because of a non-participatory observer, but only in the beginning; people get used to it in a very short time. One way to overcome this problem is to observe under disguise. For example, in a buying/selling situation an observer can act as a potential customer or a salesperson. Observations for research should be planned systematically in direct relevance to research questions. However, these observations can be simple and straightforward, quite often in a natural setting, event or occurrence. An example is observing customers in a supermarket while they make their choices in picking up a particular product category/brand.

In the case of a *mechanical* method of observation, the same observation can be done by placing a video camera overlooking a particular section of the supermarket. Another way employed by a number of companies is to use their hotline statistics to understand consumer behaviour and future trends. These calls are recorded and later analysed in terms of the type of questions asked, and the types of problems mentioned by the customers. However, a researcher has to consider

116

the ethical aspects of this method of data collection. Do the customers/subjects know that they are being observed or not? If not, then is it ethically correct, or can the recording of their behaviour in any way harm them or violate their personal integrity?

In the case of *human* observation, an observer follows his or her own values and expectations and is also limited by his or her own constraints. The subjects can catch those values and constraints by placing the researcher in some class or category. Most subjects who are alert to these issues can do so by the dress, manner or language used. For example, while studying the behaviour of a labour force, if the observer is classified as anti-working class, this can influence the behaviour of the observed (Phillips, 1966).

Some scholars agree that data collected through observation are more objective and accurate, as this method is independent of respondents' unwillingness or inability to provide the information needed by the researcher. For example, respondents are often careful in replying to sensitive or embarrassing questions. Observation of the actual behaviour as it occurs reflects respondents' behaviour more correctly (Churchill, 1999). As mentioned earlier, observation as a data collection method should not be selected just because it is easier. This choice is highly influenced by the research problem, research design, researcher's skills, capabilities and nature, and the characteristics of the subject to be observed.

8.4 Communication

For primary data, the researcher has to decide whether to communicate with the respondents/subjects or just to observe them. *Communication* does not have to be direct or face to face. We could send our questions by post or email and ask for answers to be sent back to us in the same manner. The instrument used for this type of data collection is called a survey or questionnaire. A questionnaire can be structured, unstructured or semi-structured. We could also use more personal methods and meet with the respondents/subjects face to face and ask questions.

Communication thus refers to collection of data by asking those who have experienced a particular phenomenon to explain it to the researcher. This type of data collection makes it possible to generalize the results and test theories. There are four main ways to collect data through this method:

1. postal survey
2. personal interview
3. telephone interview
4. email interview.

The most commonly used primary data collection method is through communication. Many students and business researchers collect their data through surveys or interviews. In this case, the first question to ask is how structured or standardized the questions should be. In most *structured* questionnaires, whether for a survey or an interview, the questions and the answers to be given are pre-determined. The researcher poses a question and the respondent has to select one of the pre-stated answers (e.g. in a multiple-choice manner).

In the case of *unstructured* questionnaires or interviews, the questions are only roughly predetermined. Moreover, there are no predetermined answers. The respondent can reply in his or her own words. A questionnaire where the questions are predetermined, but the respondents can use their own words and ways to answer, is a *semi-structured* questionnaire, used in a survey or an interview (Churchill, 1999).

In practice, since questions are to some extent always formulated by the researcher, methods are inevitably more or less structured. To rely completely on a structured method means that there is no room for the respondents to give their own views in a real sense, which might have been useful for the findings. Similarly, total dependence on the unstructured method may not allow accurate testing of hypotheses (Phillips, 1966).

Example

Structured: 'Do you prefer alternative A, B, C or D?'
Unstructured: 'Do you have any alternative in mind? If *yes*, 'Please explain.'

An important difference between a survey and an experiment is that the survey is not focused around an analysis of the effects of certain test stimuli on the individuals but deals with reconstruction of processes that occurred prior to the investigations (Phillips, 1966). The most obvious difference between a questionnaire and an interview is the cost. For a very large study (survey) it will be difficult and costly to interview hundreds of respondents. Moreover, an interviewer needs a lot of training, especially if it is someone other than the researcher. The questionnaire survey causes no such problems. Interviewing, on the other hand, is a much more flexible method than the questionnaire. Interviews are considered more appropriate for qualitative studies, while questionnaires are considered more suitable for quantitative types of research methodology.

8.5　Surveys

Surveys refer to a method of data collection that utilizes questionnaires or interview techniques for recording the verbal behaviour of respondents. The survey is an effective tool to get opinions, attitudes and descriptions as well as for capturing cause-and-effect relationships. However, there are several circumstances that might influence respondents and their reactions, as well as their answers. Factors that influence respondents might include:

- *Sponsor*: when a study is financed or sponsored by a particular organization, this might lead to suspicion and deter respondents from answering questions correctly.
- *Appeal*: when a researcher makes an appeal on why or how important it is for him or her to get answers to his or her questions and how it can be useful for the respondent/society if the study at hand is performed.
- *Stimulus*: when some type of reward is given to respondents. Here the decision is to be made whether the reward should be financial or non-financial.
- *Questionnaire format*: the appearance, layout, length and even the colour of the paper used have an influence on whether the questionnaire will be responded to properly or not.
- *Covering letter*: its tone and stance have an enormous impact on the respondent.
- *Stamped and self-addressed envelope*: so that the responder need not incur any expense while providing you with information, and to make it easier or more convenient for him/her to send the answers back.

Surveys and questionnaires are among the most popular data collection methods in business studies, and the major types of questionnaires are descriptive and/or analytical. Once a research problem is formulated and the purpose of the study is clearly defined, this will determine the type of survey we should undertake, whether analytical or descriptive. Different surveys lead to different problems and issues and demand different types of planning and handling. According to Gill and Johnson (1991) the planning of a survey should follow a pattern as suggested by Figure 8.6.

According to Simons (1987), with *analytic surveys* we can test a theory by taking the logic into the field, for example to understand the relationship between accounting control systems and business performance. In this type of survey, we have to put the emphasis on specifying the independent, dependent and extraneous variables. We should also give due attention to and benefit from existing literature, theory and research while conceptualizing and structuring our research. The review of literature is therefore of the utmost importance. In analytical surveys, independent, dependent and extraneous variables are controlled through statistical techniques such as multiple regression. The questions and variables included in such a survey thus need careful conceptualization and measurement scales.

On the other hand, *descriptive surveys* are concerned with identifying the phenomena whose variance we wish to describe. The survey is concerned with particular characteristics of a specific population or subjects, either at a fixed point in time or at varying times for comparative purposes. Here the focus is more on a representative sample of the relevant population than on the analytical design, as we are concerned principally with accuracy of the findings and whether they can be generalized. Even in these surveys, a review of earlier research and literature is important to determine what kind of questions are to

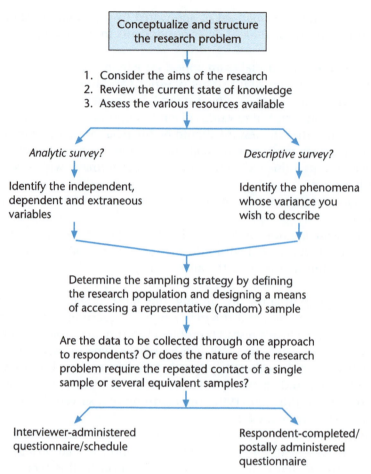

Figure 8.6 Planning a survey

Source: Gill and Johnson (1991: 76–7). Copyright © Sage Publications Ltd. Reproduced by permission of Sage Publications Ltd

be included in the questionnaire. In business studies, descriptive surveys are often used to obtain consumer attitudes towards a certain product and to ascertain views and opinions of employees in an organization (Reeves and Harper, 1981). These surveys are often used to understand behaviour of employees with regard to motivation, job satisfaction and grievances.

Figure 8.6 also illustrates that both analytical and descriptive surveys are concerned with identifying the population (the object of the study). The population would provide all the responses that would help us to answer our research questions. From this population a sample should be drawn that is representative. The research problem and objectives also dictate whether or not data are to be collected by only one approach, or whether we have to contact our sample again and again. In either case, we have to consider practicalities and access before starting to work on a questionnaire and schedule (Moser and Kalton, 1971).

The most important issue is to know what information we want to have. Both descriptive and causal research demand some a priori assumptions or hypotheses. This will direct our questions, what information we need and who should be the respondent. The development of the questionnaire may also lead us to modify or revise our hypotheses. The questionnaire for an exploratory study is often loosely structured, as we are interested in the discovery of ideas and insights and not their causal relationship.

Finally, we have to decide whether we are going to send the questionnaire by mail or email and wait for the answers, or whether we should interview the respondent face to face or by telephone. Here not only the research problem and objectives, but also issues such as sample size location, availability of funds and complexity of information required may influence the procedure and schedule. Resources are very important at this stage. For example, email and postal surveys are generally less expensive and time consuming than personal interviews. Moreover, in these surveys there is a problem with high rates of 'non-response', while in interviews there is a risk of interviewer bias (Scott, 1961; Boyd and Westfall, 1970). Also, a mail survey is not recommended for unstructured questionnaires with open-ended questions (Churchill, 1999).

8.5.1 Constructing questionnaires

In survey research where structured data collection techniques are used on a large number of respondents, instrument (questionnaire) design becomes very important.

The first step in the construction of a questionnaire is to specify what type of information is required. This depends, first, on the type of study we have at hand. In the case of descriptive and causal studies, we should have knowledge on the basis of hypotheses and propositions. We should know what is the basis of our study and what we want to achieve. Here we should also consider to whom this questionnaire is to be sent and what is to be asked.

Second, we should consider whether the questionnaire is going to be disguised or undisguised. Moreover, we must consider how it is to be administered, through mail, personal interview, telephone interview or a combination. For example, if we want to establish the relationship between behaviour and income levels (who buys BMW cars) or age, we could use either mail, telephone or interview methods. We might have other considerations, such as cost, in this choice.

Third, we should consider the construction of individual questions. Is it necessary to ask a certain question? What are the benefits of *dummy variables* and tables? Is it necessary to have several questions on one issue? Can questions be interpreted differently? Would respondents be willing to give answers to the questions? How long would it take for them to answer? Would they be in a position to answer a particular question? Is it a sensitive issue? All questions in a questionnaire should be judged according to the above.

121

☐ Less than 25 years
☐ Between 25 and 35 years
☐ Between 36 and 45 years
☐ Between 46 and 55 years
☐ Above 55 years

Figure 8.7 Categories for structured questions

Fourth, we should consider how the questions are to be answered. Should we have open-ended questions, such as: 'How old are you?', 'What is the total turnover of your company?' where no answers or alternatives to a question are provided and respondents can answer exactly as they like? Or should we have closed questions such as: 'How old are you? Please tick the appropriate box below' (see Figure 8.7). With open-ended questions we may end up with enormous variations in answers that would make coding or categorization difficult or almost impossible. On the other hand, we can get correct answers from the respondents when they do not have to limit their answers to one of the categories mentioned in Figure 8.7. We should, therefore, be aware of the type of information we need for each question, so that we can formulate the questions and expected answers accordingly.

Another aspect that should be considered here is whether or not we should have 'Don't know' or 'No comment' options. In this case we might be providing an escape route to a respondent wanting to avoid answering a question, perhaps due to its sensitive nature. The responses received for questionnaires with or without an escape route differ by up to 20–25 per cent. In case no escape route is provided, the respondents have to take a position.

The length of the questionnaire and its effect on the response rate and responses is important. A common belief is that the shorter the questionnaire, the higher the chance that it will be returned fully completed. However, there are no standards available in the existing literature regarding what is a 'short' and what is a 'long' questionnaire. The idea is that a respondent gets tired or loses interest in answering the questions as the length increases. Some guidelines for designing questionnaires are presented in the next section.

The precise wording of questions is crucial in achieving maximum validity of survey information (data) collected through asking questions. This is illustrated by the following story:

Two priests, a Dominican and a Jesuit, are discussing whether it is a sin to smoke and pray at the same time. After failing to reach a conclusion, each goes off to consult his respective superior. The next week they meet again. The Dominican says,

| Strongly disagree | Disagree | Agree in part | Agree | Strongly agree |
| ☐ | ☐ | ☐ | ☐ | ☐ |

Figure 8.8 Scale for ranking answers

'Well, what did your superior say?' The Jesuit responds, 'He said it was all right'. 'That's funny', the Dominican replies, 'my superior said it was a sin'. Jesuit: 'What did you ask him?' Reply: 'I asked him if it was all right to smoke while praying'. 'Oh', said the Jesuit, 'I asked my superior if it was all right to pray while smoking'.
(Sudman and Bradburn, 1989: 8)

The above story reveals that a small change in wording can cause large differences in meaning and therefore in responses. At this stage we should also decide whether we should have 'Yes' and 'No' questions, where the respondent has to take a position. Moreover, in questions where the respondent has to rank answers, we need to decide what type of scale we should use. For example, should we use the scale shown in Figure 8.8 or say: 'Please rank your answer on the scale of 1 to 10, where 10 is the most important or positive'?

8.5.2 Guidelines for constructing questionnaires

Considering the above, we provide some guidelines for the construction of questionnaires.

1. The questions must be asked in very *simple and concise language.* One should consider the respondent's background when it comes to educational level, cultural background, knowledge and acquaintance with the subject matter. The questions should then be adjusted and adapted to the above-mentioned characteristics of the respondents. Not only the questions but also the option answer provided (in the case of a structured questionnaire) should use clear and unambiguous language.
2. We should be rather conservative as to the level of knowledge, education, etc. necessary for the respondent to answer the question. We should not put an *unrealistic demand* on the respondent's know-how, memory and willingness to respond.
3. Each question should deal with only *one dimension* or aspect. If we mix up several dimensions or aspects of questions in one question, it will be difficult for respondents to explain their behaviour or to answer 'yes' or 'no'. In other words, one cannot ask one question about more than one variable or dimension of the study. Each variable and dimension should be covered by a separate question. It is quite common to ask several questions on one variable or to have each question cover different dimensions of the subject

123

Question: *Who are the primary users of your exported products/services?*

Industry	Individual consumers	Government	Don't know
☐	☐	☐	☐

Question: *Do you consider exporting is or will be a major business activity of your company?*

Yes	Don't know	No
☐	☐	☐

Figure 8.9 Examples of escape routes

matter. In other words, avoid '*double-barrelled' questions*, such as: 'What is the turnover of your company and how much of that comes from export?' or 'What is your educational background and how long have you been working in this position?' One way to do this is not to use 'and' in any question.

4. The questions should be formulated in such a way that there is no *escape route* in the questions. We should not offer an option such as 'Don't know' or 'No comment' (see Figure 8.9).

5. Moreover, the questions should be *specific* and not too general in nature so that the respondent does not give several answers. If we must have general questions, we should check the understanding of these questions through another question. The more specific and concise the questions are, the easier it is for us to interpret these questions and answers in different categories and then draw conclusions.

6. The questions should *not be of a suggestive nature*, directing the respondent towards an answer or a specific opinion. For example, we cannot ask a high-tech or a pharmaceutical company the following question: 'Do you consider R&D important for your type of company?'

7. Questions should be formulated in a *polite and soft* language. They should not irritate, offend or provoke the respondent. It is very important to place the sensitive questions, if any, at the right place in the questionnaire, so that the respondent can understand why that particular question is being asked. But, in any case, there must be a logical and systematic sequence of questions to avoid misunderstandings and to ensure a high response rate. We must keep in mind that the respondent, by answering the questions, is doing us a favour.

8. The language and words used in the questions should be *straightforward* and should not have double or hidden meanings, otherwise the respondents will answer the questions with a different understanding and will thereby contribute negatively to the conclusions of the study. Another risk is that the respondent, if not sure of the question's meaning, will leave the question

unanswered. For example, it will be quite difficult for a respondent to understand what you want to know by the following question: 'What type of structure does your company have for export activities?' or 'What are the major barriers to entry faced by your company in international markets?' If one is using complex wording or concepts, a note describing or clarifying the exact meaning of the text should be added to the question. Several authors (e.g. Cannell et al., 1981) have advocated that an explanation or argument as to why that particular question is being asked gives a better response rate.

9. Questions should be placed in a *'right' order*. The easy-to-answer questions and positive types of questions should be placed first. If we place the complicated or difficult questions first – for example questions for which the respondents need to consult books or managers/colleagues – they might get the impression that all the questions are of that nature and thus refrain from responding at all. The same is true for sensitive questions. There should also be a logical order from general to specific questions.

10. The layout of the questionnaire is also important. It should look *neat and tidy* as this can influence respondents' willingness to answer. The questionnaire should be formatted and printed in a way that does not look frightening, due to its length or complexity to understand and answer.

11. Last but not least, we should go through the questionnaire critically or have a friend, colleague or adviser do this and give comments. The best way to handle this is to do a *pre-test* on three to five real companies or respondents. In such a pre-test we should check whether the above-mentioned issues such as understanding, the level of difficulty, the willingness to answer sensitive questions and the time it takes to answer the questionnaire are as we wish.

8.6　Interviews

Interviews demand real interaction between the researcher and the respondent. To be able to run the interview efficiently and without any disturbances, the researcher needs to know the respondent, his background, values and expectations. At present, we have enough accumulated experience available to be able to carry out efficient interviews. Interviews are often considered the best data collection methods. This can be done via mail, telephone or in person (see Figure 8.10).

Figure 8.10 **A typology of interviews**

In research we use two types of interview. The first is survey research or *structured* interviews, where a standard format of interview is used with an emphasis on fixed response categories and systematic sampling and loading procedures combined with quantitative measures and statistical methods. The second type is *unstructured* interviews, where the respondent is given almost full liberty to discuss reactions, opinions and behaviour on a particular issue. The interviewer is there just to give lead questions and to record the responses in order later to understand 'how' and 'why'. The questions and answers are often unstructured and are not systematically coded beforehand.

In the literature there is some discussion on *semi-structured* interviews, which differ from both unstructured and structured interviews. They differ from the former in the sense that the topics and issues to be covered, sample sizes, people to be interviewed and questions to be asked have been determined beforehand. They also differ in the way in which we plan to minimize bias. In semi-structured interviews we handle bias by careful design of the technique itself: bias arising from the sequence in which we address subject matter, from any inadvertent omission of questions, from unrepresentative sampling and from an uncontrolled over- or under-representation of sub-groups among our respondents. Semi-structured and unstructured interviews differ from structured interviews in that they demand greater skills from the interviewer, as in semi-structured and unstructured interviews we often obtain information about personal, attitudinal and value-laden material, that call for social sensitivity. An advantage of structured interviews lies in the uniformity in the behaviour of interviewers, as those other than the researcher can replicate the interview in similar situations. Unstructured interviews are considered advantageous in the context of discovery. Then the researcher/interviewer who is well acquainted with the research questions/area can ask subsequent questions and enrich the data so collected (Phillips, 1966).

There is an abundance of literature available on structured vs. unstructured or semi-structured interviews when it comes to the question form and respondent understanding (e.g. Schuman and Presser, 1976; Beza, 1984; Mishler, 1986; Fowler and Mangione, 1990; Jankowicz, 1991; Yin, 2003; Bryman and Bell, 2003). Anybody interested in this discussion should consult any of the references cited, as our purpose here is to provide some guidelines for interviewing. For the purpose of this book, interviews refer to face-to-face verbal exchanges, in which one person, the interviewer, attempts to obtain information or opinions or beliefs from another person, the interviewee.

The *advantage* of in-depth interviews is that we can gain a more accurate and clear picture of a respondent's position or behaviour. This is possible because of open-ended questions and because respondents are free to answer according to their own thinking, as we have not constrained answers by only a few alternatives. This is also true in the case of complicated or sensitive issues, where the interviewer can ask for further elaboration of answers and attitudes. This method of data collection is highly suitable for exploratory and inductive types of study as it matches their purposes very well.

Example

An interviewer starts by asking: Could you please tell me about your experiences with your new computer?
Respondent: At first I had a lot of trouble.
Interviewer: What trouble?
Respondent: It was difficult to operate, it was different from my old computer.
Interviewer: How?
This hypothetical example reflects that the respondent feels unsure and uncomfortable learning to use a new computer.

The *disadvantage* of in-depth interviews is that they demand a skilled and cautious interviewer. The interviewer should have a complete understanding of the research problem, its purpose and what information is being sought. The course of the interview is decided by the skills of the interviewer when asking questions and probing further with supplementary questions. The know-how and skills of the interviewer are thus of the utmost importance. Interviews can also take a long time – longer than filling in structured questionnaires – and may even require several sessions with the same respondent (Churchill, 1999). In addition, interviews are difficult to interpret and analyse. Our own background may greatly influence the interpretations, thereby causing problems of objectivity. Depending upon which type of analysis we want to do, coding of in-depth interviews is a difficult task in spite of improved techniques and systems.

8.6.1 Preparing for an interview

The first steps in preparing for an interview are to: (1) analyse your research problem, (2) understand what information you really need to have from an interviewee, and (3) see who would be able to provide you with that information. The clearer the problem statement is, the easier it is to know what to ask. It is understood that the purpose of data collection through interviews is to obtain valid information from the most appropriate person. In other words, you should clearly know what you want to ask as well as who are the persons who can provide the most relevant and valid information on those issues (Buckley, 1983). Moreover, the interviewee should be willing to answer your questions truthfully. For example, you cannot expect everyone to be honest on very sensitive matters.

The next step is to draft an *interview guide* or *interview questions*. These questions should be compared with the research problem several times, partly to test the consistency between the two and partly to see whether these questions are thorough and correct enough to find out what you want. It is very useful to let somebody else (perhaps your supervisor) see the problem statement and the questions to be asked in the interview to check this congruence.

After the above scrutiny, a first draft of the interview questions should be prepared. This draft has to be pre-tested as a *pilot study*. While the above scrutiny dealt with the researcher's understanding of the research problem and the interview questions, this test checks the understanding of the interviewee regarding the research problem and interview questions. Such pilot research also provides first-hand insight into what might be called 'cultural endowment' of the informants. After this pilot study, where a few respondents (say three to five) have been asked to read the research problem and the interview questions, and have also answered the questions and have commented on their understanding of them, you can prepare the final draft of the interview guide and questions.

At this point, particular attention has to be given to the approach you are going to use: for instance, before contacting the interviewee you have to decide *how much time* the interview should take. The pilot study can help you to determine the time needed for your questions. You must take into account that business executives work with the belief that 'Time is money' and might refuse to offer an interview only because of the shortage of time. Our experience shows that an interview should not take more than one and a half hours; ideally it should take around an hour. However, the total meeting time can be two hours or more. In many cases the interview is preceded or followed by a factory visit or lunch. In open-ended interviews you can get a lot of information during these.

In this respect it is very important to realize that the interviewer has to *create a situation* where the respondent willingly offers time. If the respondent is not sufficiently motivated to provide you with time, there will be little innovation to answer your questions and to be an interviewee. This can jeopardize the whole purpose of the interview.

Once you have considered all aspects and *prepared the interview guide*, you should approach the person(s) you want to interview. Here you can use the telephone or write a letter, perhaps both. In the letter, for example, you can explain the purpose of your study, provide a short problem statement and describe the type of information you are interested in collecting. In this letter you may also mention that you will be calling very soon (next Monday, next week, etc.) to request an appointment for an interview. In the letter or telephone call you should also mention how much time you think the interview will take. You must

---

Box 8.1 Getting an appointment for an interview

'Hello, my name is . . . I'm working on my Master's thesis on new product development. Last week I sent you a letter with some information on my project, which I think will be of interest to your company, and I would like very much to have an interview with you.'

Manager: 'It sounds interesting, but it is very hectic here, and I'm short of time.'

Student: 'I understand the situation, but the interview will not take more than an hour.'

Manager: 'Well, let me see, can you meet me at my office on Monday at 9am?'

Student: 'Thank you, I will be there on time.'

remember that you cannot demand a certain time, day or week for the interview: you have to adapt to the interviewee's schedule and not the other way around.

One important issue that you have to be clear on before you contact the interviewee is how you are going to *record the information* you will get. There has been a lot of discussion on how to record information, and it is widely accepted that tape-recording is a useful method. The disadvantages with tape-recording are that the respondent might hesitate or even not answer some questions which are sensitive, and there is a risk that, while tape-recording, the interviewer might cease to listen carefully, believing that all the information is going on to the tape and will be listened to later in a more relaxed environment. It is therefore recommended that some note taking, together with tape-recording, is most useful (see Lofland, 1971 for further discussion).

When you make the approach for an appointment, you will have to *inform the respondent* whether or not you will be using a tape or video recorder. In fact, instead of informing, you should ask whether or not you can use the tape recorder. This issue automatically leads to the question of *confidentiality*. You will have to ask if the interview is to be treated confidentially and you will have to give your promise (undertaking or personal guarantee) that all information you receive will be kept confidential. If necessary, you may send a written assurance of confidentiality, signed by yourself and your supervisor or any other responsible person from the school, for example the director of research.

When making an appointment, you should also remember that you have *to create a reason or a reward* for the respondent – why should they answer your questions? What is in it for them? For example, you can mention that the results of the study will be provided to the respondent, or that these results would hopefully help in analysing a competitive/managerial position that he/she/the company in question would benefit from. Or perhaps the study would help the industry or the country as a whole or it would help the policy makers in their job and thereby indirectly the firm in question. Another way to show your appreciation is to take a token gift such as a pen with your school's logo or a visiting card holder with your school's logo.

Now that you have the appointment, it is time to decide who is going to do the interview: one person or more, the same person doing all the interviews or different people interviewing different companies/managers. If several interviewers are used, they have to be trained. In structured interviewing, where it is common to use a number of people as interviewers, each interviewer has to be trained. Once you have taken an appointment and cleared matters such as the amount of time to be used, tape-recording or not, etc., you should send a *confirmation letter* about the appointment, thanking the interviewee for giving you the opportunity to visit them and saying you look forward to seeing them on the agreed date. This is necessary to avoid any misunderstandings on date or timing, and also to remind the interviewee.

Before closing the preparation section, we would like to discuss what you need to do before you start making appointments and interviewing. It is very important to analyse, discuss and consider *resources available* to you for performing these interviews. You have to consider all the costs: for example travelling costs, the time necessary for the interviews, and also the time you need to process the interviews. We have seen a number of examples where the researchers start a very ambitious interview process and after a couple of interviews, or after about 50 per cent of their planned interviews, they give up due to travelling expenses, the time consumed or loss of interest. We have seen several students start their research interviewing, spending two to four hours at each interview, tape-recording everything and ending up with several hours of information. But when they started listening to the tapes (which is a very time-consuming and tedious job) they did not know what to do with all the information, and in fact reported that they had used less than half of the interviews they recorded. The best way to handle this issue is to discuss these matters with your supervisor before you start interviewing and stick to a model or interview.

8.6.2 Pre-interview

The appointment has been made with the respondent and now, together with your supervisor, you have to review the questionnaire. Here you must consider the data collection dimension, how you are going to use the responses for the analysis in your report, and how you want to present the information you are gathering. You also have to schedule your time properly. If you are having more than one interview per day, you should *plan your time*. This is particularly important when you are in a foreign environment or if you are in a strange city, as you must also consider how much time you need to arrive at the location from your hotel, especially in the rush hour. The interviewees have limited time and are always very busy. If you have already informed them that you need one hour of their time, you cannot arrive half an hour late and give the excuse that the journey took longer than you thought, or that you were stuck in traffic, or could not find a taxi.

Another important issue is one of 'social conventions', meaning how you behave in the interview, how you should dress, and so on. It is advisable to be reasonably formal. If you go in shabby clothes or worn-out jeans you may not give a positive impression to the interviewee with regard to your seriousness and the fact that you can do worthwhile research, and thereby may be of some help to the company. It is also wise not to 'party' the night before. It would not be a good idea to go for an interview smelling of alcohol or half-asleep.

Finally, we believe that interviewing is a skill you should *rehearse* or *practise* with regard to understanding, time taken, your own arguments and questions, etc. Find a 'victim', such as a friend, and *practise*. If there is the slightest risk that the respondent may misunderstand something, then they probably will. Moreover, it goes without saying that you must check and recheck the equipment you are going to use in the interview, such as the tape or video recorder.

Dress properly and check your timing, questions and recording material.

8.6.3 The interview

The first important issue here is to introduce the study and its purpose and *to orient the respondents*. The interviewer should be able to answer clearly all the questions the respondents might have, such as: Who would benefit from the study? When will the final report be ready? Will they get a report or not? Moreover, the interviewer should reinforce the confidentiality, if required, to the respondent's satisfaction. At this stage it is important to realize that the respondent is asking the questions and the interviewer has to provide satisfactory answers. These introductory five to ten minutes can be a determining factor in how the rest of the interview goes.

The language used in these early minutes and in the subsequent interaction is of great importance. The interviewer has to use *simple and understandable language*, being extra careful when using certain terminology or concepts from a particular discipline, such as finance or management. It is quite possible that business executives, although they might have been working in the field for several years, will not be familiar with textbook terminology. This point is even more important when the interview is taking place in another environment or country. In that case, it is not only the terminology you have to be careful about, but also the language as a whole. You have to be sure that the language and the level of language you are using is compatible with the respondent's knowledge and usage of the same language.

The interviewer, irrespective of questioning technique, must leave it *entirely to the informant to provide answers* to questions. In other words, the questions should not be asked in a leading or directive manner, as this puts pressure on the respondent to answer in one particular way or even to give the answer she/he thinks you want to hear. For example, do not pose questions such as: 'You must have realized that . . .' or 'How could you . . . ?' Moreover, it is important that the interviewer, every now and then, expresses an understanding of what the interviewee is saying. A nodding of the head or a 'hmm' from time to time gives the impression that the interviewer understands what is meant. For the interviewee to keep on asking and answering questions, the interviewer has to show interest and enthusiasm in the respondents and their 'story'.

Although it is advised that the interviewees are given full freedom to express personal meanings and give their own answers, it is quite important that the interviewer controls the situation so as to get the relevant information. Therefore, *control with some care* is necessary, not only to get the relevant information but also to manage the time. The interviewee has to be given reasonable time for each question and should not be interrupted every now and then. However, business executives or other respondents often like to talk at length about their experiences and know-how, especially about positive events, and should therefore be controlled, but with care.

> ### Box 8.2   Managing the interview
>
> Interviewer: 'You have allowed one hour for this interview. I've read annual reports and inspected your homepage. Could you first tell me about what you consider to be the major reasons for your company's success in the past?'
>
> Manager starts by explaining in detail the firm's history and his role.
>
> Interviewer: 'This is interesting, but could you tell me a little more about the development case you just mentioned?'

Controlling time is very important, as the interviewee has given you a certain time and may be interested in talking a lot on each and every issue. You must ensure that you have answers to all of your questions within the specified time. If the time agreed upon beforehand was between 9 and 10.30 am, it is quite possible that at 10.30 the interviewee has to go to a meeting and just stops talking and asks you to leave, or a number of people enter the room to have a meeting, giving you only one option, to leave.

You also have to, in a way, *develop a relationship* with the interviewee. That is why we stress taking great care in the opening minutes of the interview. You must be able to give the impression of a serious, trustworthy and friendly person. The relationship can also be developed by expressing interest in the interviewee's position and opinion and by appreciating his/her point of view. The better the relationship between the interviewer and the interviewee, the more open the responses and the more useful the information you get. This is also important in case you have not been able to get all the information, due to time or any other reason, or if you would like to have some additional information later on. If the interviewee enjoyed talking to you, s/he would definitely not mind having another meeting with you or offering you a factory visit or lunch. These are excellent opportunities to develop trust, friendship and a positive relationship with the interviewee.

You should be *careful about sensitive questions*. Many times it is just a question of phrasing or using the right language to make the questions less sensitive. Sometimes, the questions are of a sensitive nature but must still be asked. Here the interviewee should not be pressured to provide a definite yes or no (admit it . . .) answer. Questions regarding why a certain strategy or plan failed, about competitors and their success or about some financial issues can be of this nature. For example, while interviewing a bank manager the following question can be quite sensitive: 'Who is responsible for all the bad debts reported by your branch/ office?' The same question can be asked in another way; for example: 'What, in your opinion, are the factors that caused the bad debts reported by your branch/ office?' It is advisable to avoid any direct questions on who was responsible for a certain blunder or miscalculation. Questions regarding intra-organizational conflicts should be asked with some care and with indirect language.

8.6.4 Post-interview

After coming back from the interview, you should *write down the important points* from the interview as well as notes on the practical details. This can include whether you were able to get all the answers or how much time it took, some opinions on the respondent, such as very open or reserved person, and also your perception of your interaction and relationship with the interviewee. All these details will help you later when you listen to the recorded tape or when you sit down to write up the information you collected. Most of all, it will help you in case you need to have additional information. In case the interview was not recorded, it is recommended that you go through the notes and write a complete, descriptive report of the interview immediately (or as soon as possible) after the interview.

The second thing you have to do is to write a *'thank-you' letter* to the respondent. You may also send some further information on your research project which you might have promised or realized in the interview that they would like to have.

Reporting or transcribing an interview is an important and tedious job. As mentioned earlier, interviews that are not recorded should be written as a narrative story as soon as possible. For structured interviews, you should check your forms to see if they are completely and properly filled in. The interviews that are recorded always need some supporting material to remind you of the situation and the feeling of the interview. The best way is to first write down all the information on the tape in the same order, and later develop a descriptive report of the interview relevant for the study. In this second stage you can discard all irrelevant talk and information.

Sometimes it is useful to send this descriptive report to the interviewee for comments. You might have misunderstood something or perhaps you are not sure what the respondent really wanted to say. Depending upon your relationship with interviewees, they might like to see what they said and, quite often, they give additional information or clarify their message voluntarily.

Go through your interview notes promptly.

8.7 Focus groups

Focus groups, as a data collection method, take many different forms, such as discussion groups, focused interviews, group interviewing and group research, and are often used in business studies, for example for programme evaluation, marketing, advertising and communication. By focus group we mean a small group of people interacting with each other to seek information on a small (focused) number of issues (Stewart and Shamdasani, 1990; Bryman and Bell, 2003).

In this method the group interviewed should be a small number of individuals, normally from six to around ten people, who discuss a particular topic/issue under the direction of a moderator, who keeps the discussion on track (focused). Too small (e.g. < 5) or too large (e.g. > 10) numbers can make the focus group ineffective as the participation of individuals can become too fragmented or too little. These groups are arranged and the discussion may last from half an hour to around two hours. The moderator can then observe the interview or group, sometimes without disturbing the discussion.

The moderator plays an important role in keeping the discussion on the focus issue and also in ensuring that it goes smoothly. The role of the moderator is to secure interaction between the focus group members, and see that they address topics believed to be important. Prior to a focus group a list of topics or key words is usually prepared. The moderator's task is to secure discussion on all the topics, but not necessarily in the listed order.

He or she can introduce the topic by asking a series of questions on the topic and then make questions more and more specific as the discussion proceeds. The amount and the nature of direction provided by the moderator influence the quality and depth of data collected. In the worst case, the group discussion might not cover the topic/issue at all. The moderator must therefore properly think through the structure and the nature of direction, in relationship to his or her research questions and purpose.

Although focus groups can produce/provide quantitative data, they are mostly used for collecting qualitative data. One of the conditions is that there should be some homogeneity among the individuals in one specific focus group. In the case where data are to be collected from different groups of people it is often advised that separate focus groups be arranged for different groups/subsets of the population. A homogeneous group will encourage more in-depth and open discussion.

Focus groups normally explore a specific theme or topic, while group interviews can deal with several themes or topics. However, the difference between a focus group and a group interview is not clear cut (Bryman and Bell, 2003); perhaps that is why these two concepts are often used interchangeably. In any case, these methods are frequently used in qualitative research, as the purpose is to understand the views of the participants, which can only be done in an unstructured setting (Merton et al., 1956; Cowley, 2000).

8.7.1 Advantages/disadvantages of focus groups

One *advantage* of the focus group is that it produces very rich and in-depth data expressed in respondents' own words and reactions, which is normally difficult to obtain using other methods such as surveys. It allows the researcher to understand why people feel or behave the way they do. It allows him or her to probe into respondents' views through discussion and reasoning, as in a focus group people can argue with each other's views. This reveals how people really think about different issues.

The main advantage, however, is that it is a quick, flexible and inexpensive method of data collection. It gives the researcher a chance to observe reactions of people in open and free conversation with each other. Further advantages include the fact that it allows the researcher to interact directly with respondents, and to react and build upon the discussion as it goes. Focus groups allow the collection of data from people who are not literate, or from children. The results from data collected in this manner are easy to understand.

The *disadvantages* are that this type of data collection makes it very difficult to summarize and categorize the information gathered. And, as mentioned earlier, in the case of an unskilled moderator, it will be difficult to get really useful information. Other disadvantages include the fact that it can be difficult to gather people at a location, and the small numbers who are willing might not be representative of our population. The responses of the group members are not independent of one another and might be influenced by each other or, as can be the case in such groups, by a dominant group member. The live participation and observation may lead the researcher to have greater faith/belief than is actually warranted. The moderator may bias the respondents, knowingly or unknowingly.

8.7.2 Conducting focus groups

Normally in focus groups researchers record data on paper or notepads. It is becoming quite common to use video recorders that enable researchers to see and analyse the data later on. In the case of several focus groups, the records and notes are then analysed, for example by using content analysis. They then provide a good picture to the researcher. In business studies, focus groups can be particularly useful in the following types of study (Stewart and Shamdasani, 1990: 15):

- obtaining general background about a topic;
- generating research hypotheses;
- stimulating new ideas and creative concepts;
- diagnosing problems/success factors for a new product, service or programme;
- generating impressions of products, programmes, services or institutions/firms;
- learning how respondents talk about the phenomenon, which may help in designing questionnaires or other instruments;
- interpreting previously obtained quantitative data.

Once a clear statement of the problem is generated (see Figure 8.11), it is important to identify the sample from those who are representative of the larger population. The representativeness is most important in this case as we will observe only a few individuals. Having done this, we need to find an appropriate moderator and, with his or her assistance (or keeping that individual in mind as well as our research objectives), formulate an interview guide/questions, as well as the structure of the focus group and how exactly it will be run.

Figure 8.11 Steps in conducting a focus group

Source: Stewart and Shamdasani (1990: 20). Copyright © 1990 by Sage Publications. Reprinted by permission of Sage Publications, Inc.

Further reading

Flick, U. (2009) *An Introduction to Qualitative Research*, 4th edn, London: Sage.

Fontana, A. and Frey, J.H. (1994) 'Interviewing: the art of science', in Denzin, N.K. and Lincoln, Y.S. (eds) *Handbook of Qualitative Research*, Thousand Oaks, CA: Sage, pp. 361–76.

Mason, J. (2002) 'Qualitative interviewing: asking, listening and interpreting', in May, T. (ed.), *Qualitative Research in Action*, London: Sage, pp. 225–41.

Questions

1. When are: (1) quantitative and (2) qualitative research approaches most appropriate?

2. What do you consider to be the major reasons for doing historical reviews?

3. For what research purposes do you consider focus group interviewing appropriate?

4. What is (are) the difference(s) between single case and multiple case study designs? When do you consider: (1) single, (2) multiple case designs to be most appropriate?

5. 'Develop a relationship with the interviewee.' Comment

Exercises

1. You want to understand consumer behaviour towards usage of mobile telephones. You have decided to do that through focus group interviewing. Prepare a focus group interview plan to gain insights into how a group of people experience and use a product (e.g. mobile phones). Draft a letter to explain your plan that you will send to the target group.

2. Draft a letter that you want to send to companies you want to interview/study using the case study method for your research. Formulate a research problem and try to explain that to companies, also convincing them to participate in your study.

3. Referring to exercise (1) above: supposing you are trying to understand consumer behaviour for mobile phones through a survey. Formulate a precise research problem and develop a questionnaire that you can use for this data collection.

4. Visit a store or a marketplace. Observe how people behave and shop.

CHAPTER 9

Sampling in empirical research

9.1 Why take samples?

When the research problem is specified, and an appropriate research design and data collection instrument developed, the next step in the research process is to select those elements from which the information will be collected. One possibility is to collect information from each member of the population. Another way is to collect information from a portion of the population by taking a *sample* of elements from the larger group and, on this basis, infer something about the larger group. For quantitative studies, in particular, sampling is extremely important. A well-known example is an election poll, on the basis of a small fraction of all voters, to infer something of the voting intentions of all potential voters. There are at least two reasons for taking a sample instead of including all *units* or elements: the costs of including all units will often be prohibitive, and the time needed to do so will often be long. For example, if you want to study the problems faced by SMEs (small and medium-sized enterprises) while exporting, you cannot study each and every SME, as even in a small country such as the Netherlands there might be tens of thousands of registered SMEs. You might not have the financial resources and time to visit each of these to get answers to your questions. In this case, you will have to select perhaps a few hundred. The important issue is, however, that the companies selected should be *representative* of the whole group.

It may sound paradoxical, but in some instances samples may be more accurate than censuses. For example, the US Bureau of Census uses sample surveys to check the accuracy of the various censuses.

Population here refers not only to people, but also to firms, products and so on. For example, one may be interested in relationships, so a sample of relationships from a larger population of relationships is examined. Figure 9.1 outlines a useful procedure when drawing a sample.

Deciding on the relevant population is not always easy. The key question is to know who or what one wants information about. For example, a research project is interested in relationships. What is the population – firms or the many relationships that exist between firms, between firms and customers and so on?

A sample frame is (in principle) a listing of units from which the actual sample will be drawn. An example is a telephone book as a sample frame of

Figure 9.1 Procedure for drawing a sample

Source: Based on Churchill (1995: 557), © 1999 South-Western, a part of Cengage Learning, Inc., reproduced by permission www.cengage.com/permissions

households. Often it can be difficult to find (create) a sample frame that perfectly corresponds to the target population of interest. Another example is 'Fortune 500', a list of the 500 biggest companies in the world, compiled by *Fortune* magazine. Terminology and concepts used in this respect are explained in Box 9.1.

9.2 Sampling procedures

Sampling procedures can be divided into two broad categories, *probability* and *non-probability* samples. In probability samples each unit has a *known*, non-zero chance of being included in the sample, which allows for statistical inferences. For example, by drawing a probability sample of voters and asking them about their voting intentions, inferences about voting intention for the population of voters may be drawn.

With non-probability samples, in contrast, it is not possible to make valid inferences about the population. This implies that such samples are *not* representative. By *representative* we mean that what has been found in the sample, for example distribution of voting intentions, is valid – within certain limits – for the population (see section 9.4 and Chapter 10).

Examples of non-probability samples are as follows:

- In a *convenience* sample, often termed an accidental sample, units that we find convenient for some reason are selected. We could, for instance, interview the business executives we happen to know personally.
- In a *judgement* sample, judgement is used to try to get a sample that is representative of the population. We simply try to select units we think are representative of the population.

Box 9.1   Basic terminology in sampling

- *Population* – basically, the universe of units from which the sample is to be selected. The term 'units' is employed because it is not necessarily people who are being sampled – the researcher may want to sample from a universe of nations, cities, regions, firms, etc. Thus, 'population' has a much broader meaning than the everyday use of the term, whereby it tends to be associated with a nation's entire population.
- *Sample* – the segment of the population that is selected for investigation. It is a subset of the population. The method of selection may be based on a probability or a non-probability approach (see below).
- *Sampling frame* – the listing of all units in the population from which the sample will be selected.
- *Representative sample* – a sample that reflects the population accurately so that it is a microcosm of the population.
- *Probability sample* – a sample that has been selected using random selection so that each unit in the population has a known chance of being selected. It is generally assumed that a *representative sample* is more likely to be the outcome when this method of selection from the population is employed. The aim of probability sampling is to keep *sampling error* (see below) to a minimum.
- *Non-probability sample* – a sample that has not been selected using a random selection method. Essentially, this implies that some units in the population are more likely to be selected than others.
- *Sampling error* – the difference between a sample and the population from which it is selected, even though a probability sample has been selected.
- *Non-sampling error* – differences between the population and the sample that arise either from deficiencies in the sampling approach, such as an inadequate sampling frame or *non-response* (see below), or from such problems as poor question wording, poor interviewing, or flawed processing of data.
- *Non-response* – a source of non-sampling error that is particularly likely to happen when individuals are being sampled. It occurs whenever some members of the sample refuse to cooperate, cannot be contacted, or for some reason cannot supply the required data (for example, because of mental incapacity).

Source: Bryman and Bell (2003: 93)

- In a *quota* sample, we just make sure that certain subgroups of units, such as small firms, intermediate firms and large firms, are represented in the sample in approximately the same proportions as they are represented in the population. (For further discussion, see Churchill, 1995: 579–85.)

Non-probability samples are easy to draw, but they may give misleading results if, in spite of our judgement, they happen to be unrepresentative of the population. The major drawback of non-probability samples is that such samples give no basis for evaluating the size of the sampling variation and the error of estimation.

If possible, we should therefore use a probability sample. This is especially important if we want to estimate unknown parameters or draw valid inferences regarding the population on the basis of the sample. It is usually assumed that non-probability samples are not useful in scientific research, meaning that non-probability samples are not valid for statistical testing of hypotheses or drawing inferences regarding a larger population. Non-probability samples may, however, be useful to gain insights into a phenomenon, predominantly in qualitative research.

9.3 Probability samples

Probability samples allow for assessment of the amount of 'sampling error'. For example, if we want to know whether students at our university are satisfied with the courses and teaching methods, we might decide to interview our students to ask for their opinion and level of satisfaction. However, we have 10,000 students in the university and we cannot interview all of them. We believe that, considering the money needed and the time available, we could interview 500 students to draw a reliable conclusion. This means that we need to interview one out of every 20 students, provided each student has an equal chance of being picked for an interview. This will allow us to avoid any sampling error.

9.3.1 Simple random sampling

There are several types of probability samples. The best known is *simple random sampling*. A key characteristic of such samples is that all units in the population have the same chance (probability) of being included. To conduct a random sample the following questions must be considered (cf. Figure 9.1):

1. What is the basic unit to be examined?
2. How should the population, or more precisely the target population, be delineated?
3. What *variables* or *parameters* are of interest? Research results are very often expressed in terms of variables or parameters. *Parameters* describe aspects of variables. The population can be described in terms of variables or parameters. A *variable* can be defined as a set of values related to a population in such a way that each unit has one and only one value from the set. A *value* can be defined as a piece of information regarding a particular aspect of a unit. Typical parameters to be estimated in a sampling survey are population total, population means, population proportions, population variances and population ratios. When more than one variable is involved, additional parameters

141

of interest might be, for example, population correlation coefficients and population regression coefficients.

4. How should the sample be drawn? As noted above, in simple random sampling all units in the population have the same probability of being included. In the case of a total listing of all units, the sample can be drawn as in a lottery. Prepared tables of random digits exist as well.

5. How many units should be included? This is a question of *sample size*, which will be dealt with in section 9.4.

The advantage of simple random sampling is that the method is easy to understand and apply. Drawbacks are, however, that:

- A complete frame (a list of all units in the whole population) is needed.
- In some studies, for example surveys by personal interviews, the costs of obtaining the sample can be high if the units are geographically widely scattered.
- The standard errors of estimators can be high. This is a major reason for applying other sampling procedures, that is to reduce standard errors of estimation for the same sample size.

If the units have quite different values for a variable of interest, simple random sampling can be improved by making the probability of inclusion in the sample proportional to the value of the variable. This is called *sampling with probabilities proportional to size*. Thus, if the units are industrial plants and we want to estimate total consumption of toilet paper in the population of plants, we can make the probability that a given plant will be included in the sample in proportion to the number of workers in the plant. This should work well since consumption of toilet paper is highly correlated with the number of workers.

9.3.2 Systematic sampling

A systematic sample involves selecting every *n*th unit after a random start. For example, a firm wants to estimate the average order size, so it selects a number between 1 and 10 at random, say 7, and then selects every tenth unit: 7, 17, 27 and so on.

A prerequisite for applying systematic sampling is that the units in the population can be ordered in some way. Examples are as follows:

- records that are ordered in a file;
- names that are ordered alphabetically in a telephone directory;
- houses that are ordered along a road;
- customers who walk one by one through an entrance, and so on.

Thus the units in the population can be numbered from number 1 (the first unit) up to unit number N (the last unit). A 10 per cent systematic sample is obtained by drawing every tenth unit in the ordered population. Usually the starting unit is determined by drawing at random one of the first ten units in the population. If we use a percentage other than 10, the procedure is similar.

Advantages: The method is simple, but probably the most important advantage is that a frame is not always needed. The method can therefore be used, for instance, to interview a sample of persons passing by a corner during a particular day. The units in the sample will be spread evenly over the ordered population. Sometimes this will increase precision.

Drawbacks: The most important potential drawback is the danger of hidden periodicities, for example that a deficiency in producing a specific product occurs at specific intervals. If one happens to get an unfortunate starting point the whole sample could consist of defective products.

9.3.3 Stratified sampling

A *stratified sample* is a probability sample, where:

- The parent population is divided into a mutually exclusive and exhaustive subset.
- A simple random sample of units is chosen independently from each subset.

An important reason for stratified sampling is that variability, and thus standard error of estimates, may be reduced.

A *stratum* (plural, strata) is simply a part or subdivision of the population. A stratified random sample is obtained by taking a simple random sample from each stratum. The idea of stratified sampling is to ensure that every part of the population, that is every stratum, gets a better representation. This is especially important if the means (or proportions or whatever we want to estimate) are very different in the different strata. The result will be a smaller sampling variation, that is more stable results in repeated samples than we would get by using simple random sampling.

Proportional allocation means that the proportion of units included in the sample is the same for each stratum.

Example

A company consists of three divisions: A = 1000 employees, B = 500, and C = 750 employees. To study employees' work satisfaction a study is conducted among a sample of 10 per cent of the employees. The study includes 100 employees from A, 50 from B and 75 from C, that is a total sample of 225.

This principle is simple to apply and often satisfactory. It is also possible to take into account the costs of getting observations and to take few units from the strata where the costs are high – for instance because of travelling costs.

Usually a population can be divided into strata in several alternative ways. When applying stratification, it is important to stratify in a fashion that makes the means (or other parameters) rather different in different strata: the more different, the better. Stratified random sampling, as with other sophisticated sampling designs, is usually compared to simple random sampling, which forms a kind of standard.

Advantages: Stratified random sampling can give higher precision with the same sample size or, alternatively, the same precision with a smaller sample. Stratified sampling can also give separate results for each stratum. Stratified sampling also simplifies data collection.

Drawbacks: A complete frame is needed. Depending on the allocation principle applied, additional information, such as knowledge of standard deviations and costs, may be needed for each stratum.

> **If the population can be divided into strata that are homogeneous within but heterogeneous between, precision can be increased or costs lowered.**

9.3.4 Cluster sampling

In *cluster sampling* the population is divided into mutually exhaustive subsets. A random sample of the subsets is selected. If the researcher examines all units in the selected clusters, the procedure is called *one-stage* cluster sampling. If a sample of units is selected probabilistically from the selected subsets, the procedure is known as *two-stage* cluster sampling.

Note the similarities and differences between cluster sampling and stratified sampling. The key ingredient that distinguishes the procedures is that with stratified sampling a sample of units is selected from each subgroup. With cluster sampling one chooses a sample of subgroups. Because one chooses a sample of subgroups with cluster sampling, it is desirable for each subgroup to be a small-scale model of the actual population. Thus in cluster sampling the subgroup should be formed to be as heterogeneous as possible. It is well known that students vary in interests, talents and preparation. In a study on students' working habits, school classes may be considered as clusters.

Advantages: The major advantage of cluster sampling is that we do not need a complete frame of the secondary sampling units. We do need a frame of the clusters, however. Another important advantage in many kinds of cluster sampling such as area sampling is the geographical concentration of the units to be interviewed.

Drawback: If there is large variation between clusters in the variables to be examined the method may yield poor precision.

9.4 Determining sample size

An important and frequently asked question is: What is the sample size needed? As always, the answer is: It depends . . . , or more precisely it depends on the desired *precision* from the estimate. Precision is the size of the estimating interval when the problem is one of estimating a population parameter. For example, a researcher investigating average income wants the sample estimate to be within ±£100 of the true population mean. This is more precise than a requirement to be within ±£200 of the true value.

The concept of *standard error* (of the mean) is central to sampling theory and to determining the size of a sample. The formula for the standard error (*SE*) is:

$$SE = \frac{SD}{\sqrt{n}} \tag{9.1}$$

where

SD = standard deviation (of mean)

n = sample size

Inspection of formula (9.1) shows that to know *SE* we first must know or estimate the standard deviation (for more detailed discussion of the concept of standard deviation, see Chapter 10).

When determining sample size, the degree of *confidence* associated with the estimate also needs to be taken into account. There is a trade-off between degree of confidence and degree of precision with a sample of fixed size. In addition, often budgetary constraints must be taken into account.

Example (population variance known)

Assume that a researcher wants the estimate to be within ±£25 of the true population value. Further, s/he wishes to be 95 per cent confident that the interval ($25\bar{x} \pm 25$) will contain the true population mean. This implies constructing an interval $\pm zSD$ around the observed mean, in which z is approximately 2.[1]

We now see that this can be expressed as

$$H = z \cdot SE \tag{9.2}$$
$$= z\frac{SD}{\sqrt{n}}$$

where H is half of the interval, i.e. 25.

Also assume that early studies have demonstrated the standard deviation to be around 100. Thus:

$$25 = 2 \times \frac{100}{\sqrt{n}}$$

$$\sqrt{n} = 2 \times \frac{100}{25}$$

$$n = 2^2 \times \frac{100^2}{25^2} = 64$$

Note what happens if the estimate must be twice as precise, that is a desired interval $\bar{x} \pm 12.5$:

$$n = \frac{2^2 \times 100^2}{12.5^2} = 256$$

145

Thus, doubling the precision, that is halving the total width of the interval, increased the required sample size by a factor of four.

In our case the standard deviation, SD, and thus the population variance, SD^2, was assumed to be known from a previous study. If this is not the case, the SD must be estimated (see Chapter 10).

Example (proportions)

Often the population proportion, π, is another parameter of interest, for example percentage of voters, percentage with a specific interest and so on.

The distribution of sample proportions (π) is centred about the population proportions. The standard error of a proportion SD_p is given by:

$$SD_p = \sqrt{\pi(1-\pi)/n} \tag{9.3}$$

To estimate the required sample size, we need, as in the former case, to decide on the precision and confidence wanted:

$$H = zSD_p \tag{9.4}$$

(where H is half of the interval, that is 25)

$$= z \cdot \sqrt{\pi(1-\pi)/n}$$

Let us assume that a political party wants to conduct a poll to estimate the percentage voting for the party within ±2 percentage points and that the party wishes to be 95 per cent confident of the result. Also assume that the percentage voting for the party is believed to be 40 per cent. To estimate the required sample size, an estimate of the proportion is also needed. To estimate the sample size, we apply formula (9.4) and solve the equation. As H only represents the half of the interval, it must be multiplied with 2.

$$n = \frac{2^2}{H^2}\pi(1-\pi)$$

By using our information we get:

$$n = \frac{2^2}{0.02^2}(0.40)(1-0.40)$$

giving $n = 2400$.

Closer examination of this example shows that required sample size is influenced by desired precision. Table 9.1 illustrates this.

As you have probably noticed, in our calculation of sample size the size of the population was not taken into account. This is because the sample represents a small fraction of the total population. This can be seen by inspecting the formula for standard error taking the finite population factor into account.

$$SE = \frac{SD}{\sqrt{n}} \cdot \sqrt{\frac{N-n}{N-1}}$$

Table 9.1 Sample size is influenced by the desired precision

Observed proportion	50 per cent	
Interval	± 2 SD	Sample size
	± 10	100
	± 5	400
	± 2.5	1600

where N = population and n = sample size. The factor $(N - n)/(N - 1)$ is the finite population correction factor. When the sample represents a small or modest fraction of the population the estimates become correct. We also see by employing the correction factor that the standard error becomes smaller.

Non-response

We should always remember that results from probability samples are uncertain, and that the reliability of such results can be calculated and will improve with the sample size. Sudman (1976: 87) gives a table showing typical sample sizes that have been used in various kinds of investigation (see Table 9.2).

A serious potential threat to the validity of results from sampling surveys is *non-response*. When some units that have been drawn for inclusion in the sample do not respond to our questions, the effective sample size is *reduced*. But this is not the main problem, since it can easily be remedied. Thus, if we need a sample of 400 units and we expect a 50 per cent response rate, we could take a sample of 800 units to counteract the non-response.

The real problem with non-response is that those who do not respond are usually *different* from those who do respond, and thus there will be no guarantee that the sample is representative for the population. To take an extreme example, suppose we use a mail questionnaire to learn something about consumption patterns for alcoholic beverages. The majority of the real drinkers will probably not respond for several reasons, but they make up an important part of the whole picture. Therefore it is very important to get responses also from the drinkers who

Table 9.2 Typical sample sizes for studies of human and institutional populations

Number of subgroup analyses	People or households		Institutions	
	National	Regional or special	National	Regional or special
None or few	1000–1500	200–500	200–500	50–200
Average	1500–2500	500–1000	500–1000	200–500
Many	2500+	1000+	1000+	500+

Source: Sudman, S. (1976: 87). Copyright © 1976, with permission from Elsevier have been picked out by our sampling procedure. For further details regarding how to deal with the problem of non-response, see Churchill (1995: 652–88). Non-response and other non-sampling errors are often more threatening than statistical errors.

9.5 Sampling in qualitative research

Sampling is primarily associated with quantitative research, emphasizing estimation of various parameters, testing hypotheses and so on. Samples consisting of one or more units of observations (and analysis) are, however, always applied in qualitative research. In quantitative empirical research an important purpose is to arrive at statistically valid conclusions, for example that on a statistical basis we can conclude that 'X' and 'Y' covary. In other words, statistical conclusion validity plays a major role in quantitative research. For example, if a study of the effectiveness of a new medical drug cannot demonstrate that the drug is effective (or more effective than another drug), no conclusions can be drawn on either internal or external validity.

In qualitative research the purpose is seldom to arrive at statistically valid conclusions (even though it is possible), but rather to understand, gain insights and create explanations (theory). However, in qualitative research sampling issues are also important, such as who and how many should be included.

Example (understanding purchase decisions)

In a qualitative study the objective is to gain insights into who influences purchase decisions. To obtain these insights the researcher has to consider who is involved, and who possesses (and is willing to share) the needed information, which implies selecting the most relevant respondents (subjects). In this effort the researcher may start with one person, for example the manager of the research department, and by asking about specific purchases, and also asking: 'Were other people involved?', will thus gradually uncover participation and influences in buying decisions.

Example (opinions)

Focus groups are often used to gain insights into various perspectives and opinions. How many focus group interviews should be conducted? Let us assume that the researcher starts with one focus group, and the data are transcribed and analysed. Then s/he conducts another focus group interview, and that also uncovers points of view not present in the first one. The researcher continues the procedure until no new opinions/points of view are uncovered.

This way of reasoning corresponds to the idea of *sequential* sampling: that is, one continues to add observations until a (final) conclusion is arrived at.

Theoretical sampling

In any study variability is needed. Consider a study designed to examine the (potential) relationship between organizational form and innovativeness. In order to study this research question variability of organizational forms of the firms (organizations) included is needed. Let us also assume that the researcher, based on a review of the literature, knows that forms, $F_1, F_2 \ldots$ exist. This insight is then useful when deciding on which firms (organizations) should be included. We see here that the sample units are chosen for theoretical reasons. Our discussion above also reveals that purposeful, non-probability samples are often applied in qualitative research.

Note

1. By inspecting a table of the normal distribution it is seen that the correct value is 1.96 to capture the 95 per cent interval.

 Further reading

Churchill, G.A. and Iacobucci, D. (2002) *Marketing Research: Methodological Foundations*, 8th edn, Mason, OH: Thomson Learning (Chapter 10).

Saunders, M.N.K., Lewis, P. and Thornhill, A. (2000) *Research Methods for Business Students*, 2nd edn, Harlow: Prentice Hall.

 Questions

1. What distinguishes probability and non-probability sampling?

2. Explain what is meant by a: (1) convenience and (2) quota sample.

3. What is a stratified sample?

4. Sampling is often associated with quantitative and survey research. Is it important in qualitative research based on in-depth interviews? If yes, give examples; if not, why not?

Exercises

1. A grocery store wants to know where it attracts customers from. It has no register of its customers. Suggest a sampling procedure allowing insight into this question.

2. Suggest, step by step, how you would select:
   (a) a sample of 150 students at your college and university;
   (b) a sample of male and female workers to compare hourly wages in (select job/work).

CHAPTER 10

Preparation and analysis of data

Teach us to count our days that we may learn to be wise.

(Psalms, 90 v. 12)

In this chapter we explain how to prepare and analyse data. The purpose of analysis is to obtain meaning from the collected data. All previous steps in the research process have been taken to support the search for meaning. The specific proced-ures to be used are closely related to the preceding steps. Ideally, the type of data required and how they will be used should be clarified before collecting them in primary research. This is particularly so when the research problem is structured.

Define your research problem, then collect and analyse the data.

10.1 Editing and coding

The search for meaning can take many forms. However, preliminary steps such as editing and coding are common to most studies.

10.1.1 Editing

The basic purpose of editing is to secure a quality standard for the data. Editing involves *inspection* and, if necessary, correction of questionnaire or observation forms.

For example, careful editing of a questionnaire will sometimes show that an answer to a question is obviously incorrect. How the questionnaire is completed may also reflect whether the respondent has really read and taken the task of answering the questionnaire seriously. A subject who has ticked the extreme positions, for example '1' or '5' on a five-point scale, for all 30 questionnaire items has probably not taken the task seriously, and the value of the submitted information is probably limited.

Inspection of questionnaires or interviews may also reveal conflicting infor-mation. If, for example, a subject is asked whether s/he knows about so and so, and the answer is 'Yes', but later in the interview it is evident that the subject really does not know, the correct answer to the first question is probably 'No'.

10.1.2 Coding

Classification and comparison are essential parts of any type of data analysis. *Coding* can be seen as some sort of classification. The first step in coding is specifying the categories or classes into which the responses are to be placed. There is no definite or 'right' number of categories. Rather, the number of categories will depend on the research problem and the actual data.

The following rules for coding should be followed:

1. The classes (categories) should be mutually exclusive and exhaustive. Every response should fall into one category only.
2. A second step involves assigning numbers to the classes. This is particularly important if the data are to be analysed statistically (see sections 10.3–10.4 and Chapter 11). For example, sex may be assigned as M for male and F for female. Alternatively the classes could be denoted 1 = male and 2 = female.
3. It is usually better to treat numerical data in their reported form than to collapse interval or ratio scales into categories. It is always possible to construct aggregated categories later in the analytical process, but the reverse is not possible. For example, assume that the following categories are used in a questionnaire to code years of age: 1 = under 20, 2 = 20–39, 3 = 40 or more. Let us assume that most of the responses fall into category 2, which does not allow the examination of the potential impact of age. By using the original numerical data one might detect great differences within the age interval 20–39.
4. Coding of closed questions and most scales is simple because the coding is established. The coding of open-ended questions can be difficult, and categories (classes) must be established.
5. For statistical analysis of data to be done by computer it is advisable to follow certain conventions:
   (a) Use only one character per column.
   (b) Use numeric codes only.
   (c) The field or portion of the record assigned to a variable should consist of as many columns as necessary to capture the variable. If the variable is such that the codes from 0 to 9 are not sufficient to exhaust the categories, then two (or more) columns are needed.
   (d) Use standard codes for 'no information', so this can be distinguished from the answer 'don't know'.
   (e) Code on *respondent identification* on each record. For example, the identification 069 on the first record allows the research to link data with data from the second record with this identification.

Developing a *code book* is an important step in the coding process. The code book contains the general instructions on how each item of data was coded (see Table 10.1).

When applying open-ended questions, several answers are often reported. The respondents may give one or more answers, and the combinations of answers

Table 10.1 **Code book format**

Variable name		Column numbers
ID number	Respondent number	1–3
City	City 1 = Chengdu 2 = Guangzhou	4
Q3	Type of store 1 = Supermarket 2 = Seafood retailing 3 = Department store	5
Q4	Outlet part of a chain? 1 = Yes 2 = No	6
Q5	Ownership 1 = Individually owned 2 = Collectively owned 3 = State owned	7

may vary across respondents. For example, assume the following question to a sample of retailers: 'What are you emphasizing in your choice of supplier?' Each answer can be given the codes 1 = present, 0 = absent. Thus the answers to the questions are treated as multiple variables (which can be combined in the subsequent data analysis).

Reliability in coding

Coding should be reliable. In order to examine to what extent this is the case, two (or more) individuals should do the coding of the same data independently. When the amount of data is large it is common to take a sample of the total set of data, say 10 per cent of the completed questionnaires, to be coded independently by two (or more) persons. The *degree of agreement* between the coders is a measure of reliability in coding.

> **Make up a detailed plan of what to do with the data before you code them and put them into data files.**

10.2 The role of statistics

The field of statistics involves methods for describing and analysing data and for making inferences (decisions) about phenomena represented by the data. Methods in the first category are referred to as *descriptive* statistics; methods in the second category are called *inferential* statistics.

Descriptive statistics enable the researcher to summarize and organize data in an effective and meaningful way. Inferential statistics are used to make inferences by interpreting patterns. For example, if we hypothesize that blue-collar workers are less politically conservative than professionals, given that adequate data were collected, we would employ inferential statistics to determine whether differences between the groups support our expectations.

10.3 Analysing one variable

After data have been coded and prepared for processing they are ready for analysis. The researcher's first task is to construct frequency distributions to examine the patterns of responses to each of the variables under investigation. A frequency distribution of a single variable, known as a *univariate frequency distribution*, is a table that shows the frequency of observations in each category of the variable. To construct a frequency distribution the researcher simply lists the categories and counts the number of observations in each.

Table 10.2 shows the distribution of auditing firms by their location. In this case 140 firms have been surveyed. Most firms are found in region D. By dividing by n_0, that is the sample size, the absolute distribution is turned into percentages. For example, for region A the percentage is $15/140 \infty 100 = 10.7$ per cent. Table 10.2 reports the frequency distribution of a categorical or nominal scaled variable (see section 6.2). Frequency tables can of course also be calculated for variables at other measurement levels.

In the above study (see Table 10.2) the firms were also asked about their opinion of 'their most important customer'. One (of several) statements the firms were asked to answer was: 'Information and documentation from this customer is often difficult to understand'. The response format was:

1	2	3	4	5	6
Strongly agree					Strongly disagree

Table 10.2 Frequency distribution of customers' location

(1) Region	(2) Frequency	(3) Percentage
A	15	10.7
B	8	5.7
C	28	20.0
D	79	56.4
E	10	7.1
Total	140	100.0

Table 10.3 **Frequency distribution of degree of agreement**

(1) Degree of agreement		(2) Frequency	(3) Per cent	(4) Cumulative per cent
Strongly agree	1	23	16.4	16.4
	2	71	50.7	67.1
	3	19	13.6	80.7
	4	14	10.0	90.7
	5	11	7.9	98.6
Strongly disagree	6	2	1.4	100.0
	Total	140	100.0	

In Table 10.3 the reported data are at the ordinal level (see section 6.2), which implies that the observations can be ranked. Inspection of Table 10.3 shows that the observations are skewed towards agreement. For example, when inspecting the cumulative distribution it is seen that 67.1 per cent of the observations fall into categories 1 and 2.

10.3.1 Using graphs to describe distributions

Frequency distributions are a useful way to communicate information about their data, for example to the users. In Tables 10.1 and 10.2 the presentation form was numerical. An alternative way of presenting the data is by using graphs. Three of the graphs most commonly used are the pie chart, the bar chart and the histogram. Both the pie chart and the bar chart can be used at the nominal and ordinal levels. The histogram is used to display measure at interval or ratio levels.

The *pie chart* shows differences in frequencies or percentages among categories of nominal or ordinal scaled variables by displaying the categories as segments of a circle. In a survey the following statement was offered: 'The hotel offers value for money'. Responses were given on the scale 1 = to a modest degree, to 4 = to a large extent. The frequency distribution is as follows:

Agree	3
Neither agree nor disagree	17
Disagree	74
Disagree strongly	94
Missing	1
Total	189

This distribution is shown in Figure 10.1.

Like the pie chart, the *bar chart* is a tool for displaying nominal or ordinal data. Bar charts are constructed by labelling the categories of the variables along the

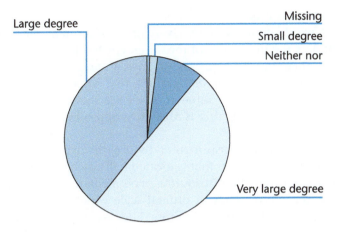

Large degree

Missing

Small degree

Neither nor

Very large degree

Figure 10.1 **Degree of agreement**

Figure 10.2 **Change in performance**

horizontal axis and drawing rectangles of equal width for each category. The height of each rectangle is proportional to the frequency of the category.

Histograms are used to display frequency distributions of interval or ratio level data. A histogram looks like a bar chart with no spaces between the rectangles. Unlike the bar chart, a histogram cannot display information for more than one variable. An example is shown in Figure 10.2. This figure reports answers on the question posed in a survey: 'Has the firm's performance become weaker, the same or better compared with last year's performance?'

Descriptive measures

When only a short summary of the data is needed the entire distribution need not be presented. Here some of the most descriptive measures are discussed.

Measures of central tendency

In section 6.2 we described various levels of measurement. Review Table 6.1, which summarizes the discussion of measurement levels. From this table we see three measures of central tendency: mode, median and mean.

The *mode* is the category or observation that appears most frequently in the distribution. Going back to Table 10.2, we see that region D represents the mode. At the nominal level, this is the only appropriate measure of central tendency.

The *median* is a positional measure that divides the distribution into two equal parts, defined as the observation that is located halfway between the smallest and the largest observation in the distribution. The median is most frequently used to describe the central tendency of ordinal scale variables. For an odd number of cases, the median is the observation $(N + 1)/2$, where N is the total number of cases. For an even number of observations, the median is located halfway between the two middle observations and is calculated as the average of observation $N/2$ and observation $N/2 + 1$.

For Table 10.2 the median is:

$$\frac{140/2 + 140/2 + 1}{2} = 70.5$$

The *mean* (or arithmetic mean) is the most frequently used measure of central tendency. This measure is appropriate for data at the interval and ratio scale levels. The arithmetic mean is defined as the sum of all observations divided by their number, that is:

$$X = \frac{x_1 + x_2 + \ldots + x_n}{N} = \frac{\Sigma x_i}{N} \qquad (10.1)$$

where

X = the arithmetic mean
Σx_i = the sum of all observations
N = the number of observations.

10.3.2 Measures of dispersion

A complete description of any distribution requires that we measure the *dispersion* (or variation) about the central value. Many measures of dispersion exist, valid for both metric (i.e. interval and ratio scaled) and non-metric (i.e. nominal and ordinal scaled) variables. For an excellent discussion, see Weisberg (1992) and Frankfort-Nachmias and Nachmias (1996). Here we will focus on measures of dispersion based on the mean only.

The simplest way to obtain a measure of deviation is to calculate the *deviation* from the arithmetic mean:

$$\text{Average deviation} = \sum \frac{(x_i - X)}{N} \qquad (10.2)$$

where

x_i = each individual observation
X = arithmetic mean
N = number of observations

However, the sum of deviations from the mean is always equal to zero. To compensate for this property of the mean, when squaring the deviations in the above formula, we obtain the *variance, Var*:

$$Var = \frac{\Sigma(x_i - X)^2}{N}$$

The variance expresses the average dispersion in the distribution, not in the original units but in squared units. By taking the square root of the variance we can bypass this problem. This is the *standard deviation (SD)*, expressing dispersion in the original units of measurement. Symbolically, the standard deviation is expressed as:

$$SD = \sqrt{\frac{\Sigma(x_i - X)^2}{N}} \qquad (10.3)$$

When comparing distributions with very different means, we cannot compare the absolute magnitude of the standard deviation. A standard deviation of 3 conveys something different in relation to a mean of 7 as opposed to a mean of 100. Therefore we need to calculate the degree of dispersion relative to the mean, which is reflected in the *coefficient of variation, V*:

$$V = \frac{SD}{X} \qquad (10.4)$$

where

V = coefficient of variation
SD = standard deviation
X = arithmetic mean.

10.3.3 Types of frequency distributions

The next step in describing a distribution is to identify its general form. Distributional forms are multiple. For example, for a dice the distribution is rectangular with the expected occurrence of '1' = 1/6, '2' = 1/6, and so on.

One type of symmetrical distribution, the *normal curve* (see Figure 10.3), is very important in the field of statistics.

The properties of the normal curve are:

- It is symmetrical and bell-shaped.
- The mode, median and mean are at the centre of the distribution.

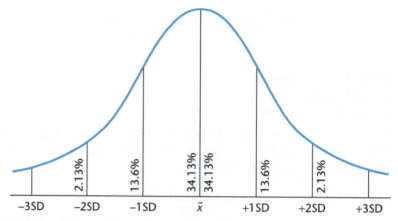

34.13% 34.13%

13.6% 13.6%

2.13% 2.13%

−3SD   −2SD   −1SD   x̄   +1SD   +2SD   +3SD

Figure 10.3 Portions under the normal curve

- The curve is based on an infinite number of observations.
- A single mathematical formula describes how frequencies are related to the values of the variable.

We can use the normal curve to evaluate the proportion of observations included within a desired interval, but the raw scores must be converted to standard deviation units to use the available table reporting areas under the normal curve. (This table is found in any statistical textbook.)

To do so, we calculate the *standard score* by applying the following formula:

$$Z = \frac{x - X}{SD} \tag{10.5}$$

where

Z = number of standard units
x = any observation
X = the arithmetic mean
SD = the standard deviation

Z is often termed the *standard score* and expresses the distance between a specific observation (x) and the mean in terms of standard deviation units. A Z of 2 means that the distance between the mean of the distribution and x is two standard deviations. The proportion included between the mean and Z is given by the following table:

Z	Area
1	0.3413
2	0.4773
3	0.4986

Table 10.4 **Descriptive measures of employment**

Descriptive measures	Employees
Mean	13.29
Median	5.00
Mode	2.00
SD	51.45
Minimum	1.00
Maximum	600.00

Because the normal curve is symmetrical, the table of the curve is only half of the curve's proportions. Thus X ± 1SD covers 0.3413 × 2 = 0.6826 or 68.26 per cent of the area.

Normally distributed variables are assumed in many statistical tests. Measures to capture deviations from the normal curve exist. One is *skewness*, that is whether the distribution is skewed to the left or right. Another is *kurtosis*, capturing whether the actual distribution is more peaked or flatter than the normal curve. The extent to which various statistical tests are sensitive to deviations from the assumption about normally distributed variables differs. Inspect the literature and consult with a statistician when needed. It should also be noted that distributions are multiple, for example the binomial distribution, the *t*-distribution, the χ^2 distribution and so on. Adequate statistical tests for the various distributions are available and are dealt with in statistical textbooks.

In the study referred to above (see Tables 10.2 and 10.3), information about the number of employees for the various firms surveyed was also obtained. Table 10.4 reports various descriptive measures for this variable.

What does Table 10.4 tell you?

10.4 Cross-tabulation

Two (or more) variables are often analysed simultaneously. Suppose, for instance, that we want to study the possible relationship between the level of education of customers and the interest in a certain product. The data can be cross-tabulated as shown in Table 10.5. Here the level of education and the interest in the

Table 10.5 **Product interest by level of education**

		Level of education		
		Low	High	Total
Interest in product	High	53% (40)	48% (60)	50% (100)
	Low	47% (35)	52% (65)	50% (100)
	Total	100% (75)	100% (125)	100% (200)

product have been classified into the two categories 'low' and 'high'. (More categories could have been used for each variable.) Notice that the figures in Table 10.5 are very specific and have been chosen to demonstrate important features.

We want to investigate interest in the product. This variable is therefore the *dependent* variable. Level of education is regarded as an *independent* variable, since it is used to *explain* the interest in the product. In Table 10.5 there is only one independent variable.

For categorical variables, or continuous variables that have been put into categorical form, cross-tabulation is one commonly used method of analysis. In its simplest form, only two variables are involved, so the table becomes a simple two-way table like Table 10.5. Typically, the categories of the dependent variable are assigned to the rows of the cross-tabulation, while the categories of the independent variables are assigned to the columns. If the categories of the variables can be quantified (or ordered), they are often arranged in decreasing order down the page and in increasing order from left to right (the same directions as in a common coordinate system with two axes).

In the cells of Table 10.5 the percentages that sum to 100 for each category of the independent variable give the most important information. Also the counts (frequencies) are shown in parentheses, since they will aid our discussion here. But the total count (total sample size) should always be recorded, since it is needed for judging reliability and performing statistical tests. The cross-tabulation can be interpreted by analysing the pattern of percentages across each row. In the first row, we see that 53 per cent of the persons with low educational level show high interest in the product, while only 48 per cent of the persons with a high educational level show high interest. In the second row, the tendency is the opposite. It is very important, however, to notice that an observed association between variables may be *spurious*, meaning not valid, even if it is statistically significant. This may especially occur if the dependent variable is not logically related to the independent one.

If a second independent variable is added to the analysis, a new table can be constructed and the situation may appear different. Suppose, for instance, that the variable 'sex' is included in Table 10.5. It is then conceivable (although unlikely) that the figures shown in Table 10.6 would be obtained. Notice that

Table 10.6 Product interest by level of education and sex

| | | Female | | Male | | |
| | | Level of education | | Level of education | | |
		Low	High	Low	High	Total
Interest in product	High	80% (20)	80% (20)	40% (20)	40% (40)	50% (100)
	Low	20% (5)	20% (5)	60% (30)	60% (60)	50% (100)
	Total	100% (25)	100% (25)	100% (50)	100% (100)	100% (200)

here, the level of education seems to have no influence on the interest in the product. Sex now explains all the differences.

> **Conclusions based on a cross-tabulation may appear untenable when additional variables are introduced.**

Our example is very specific. In most cases both independent variables will seem to have some effect on the dependent variable. In addition, there may be *interaction* between the independent variables. Interaction means that the effect of a level of one variable (the effect of a high level of education) depends on the particular level of the other variable (whether males or females are considered).

Further splitting of the tables is possible with more independent variables but, usually, at most three or four variables altogether are used. The main reason for this is that the cell counts of some cells will otherwise often be very small or zero because more and more unique cells are being created.

10.5 Test of hypotheses

In research we are often preoccupied with the testing of hypotheses, that is whether an assumed relationship or covariation between variables holds 'true'. For example, in Table 10.5 we assumed a relationship between education and product interest. Testing of hypotheses is particularly relevant in quantitative research, but can take place in qualitative research as well.

To test a hypothesis, for example the assumed relationship between education and product interest (often termed the *alternative hypothesis*, H_A), we confront H_A with the *null hypothesis*, H_0. From this we see that we do not confirm hypotheses per se, but we accept them through falsification: that is, if the null hypothesis is falsified, we accept (at least for a while) the alternative hypothesis.

In the testing of hypotheses we may commit two types of errors: (1) reject the null hypothesis when it is true (Type I error) or (2) accept the null hypothesis when it is false (Type II error) (see Table 10.7).

The probability, α, of rejecting the null hypothesis when it is true is often termed the *significance level*. If the significance level α is $p \leq 0.05$, then we are rejecting the null hypothesis in 5 per cent of the cases when it is correct. The

Table 10.7 Types of errors in hypothesis testing

	True situation: null hypothesis is:	
Conclusion	True	False
Do not reject H_0	Correct decision Probability = $1 - \alpha$	Error: Type II Probability = β
Reject H_0	Error: Type I Probability = α	Correct decision Probability = $1 - \beta$

probability $1 - \beta$ (see Table 10.7) is termed the *power* of the test and reflects a test's ability to reject the null hypothesis when it is false.

A typical procedure for test of a hypothesis is:

1. Specify the null hypothesis after analysing the research problem.
2. Choose an appropriate statistical test, which depends on research design and sampling distribution.
3. Specify significance level (α).
4. Collect data and compute the value of the appropriate test statistic.
5. Determine the probability of the test statistic under the null hypothesis.
6. Compare the obtained probability with the specified significance level, and then decide whether or not to reject the null hypothesis.

Go back to Table 10.5: are the differences in product interest after education statistically significant? The χ^2 (chi-square) test is adequate to examine this. The general formula for this simple test is:

$$\chi^2 = \sum_i \frac{(O_i - E_i)^2}{E_i}$$

where

O_i = number of observations (in category i)
E_i = expected number of observations (in category i)

When looking at the total column, we see that 100 are high and 100 are low in product interest, that is 50 per cent in each category. If we knew only the distribution in the total column and the total in the other categories, what would have been our best bet for the distribution of high and low product interest for low and high education? The answer is:

$$\chi^2 = \frac{(40 - (75 \times 0.5))^2}{75 \times 0.5} + \frac{(35 - (75 \times 0.5))^2}{75 \times 0.5} + \frac{(60 - (125 \times 0.5))^2}{125 \times 0.5}$$

$$+ \frac{(65 - (125 \times 0.5))^2}{125 \times 0.5} \approx 0.533.$$

When using the χ^2 table, degrees of freedom (d.f.), that is the number of cells -1, must be taken into account. For a cross-table this is:

$$(\text{columns} - 1) \times (\text{rows} - 1)$$

that is here:

$$(2 - 1) \times (2 - 1) = 1.$$

Assume that the selected significance level here was $\alpha = 0.05$. Inspecting the χ^2 distribution at the 0.05 level for one degree of freedom, we find the value 3.841. We thus accept the null hypothesis, because $3.841 > 0.533$.

Calculate the χ^2 statistics for Table 10.5. Are the findings significant at the 0.05 level? Observe when we calculate the χ^2 statistic that this is based on the *absolute values*, *not* on percentages. The χ^2 test has many applications, and can also be applied to tables with several columns and rows. Many tests exist to test hypotheses, and hypotheses come in many forms.

Example: the blind test

Assume that a producer wants to compare a new flavour of soft drink with that of the most popular one in a *blind test*. A sample of five subjects receive the new product, marked XZY, and the most popular one, labelled XYZ. Apart from the two almost identical labels, the only difference is the taste, which is the variable to be tested. All five subjects report that they prefer XZY, the new flavour. With no prior information, we assume that for each subject the probability of selecting the new product is $P = 0.5$. The probability that all five subjects should independently select the new product is $P(B = 5) = P^5(i - P)^0 = .5^5 \cdot .5^0 = .03125$. If the chosen significance level was 0.05, the null hypothesis (no significant difference between the products) would be rejected, and the alternative hypothesis (the new product is superior in the test) accepted. You should, however, be aware of the specific assumptions underlying tests such as this. Are there any other factors you would consider before recommending the producer to introduce the new flavour?

10.5.1 A word of warning

Any difference, for example between groups and any covariation between variables (measures) will be detected if measures are adequate and samples are sufficiently large. For example, a correlation between two variables of $r = 0.05$ is statistically significant at the 5 per cent level when the sample size is around 2000. A correlation of $r = 0.05$ counts for $0.05^2 = 0.0025$ of the variance of the variable to be explained/predicted. Is such a small explanatory power at all of interest?

Significance tests are often most interesting when the sample size is small or moderate. When the sample size is large it is often most useful to examine the explanatory power of the variable(s) included (see Chapter 11).

10.6 Use of computers in research

All of us are affected by, and are familiar with, computers. In research, computers play an important role. Even though computer technology has changed dramatically over time, the rationale for the use of computers has remained the same. Computers are tools that help us to *store*, *process*, *access* and *analyse* data more quickly and easily.

Using statistical methods today generally means applying a statistical computer program. Many excellent statistical packages are available both for mainframe and for personal computers. Among the widely used packages are SPSS, SAS, Minitab and many others. Unless you are an advanced user or have very special needs, which is unlikely, it does not matter much which package you are using. Probably the most widely used package today is SPSS (Statistical Package for the Social Sciences). Also notice that the manuals of the major packages contain very useful guidance for the use of the various methods. An example is Field (2000).

Computer-assisted data analysis is time saving and allows for more advanced data analysis.

There are three types of packaged computer applications that are particularly useful:

1. Applications that help to *input your data* in a convenient way in a format suitable for subsequent analysis (see Section 10.1 on coding).
2. Programs that will *carry out the analysis*.
3. Packages that help you to *report* your findings in a written way, either in a written/tabulated form or with the help of fancy graphics.

Data input

An example of a data entry package is *SPSS Data Entry*, which includes user-friendly facilities for data input and editing. In addition to data input itself, this package also makes definition of your variables simpler.

Data analysis

Computer packages handling the actual statistical analysis come in two basic forms: specialised programs, focusing on a particular application, and general programs, offering a wide variety of facilities. There are different versions of most of the well-known programs for mainframe computers and PCs and for different operating systems.

Data presentation

Research findings must be reported. Pages and pages of computer printout are not easily readable. Above we have given examples of how tables and figures can be presented.

Look out: always find out whether your analysis program: (1) can read the data in the format you have used/intend to use, and (2) has the capacity to analyse the number of cases and variables in your data set.

Several of the newest versions of data analysis software are *integrated packages*, for example *SPSS for Windows*, including data definition and input, statistical analysis, and graphics. The advantage is that you need only one piece of software.

Always make back-up copies of your important files.

A word of warning: with computers and program packages available, you will always get computer output. But to get reasonable and useful research results you must have command over the methods you are using and should also know your data well. When you can choose between two or more methods, always use the simplest one that satisfies the research purposes.

Do not make use of methods you do not understand!

 # Further reading

Diamantopoulos, A. and Schlegelmilch, B. (1997) *Taking the Fear out of Data Analysis*, London: Dryden.

Huberman, A.M. and Miles, M.B. (1994) 'Data management and analysis methods', in Denzin, N.K. and Lincoln, Y.S. (eds), *Handbook of Qualitative Research*, Thousand Oaks, CA: Sage, pp. 428–44.

Robson, C. (1993) *Real World Research*, Oxford: Blackwell (Chapter 11).

 # Questions

1. What do you consider to be the key challenges in coding data from an open-ended interview?

2. Explain the concepts of mean, median, mode and standard deviation.

3. Why do questions permitting several responses require special attention during coding?

Exercises

1. A study was designed to estimate the use of a service among a sample of users. The following was found:

Length of use	Assigned value	Frequency
Less than 1 year	1	36
1 to less than 2 years	2	16
2 to less than 5 years	3	26
5 years or more	4	193
Total		221

Calculate mean, median and mode. Also convert into percentages.

2. In a study the following open-ended question was asked among a sample of customers:
'Have you tasted the new cereal brand "X"?'

☐ Yes   ☐ No → Stop
↓

'What do you like about the new brand?'

Establish response categories and codes for the question, and code the following responses:
(1) 'The raisins and nuts add a nice flavour.'
(2) 'It is reasonably priced compared with other brands.'
(3) 'The package is attractive and easy to spot in the store.'
(4) 'The crispness and lightness of the cereal improve the taste.'

PART III

Implementation

Part III deals with the actual processes of conducting data analysis, examining case studies and writing up the report. The chapters (11–14) take you through step by step, providing examples and guidelines. As such, this part can be used as a manual while carrying out the respective activity.

CHAPTER 11

Quantitative data analysis

'You torture the data until they confess.'

(Market researcher)

This chapter deals with some methodological approaches frequently applied to data analysis in business studies as well as other types of research. We first introduce tests of hypotheses about differences. Then we examine whether variables covary and the prediction of relationships. In addition, we discuss methods for data reduction and the extraction of underlying dimensions.

11.1 Examining differences

The question we are asking is whether the research findings can be statistically questioned in business as well as other types of research. For example, if 81 per cent of the sample of 100 customers are satisfied with store A and 71 per cent with store B, is store A more liked?

11.1.1 Hypotheses about one mean

In research we often have to make statements about the mean. We have explained what is meant by standard deviation and Z-score (see section 10.3). When the population variance is unknown, the standard error of the mean is also unknown. The standard error of the mean must be estimated from sample data. The estimate is:

$$SD_X = SD'/\sqrt{N} \tag{11.1}$$

where

SD_X = standard error of mean
SD' = estimated standard deviation
N = sample size

$$SD' = \sqrt{\frac{\sum_{i=1}^{N}(x_i - X)^2}{N - 1}} \tag{11.2}$$

169

The test statistic is t distributed with $N - 1$ degrees of freedom and approaches the normal distribution as the number of observations increases.

Example

For a supermarket chain to add a new product, at least 100 units must be sold per week. The new product is tested in ten randomly selected stores for a limited time. A one-tailed test, that is a test when direction of findings is hypothesized, is appropriate, because it is only when the sales per store are at least 100 that the product will be introduced on a national scale. The null and the alternative hypotheses are:

$$H_0 : X \leq 100$$
$$H_A : X > 100$$

Assume the significance level to be $\alpha = 0.05$: that is, we reject the null hypothesis (H_0) when the probability for the null hypothesis is correct at 5 per cent ($\alpha = 0.05$). The significance level thus tells us at what probability we are likely to commit a wrong decision, that is, accepting the alternative hypothesis when in fact the null hypothesis is true.

By calculation we find that the mean X = 109.4 and the standard deviation $SD = 14.90$.

We also see that the standard error of the mean $SD_X = SD'/\sqrt{N} = 14.90/\sqrt{10 - 1} = 4.55$.

Calculating t we find:

$$t = \frac{X - \mu}{SD_X} = \frac{109.4 - 100}{4.55} = 2.07$$

Critical t (i.e. the required t-value to reject the null hypothesis) as read from the t-table with one degree of freedom is 1.833 ($\alpha = 0.05$).

Here the t test is applied. The t test assumes normally distributed variables, but has been found to be rather robust. When N becomes large, i.e. $N > 30$, the t distribution approaches the normal distribution.

Box 11.1 Hypotheses

Hypotheses play a major role in research. They imply assumptions or beliefs, and are often stated as questions. Is A larger than B? Will the new product sell more than 100 units per week? Hypotheses can (in principle) be tested. In doing so we contrast the hypothesis, for example A is better than B, with the null hypothesis, there is no difference between A and B. To do so we need data on the performance of A and B. If sufficient difference exists we reject the null hypothesis and accept the alternative hypothesis. Thus, we gain insights, through falsification, that is we test our assumption or belief.

11.1.2 Hypotheses about two means

Researchers are often confronted with questions such as: Are the tastes in region A different from the tastes in region B? Does customer segment 1 react in a different way from customer segment 2? Is one promotional campaign more effective than the other? The formula for testing differences between means that are normally distributed, and thus whose differences are also assumed normally distributed, is:

$$Z = \frac{(X_1 - X_2) - (\mu_1 - \mu_2)}{SD_{X_1-X_2}}$$ (11.3)

where:

X_1 = the sample mean for the first sample
X_2 = the sample mean for the second sample
$SD_{X_1-X_2}$ = the standard error of differences in means

μ_1 and μ_2 are the unknown population means.
The general estimate of:

$$SD_{X_1-X_2} = \sqrt{SD_{X_1}^2 + SD_{X_2}^2} = \sqrt{\frac{SD_1^2}{N_1} + \frac{SD_2^2}{N_2}}$$

In assuming the two population variances to be equal, the common population variance can be generated by pooling the samples. When the variances are unknown and the standard errors of means must be estimated, then the t represents an adequate test statistic, distributed with $v = N_1 + N_2 - 2$ degrees of freedom.

Example

A manufacturer has developed a new product and wonders whether the label of the package should be red or blue. The new products with two different labels are tested in ten randomly selected stores. The mean sales obtained for the red package are 403.0 and for the blue package 390.3. The standard error of estimate for the differences in means is 8.15.

Calculate $t = \dfrac{(X_1 - X_2) - (\mu_1 - \mu_2)}{SD_{X_1-X_2}} = \dfrac{(403.0 - 390.3) - 0}{8.15} = 1.56$

This value is referred to a t table for $v = n_1 + n_2 - 2 = 10 + 10 - 2 = 18$ degrees of freedom. The test is *two-tailed* because the null hypothesis is that the two colours are equally appropriate. For $\alpha = 0.05$, and 18 degrees of freedom, critical $t = 2.101$. This means that the null hypothesis is accepted. In the above example we see that $(\mu_1 - \mu_2) = 0$. This is because the two unknown population means are assumed to be the same.

NB: Be aware that in the above example the two samples were assumed to be unrelated, that is drawn independently from each other.

11.1.3 Related samples

Suppose we want to find out whether income has increased from the last year to the present on the basis of variables capturing last year's and this year's income in a sample:

(1) Person	(2) Income last year	(3) Income this year	(4) DIF
1	228	224	−4
2	213	225	+12
3	257	271	+14
⋮			
30	260	292	32

This is often called a two-sample problem with *paired observations*. They are paired because the observations occur in pairs for each individual. To solve this problem we can subtract the values for income last year (2) from this year's income (3) and, as here, create a new variable, denoted differences, *DIF*, placed in column (4).

Notice that the differences, *DIF*, are comparable to the one-sample observations discussed earlier, so the same methods apply.

The null hypothesis, H_0, is that the population mean of differences, the 30 differences in column (4), is equal to zero. The alternative hypothesis, H_A, is that the population mean is greater than zero.

The computer printout from a student's project *t*-test shows that:

$$\text{mean} = 8.13$$
$$SD = 10.91$$
$$\text{St. error mean} = 1.99$$
$$t = 4.08$$
$$p = 0.0002$$

The computed *t*-statistic is 4.08. The corresponding *p*-value, 0.0002, is substantially smaller than 0.05, and therefore H_0 is rejected. In (most) computer programs both the value of the test statistic and the corresponding *p*-value are shown, so we do not have to look it up in the table for the corresponding statistical distribution.

Several useful *non-parametric methods*[1] are also available as alternatives to the classical *t*-methods. These have the advantage of requiring less in terms of assumptions. But if the assumption necessary for using the *t*-test is valid, then it may be preferable, since this test often is more *powerful* by, for instance, giving narrower confidence intervals than the corresponding non-parametric methods. Notice that methods based upon the *t*-distribution are concerned with means, while non-parametric methods are often concerned with *medians*. But if a distribution is symmetric, the mean and the median will coincide.

A simple non-parametric test applicable for the above income problem is the *sign test*. Assume that in the above case of 30 differences, 7 differences were below and 23 above the median. A sign test of the median yields $p = 0.0026$. The p-value indicates a significant difference between this year's and last year's income. The sign test in this example is based on the fact that 7 of the differences are negative and 23 are positive. No other information is utilized. The sign test throws away some of the information contained in the data, as it only takes direction into account (above, below). A parametric test, e.g. the t-test, also takes the absolute differences in scores into account.

> **In problems involving one or two population means, t-methods are usually appropriate, but often non-parametric methods are good alternatives.**

11.1.4 Comparison of more than two groups

In research we are often confronted with comparisons of more than two groups simultaneously. To handle such situations *analysis of variance* (ANOVA) is frequently used. Before explaining this method, we will mention why carrying out several t-tests to compare all combinations of groups is not very appropriate.

Imagine that we are interested in differences between three groups. If we are to carry out t-tests on every group, we must compare groups 1 and 2, groups 1 and 3, and groups 2 and 3. If each of these t-tests uses a 0.05 level of significance, then the probability of falsely rejecting the null hypothesis is 5 per cent and, therefore, the probability of no type I errors is 0.95 in each test. When assuming that the tests are independent, the probability of no type I errors is $(0.95)^3 = 0.95 \times 0.95 \times 0.95 = 0.857$. Now the probability of committing a type I error is $1 - 0.857 = 0.143$, or 14.3 per cent. (This error rate across statistical tests conducted on the same experimental data is known as the experimentwise error rate.)

Analysis of variance rests on comparing the ratio of systematic variance to unsystematic variance. Imagine an experimental study involving the examination of three instructional methods. If the methods vary in effectiveness, one would probably expect less variation in a group having being exposed to a specific type of instruction than across groups. In analysis of variance the following is computed:

1. *total* variation by comparing each observation with the grand mean;
2. the *between-group* variation, computed by comparing the treatment means with the grand mean; and
3. the *within-group* variation, computed by comparing each score in the group with the group mean.

The separate estimates of population variance on the associated mean squares are:

$$MS_T = \frac{SS_T}{df_T} = \frac{SS_T}{N-1}$$

$$MS_B = \frac{SS_B}{df_B} = \frac{SS_B}{k-1}$$

$$MS_W = \frac{SS_W}{df_W} = \frac{SS_W}{N-k}$$

where:

MS_T = the total variation, computed by comparing each observation with the grand or total mean

MS_B = the between-group variation, computed by comparing the means for each treatment group with the total mean

MS_W = the within-group variation, computed by comparing each score within the group with the group mean

Example

Imagine three advertising campaigns tested in 24 randomly selected cities, comparable in size and demographics. Assume the following results from the computer run:

Source of variation	Sum of squares	Degrees of freedom	Mean squares	F ratio
Between group	49.0	2	24.1	5.88
Within group	87.5	21	4.17	
Total	136.5	23		

Degrees of freedom are calculated as follows: total $(24 - 1) = 23$, between group $(3 - 1) = 2$, within group $(23 - 2) = 21$.

The null hypothesis is that the group means are the same, i.e. $X_{G^1} = X_{G^2} = X_{G^2}$, and the critical value is $\alpha = 0.05$. To test the hypothesis, an F-test (based on the F-distribution) is appropriate. The F-test can be considered as a generalization of the t-test and allows for comparison of more than two group means at a time. The F-value is calculated by dividing the between mean squares by the within mean squares, that is $24.5/4.17 = 5.88$. When inspecting a table of the F-distribution, we look up degrees in the numerator (here 2) and the denominator (here 21) and find the value 3.47. Because 5.88 is greater than 3.47 we reject the null hypothesis, that is, the group means are equal, and accept the alternative hypothesis, that is, that the advertising campaigns vary in effectiveness. If we inspect the mean effectiveness score for each of the three campaigns we would also observe which one is the most effective.

NB: In analysis of variance, the dependent variable, here advertising effectiveness, is assumed to be metric, that is interval- or ratio-scaled. The independent variable (here different advertising campaigns) is categorical.

The above is an example of a simple or *one-way* analysis of variance. Only one factor, how advertising campaigns vary, is analysed. Analysis of variance can be extended to include two or more independent categorical variables: for example, students' performance (dependent variable) could be studied as the outcome of different methods of instruction and the instructor's educational background (independent variables). Analysis of variance can also be extended to examine the impact on more than one dependent metric variable simultaneously, termed multivariate analysis of variance (MANOVA) (see Hair et al., 1998 for a detailed description).

11.2 Relationship (covariation) between variables

In research we are often preoccupied with whether there is a relationship or whether two or more variables covary. Several measures of covariation or association exist (see, for example, Frankfort-Nachmias and Nachmias (1996) for an overview of some common measures of associations).

11.2.1 The correlation coefficient

An important measure is the correlation or, more correctly, Pearson product-moment correlation coefficient, r – also mentioned in earlier chapters. The Pearson product-moment correlation assumes (in principle) interval-scale variables. Like other measures of covariation, it considers the joint variation in two measures. The Pearson product-moment correlation examines the strength of the linear relationship between two variables, for example X and Y.

Theoretically, the correlation coefficient can take the values from -1 to $+1$ ($-1 \leq r \leq +1$). A correlation coefficient of $+1$ tells us that two variables perfectly covary positively. A correlation coefficient of -1 shows that two variables are perfectly inversely related. A correlation coefficient close to zero indicates that the variables are unrelated. The formula for the Pearson product-moment correlation is:

$$r_{xy} = \frac{\Sigma(x_i - X)(y_i - Y)}{\sqrt{\Sigma(x_i - X)^2(y_i - Y)^2}} \tag{11.4}$$

where the symbols X and Y represent the sample means of X and Y, respectively.
An alternative way of expressing the correlation formula is:

$$r_{xy} = \frac{\sigma_{xy}}{\sqrt{\sigma_x^2 \sigma_y^2}}$$

where:

σ_x^2 = variance of X
σ_y^2 = variance of Y
σ_{xy} = covariance of X and Y

> A correlation coefficient shows covariation between two variables, and *not* that the variables are causally related.

The square of the correlation coefficient is the *coefficient of determination*, where:

$$R^2 = \frac{\text{Explained variation}}{\text{Total variation}}$$

This implies that if the squared correlation coefficient between X and Y is $R^2 = 50$ per cent, then 50 per cent of the variation in Y is accounted for by variation in X.

Correlations are often used as bivariate tests of hypotheses, that is tests of hypothesized relationships between two variables. From this we see that whether a correlation coefficient is statistically significant depends both on the size of the correlation coefficient and on the number of observations. The standard deviation for the correlation coefficient is $\sqrt{\dfrac{1}{N-1}}$.

Example

In a quasi-experimental study among two groups examining whether the recognition of an advertisement was influenced by advertising appeal (1 = positive, 0 = negative appeal), belief in the advertised product, and sex (1 = women, 0 = men) and where the number of observations = 60, the results shown in Table 11.1 were observed.[2] Inspection of them shows that women are less inclined to recognize the advertisement (see coding), and that women also are less likely to believe in the advertised product. We also see that these findings are significant in the bivariate analysis (the analysis of two variables). In addition, we notice that the positive appeal is more likely to be recognized than the negative one (significant at the 0.05 level).

Table 11.1 Overlap between advertising recognition, sex, belief in the producer, and appeal (r)

	Advertisement recognition	Sex	Belief	Appeal
Advertisement recognition	–	−0.33*	0.25**	0.24**
Sex		–	−0.36*	0.09
Belief				0.14
Appeal				–

* $p \le 0.01$, ** $p \le 0.10$.

11.2.2 Partial correlation

In Chapter 10 (as well as demonstrated in Chapter 5) we discussed how we could exert control with regard to the observed relationship between variables by controlling for a third (or more) variables. This can also be done in correlational analysis, that is *partial correlation*. The formula for the partial correlation coefficient $r_{12 \cdot 3}$ (read the partial correlation between (variable) 1 and 2 'dot' 3) is:

$$r_{12 \cdot 3} = \frac{r_{12} - (r_{13}) \times (r_{23})}{\sqrt{1 - r_{13}^2} \sqrt{1 - r_{23}^2}} \qquad (11.5)$$

The formula is iterative, and thus after controlling for variable 3 subsequent variables can be controlled for.

Example

Is the observed relationship between advertisement recognition and appeal influenced by controlling for sex? In using formula 11.5 we found:

$$r_{Ad.rec.ad.appeals\ sex} = \frac{0.24 - (-0.33) \times (0.09)}{\sqrt{1 - (0.33)^2} \sqrt{1 - 0.09^2}} \approx 0.29$$

This shows that by controlling for sex the observed relationship between advertising recognition and advertising appeal (positive) is strengthened.

11.3 Explaining and predicting relationships between variables

Describing, explaining and predicting relationships between variables are important tasks in business research. For example, a manager might be interested in the relationship between the amount of money spent on advertising and sales, or the relationship between number of sales visits and sales. Such information is important in business because it can lead to better decisions, for example more certainty about how much to spend on advertising.

One of the most applied and useful approaches to examining relationships between variables is regression analysis. In regression analysis we have one dependent variable (i.e. the variable to be explained) and one or more independent variables. Both dependent and independent variables are usually assumed to be metric (i.e. interval- or ratio-scaled). As will be discussed below, so-called dummy variables can also be used as independent variables. In regression analysis (as in many other types of analysis) we want to fit a model that *best* describes the data, which is done in regression analysis by applying the *method of least squares*. More precisely, this is done by fitting a straight line that minimizes the squared vertical deviations from that line as shown in Figure 11.1.

11.3.1 Simple linear regression

It is well known that any straight line can be drawn if you know two things: (1) the slope (or gradient) of the line, and (2) the point at which the line crosses the vertical axis of the graph (known as the intercept of the line).

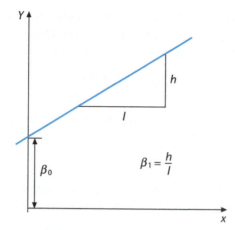

Figure 11.1 The linear model

The equation of a straight line is:

$$Y = \beta_0 + \beta_1 x_i + \varepsilon_i \tag{11.6}$$

Y is the outcome variable we want to predict; x_i is the ith subject's score or the predictor variable; β_1 is the gradient of the straight line fitted to the data, and β_0 is the intercept of that line; ε_i represents the difference between the score predicted by the line for subject i and the score that subject i actually obtained, often termed the *residual*. In regression analysis the estimated regression line reflects the predicted values. If all observed values fall on the predicted line, there are no differences between predicted and obtained values, as shown in Figure 11.1.

Assume a car dealer collects data for six months on four variables: TV advertising, printed advertising, competitors' advertising, and sales, Y. The car dealer expects CarSales to be positively correlated with TV-Ads and Print-Ads. The correlation between CarSales and Comp.Ads is probably negative. But if the advertising of the competitors expands the whole market rather than just changing market shares, the correlation might be positive. The values of the four variables are shown in Table 11.2.

Table 11.2 Data matrix

Row	TV-Ads	Print-Ads	Comp.Ads	CarSales
1	0	1	2	1
2	1	0	0	1
3	2	2	4	2
4	2	3	6	3
5	3	3	3	4
6	4	3	0	4

Table 11.3 **Simple mean regression**

Predictor	Coef.	St.dev.	t-ratio	P
Constant	0.7000	0.4453	1.57	0.191
TV-Ads	0.9000	0.1871	4.81	0.009

$s = 0.5916$ R-sq = 85.3%   R-sq(adj) = 81.6%
The regression equation is thus
CarSales = 0.7000 + 0.9000 TV-Ads

First, we explain the essentials of simple linear regression by assuming that only TV-Ads and CarSales have been observed. We regard CarSales as the dependent variable and TV-Ads as the independent variable. Next, we estimate the simple linear regression function of CarSales on TV-Ads. Table 11.3 gives the results from a computer analysis.

The estimated constant term 0.7000 shows that, if the dealer does not use TV advertising at all (TV-Ads = 0), the estimated expected value of CarSales is 0.7 units, that is seven cars. The estimated regression coefficient of Sales on TV-Ads is 0.9000. This coefficient shows that, if the variable TV-Ads is increased by 1 unit, the estimated expected value of CarSales increases by 0.9 units, that is nine cars. This is useful information to the car dealer. But he should be reluctant to extrapolate: that is, he should preferably not use this information for values of TV-Ads outside the interval from 0 to 4 which is covered by the sample (see Table 11.3).

The result, R-sq, i.e. R^2 = 85.3 per cent, shows that the sample determination coefficient R^2 is equal to 0.853. Practically speaking, this means that the variation in the variable TV-Ads has explained 85.3 per cent of the variations in the variable CarSales in our sample. R^2 is the square of the sample correlation coefficient, r. The P-value, 0.009, of the estimated regression coefficient, β, of Sales on TV-Ads is smaller than $\alpha = 0.05$, which we assume is our conventionally chosen level of significance. This means that we can reject the null hypothesis, H_0, that the corresponding population regression coefficient, β, is equal to 0, using a two-sided alternative, $A_2 : \beta \neq 0$. (A two-sided alternative is the default of the computer program used.)

The conclusion, then, is that TV-Ads and Sales are significantly related to each other. Since it is close to impossible that increased advertising will result in decreased sales, it is indeed appropriate to use a one-sided alternative, $A_1 : \beta > 0$ here. This means that the p-value computed by the computer program should be divided by 2. Thus the relevant p-value is (0.009/2) = 0.0045. This represents even more evidence that there is a relationship between TV-Ads and CarSales. In certain cases, as we shall see later, a coefficient may not turn out to be significantly different from zero when we use a two-sided alternative, although it proves to be significantly different from zero if a one-sided alternative is stated. Thus it *is* important to choose a one-sided alternative when appropriate (see section 10.5). Table 11.4 illustrates several variables related to this problem.

179

Table 11.4 Residuals and fits

Row	Sales	TV-Ads	StandRes	Fit	Residual
1	1	0	0.77033	0.7	0.3
2	1	1	−1.18431	1.6	−0.6
3	2	2	−0.92582	2.5	−0.5
4	3	2	0.92582	2.5	0.5
5	4	3	1.18431	3.4	0.6
6	4	4	−0.77033	4.3	−0.3

> **A variable is useful if its p-value is smaller than α. Using a one-sided alternative instead of a two-sided means that the actual p-value will be halved.**

The *fits* are the *estimated expected* car sales or predicted car sales corresponding to the values of the independent variable TV-Ads found in the sample. The *residuals* are the corresponding deviations from the estimated regression line. Notice that the equation Fit + Residual = CarSales is valid for each month (each observation). We like the fits to be close to Sales and the residuals to be close to 0. Then R^2 will be close to 1.

Assumptions in regression analysis

Regression analysis is based upon certain assumptions, including:

1. The expected value of the error term is zero, i.e. $E(\varepsilon_i) = 0$.
2. The variance for the error term for each x_i is constant. This is termed *homoscedasticity*. If the variance to ε_i varies with x_i it is termed *heteroscedasticity*.
3. The errors for the observations are uncorrelated.
4. ε_i should be normally distributed for each x_i.
5. The error term should not be correlated with x_i, i.e. $Corr(\varepsilon_i, x_i) = 0$.
6. It is also a common assumption that the regression model should be linear in its parameters.

It is sound practice to check these assumptions. Your results may be useful even if the standard assumptions are not all met, but then the results are typically more uncertain than the various statistics indicate. The most important thing is that you use sound judgement at all stages and that you know what you are doing.

Let us briefly show how some of the assumptions may be checked in the previous case. It should be remembered, however, that we have too few observations to get a realistic situation. The assumption of a *linear* model may be checked visually by looking at the plot offered in (most) computer programs. Several assumptions can be related to the unobservable disturbances that are 'estimated' by the residuals. The residuals can be plotted in several ways – for instance against the independent variable. We may check visually the assumption of *homoscedasticity*: that is, we check that the variance of the disturbance term does not change when the value of the independent variable changes. We would like to see a picture where the variation up and down in the diagram is roughly the same in, say, the left, the middle and the right part of the diagram.

To get some idea of the appropriateness of the assumption of normally distributed disturbances, you can, if you have more observations than we have, examine whether the resulting histogram of the residuals has some resemblance to the normal density. You can also use a normal probability plot. If the points in the resulting diagram of normal scores fall roughly in a straight line, the residuals (and hopefully also the disturbances) seem to come from a normal population. The correlation coefficient tells how straight the line is. If, as here, the data are time series data, there may be *autocorrelation* in the disturbances. An appropriate test for autocorrelation is 1. If the D-W statistic is close to 2, as here, there is no danger of autocorrelation. If it is closer to 0, there may be positive autocorrelation. If it is closer to 4, there may be negative autocorrelation occurring (more seldom) (for more details see Field, 2000).

Choice of variables

If we want to use simple linear regression we may, in our example, regress Y on x_1, as already done. But we may also regress y on x_2 or y on x_3. In choosing between various regression functions in situations like this it is useful to look at the correlation coefficients. Here the correlation coefficients are shown in Table 11.5.

We notice that among the three independent variables, TV-Ads is the one which has the highest sample correlation with the dependent variable Sales. Previously we found that the corresponding regression function seems to be satisfactory in all respects. Therefore, if we decide to use only one independent variable, TV-Ads is chosen. Inspecting the correlations above, we also see that TV-Ads also correlates strongly with Print-Ads, and that Print-Ads correlates strongly with Sales as well. The high correlation coefficient between TV-Ads and Print-Ads indicates a high degree of *multicollinearity*, which is likely to obscure the estimate, also indicating that this variable (Print-Ads) influences the dependent variable.

Assessing goodness of fit

How well does the estimated regression model fit the data? (This is often termed 'explained variance'.) As noted above, the intercept β_0 and the regression coefficient β_1 must be estimated.

Table 11.5 Correlation coefficients

	TV–Ads	Print–Ads	Comp.Ads
Print-Ads	0.783		
Comp.Ads	−0.060	0.472	
Sales	0.923	0.918	0.155

When summing over all i it can also be shown that:

$$\underbrace{\sum_{i=1}^{n}(Y_i - \bar{Y})^2}_{\text{TSS}} = \underbrace{\sum_{i=1}^{n}(\hat{Y}_i - \bar{Y})^2}_{\text{RSS}} + \underbrace{\sum_{i=1}^{n}\varepsilon^2}_{\text{ESS}} \tag{11.7}$$

As can be seen from the above equation, we have three sums here. The first one, TSS, is the total sum of squares. The second, RSS, is the regression sum of squares, that is the variation in the dependent variable explained by the regression model. The last term, ESS, error sum of squares, is the sum of the squared residuals. The fraction RSS/TSS is the part of the variance in the dependent variable explained by the regression model, often termed the coefficient of variation, R^2, as mentioned above.

The standardized regression coefficient

The regression coefficient β_1, as shown in the above example, is easy to interpret if the measurements for X and Y are meaningful. This is often not the case, making it difficult to assess the strength in the linear relationship. When we have more independent variables, this may be particularly so. In such cases, we can standardize the regression coefficients by multiplying the regression coefficient(s) by the fraction standard deviation of X over the standard deviation of Y.

11.3.2 Multiple regression

In multiple regression two or more independent variables are applied to explain/predict the dependent variable. The purpose is to make the model more realistic, control for other variables, and explain more of the variance in the dependent variable (and thus to reduce residuals). The general multiple regression model can be written as:

$$Y_i = \beta_0 + \beta_1 X_{i^1} + \beta_2 X_{i^2} + \ldots + \varepsilon_i \tag{11.8}$$

Compared with (11.6) we see that the only difference is the inclusion of more independent variables.

Example

Firms are often interested in exploiting their well-established brands by extending them into new product categories. Past research has shown that the success of this strategy is influenced by, among other things, factors such as the reputation of the brand to be extended and the perceived similarity of the new product category and the existing brand. It is also believed that factors such as consumers' knowledge about the new product group, and the potential negative consequences as well as perceived uncertainty may influence consumers' willingness to accept a brand extension (see e.g. Keller, 1998). A manufacturer conducted a study to examine the willingness among consumers to accept a brand extension (*ACC*). More precisely, the manufacturer examined the explanatory power of the following variables, that is brand reputation (*REP*), similarity (*SIM*), consumer knowledge of the new product category (*PKNOW*), perceived consequences (*CONC*) and perceived uncertainty (*UNCERT*). The manufacturer also believed that consumer knowledge might *interact* with perceived uncertainty (i.e. consumer knowledge might reduce perceived uncertainty), *UNCERT* ∞ *PKNOW*. Thus the model to be tested is:

$$ACC = x_1 REP + x_2 SIM + x_3 CONC + x_4 UNCERT + x_5 PKNOW$$
$$+ x_6 UNCERT \times PKNOW$$

The results, as reported in the SPSS computer output, are shown in Table 11.6, which first shows a model summary. We here see that the explained variance R^2 is 0.384 and is adjusted somewhat lower to 0.372. R^2 tells us how much of the variance in *Y* is accounted for by the regression model from our sample; the adjusted value tells us how much variance in *Y* is accounted for if the model

Table 11.6 Multiple regression – output from SPSS

Model summary

Model	R	R square	Adjusted R square	Std. Error of the estimate
1	.620[a]	.384	.372	1.0053

[a] Predictors: (constant), *PKNOW, REP, CONC, SIM, UNCERT, UNCERT × PKNOW*

ANOVA[b]

Model	Sum of squares	df	Mean square	F	Sig.
1 Regression	192.691	6	32.115	31.775	.000[a]
Residual	309.275	306	1.011		
Total	501.966	312			

[b] Dependent variable: *ACC*

Coefficients[c]

Model	Unstandardized coefficients		Standardized coefficients	t	Sig.
	B	Std.Error	Beta		
1 (Constant)	6.245E-02	.475		.132	.895
REP	.359	.055	.300	6.491	.000
SIM	.516	.050	.481	10.291	.000
CONC	6.796E-02	.075	.045	.905	.366
UNCERT	.106	.103	.103	1.025	.306
UNCERT × PKNOW	−3.232E-02	.034	−.111	−.952	.342
PKNOW	7.496E-02	.141	.067	.532	.595

[c] Dependent variable: *ACC*

had been derived from the population from which the sample was taken. Next, analysis of variance (known from section 11.2) is reported. When going back to (11.8) this is not surprising. Regression analysis and analysis of variance are related. By calculating the fraction of variance explained by the regression model over the total variance, we get 267.149/777.129 = 0.344.

By inspecting the significance level, we also see that the regression model is highly significant, indicating that the model has explanatory power, and that the null hypothesis, that is, that the regression model does not improve prediction, can be rejected. The last part of Table 11.6 shows the estimated regression coefficients, standard errors of the estimates, t-values and significance level. Both standardized and unstandardized coefficients are reported. 6.245E-02 is $6.245 \infty 10^{-2}$, that is 0.06245. Note that the intercept (β_0) is not reported when standardized regression coefficients are estimated. Inspection of the standardized regression coefficients shows that SIM is the variable possessing the highest explanatory power. The reported value (0.481) means that a change of one standard unit in REP will result in a change of 0.481 standard unit in the dependent variable.

11.3.3 Dummy variables

Often categorical variables are included as independent variables. For example, the demand for a product or service may change with the seasons. We can, for example, divide the year into summer, autumn, winter and spring. This is a nominal scaled variable that cannot be ranked. To be applied in a regression (and other quantitative) analysis, the seasons need to be assigned numbers (see Table 11.7).

Inspection of Table 11.7 shows three new variables, A, B and C. We see that if the sales are in the summer, a 1 is coded in variable A, and zero in variables B and C. Table 11.7 also shows that the four seasons are different combinations of zeros and ones. Assume that the following regression model for sales of women's clothing, where the price (in £) is also included, has been estimated:

$$\text{Sales} = 1000 - 0.5 \times \text{Price} + 100\,A - 20\,B - 50\,C$$

The equation tells us that sales are by far the highest in the summer (A = 1, B = 0, C = 0).

Table 11.7 Coding of dummy variable

Season	A	B	C
Summer	1	0	0
Autumn	0	1	0
Winter	0	0	1
Spring	0	0	0

By including dummy variables, shifts in the regression line occur. Assume the price is £200. The sales in the summer are then:

$$1000 - 0.5 \times 200 + 100 \times (1) - 20 \times (0) - 50 \times (0) = 1000.$$

In autumn the sales when keeping the same price are:

$$1000 - 0.5 \times 200 + 100 \times (0) - 20 \times (1) - 80 \times (0) = 880.$$

11.3.4 Discriminant analysis

Regression analysis assumes metric, that is, interval- or ratio-scaled, dependent variables. Often, however, the dependent variable is categorical. One may, for example, be interested in explaining how and why successful firms differ from unsuccessful ones, what distinguishes adopters from non-adopters of a new product and so on. To do so discriminant analysis is appropriate. The objective in discriminant analysis is to derive a *variate*, the linear combination of two or more independent variables that will best discriminate between two (or more) a priori defined groups. Discrimination is achieved by setting the variate's weights for each variable to maximize the between-group variance relative to the within-group variance. The linear combination for a discriminant analysis, known as the *discriminant function*, is derived from an equation that takes the following form:

$$Z_{jk} = a + W_1 X_{1k} + W_2 X_{2k} + \ldots \tag{11.9}$$

where:

Z_{jk} = discriminant Z score for discriminant function j for object k
a = intercept
W_i = discriminant weight for independent variable i
X_{ik} = independent variable i for object k

By averaging the discriminant scores for all individuals with a particular group, we arrive at the group mean, referred to as a *centroid*. The weights W_i can be interpreted very much like regression coefficients (β) in regression analysis. Most computer programs report both unstandardized and standardized discriminant weights. The discriminating (predictive) power can be assessed as improvement in correct over by-chance classification.

Example

Assume that a manufacturer has conducted a study to examine whether it is possible to find out what discriminates buyers and non-buyers. More precisely, the manufacturer is interested to know whether age and income possess discriminating power. The dependent variable is categorical (buy = 1, not buy = 0) while the independent variables are metric. The computer output from this two-group discriminant analysis is shown in Table 11.8. Inspection of part (a) shows that 28 of the 30 observations are applied in the analysis, and two observations are excluded due to missing data. We also see that group 0 includes 19 subjects

Table 11.8 Two-group discriminant analysis

(a) Cases

Group	0	1
Count	19	9
28 cases used	2 cases contain missing values	

(b) Summary of classification

Put into Group	. . . True 0	Group . . . 1
0	19	0
1	0	9
Total N	19	9
N Correct	19	9
Proportion	1.000	1.000

N = 28 N Correct = 28   Prop. Correct = 1.000

(c) Squared distance between groups

	0	1
0	0.00000	7.42431
1	7.42431	0.00000

(d) Linear discriminant function for group:

	0	1
Constant	−18.127	−31.758
Age	0.225	0.052
Income	0.120	0.203

and the other group 9 subjects. From part (b) we see that the analysis has put all units into the groups where they truly belong. This is not usually the case.

Part (d) shows that the following two linear discriminant functions have been computed. For group 0: $F_0 = -18.127 + 0.225$ Age $+ 0.120$ Income. For group 1: $F_1 = -31.758 + 0.052$ Age $+ 0.203$ Income. These two can be used to predict whether a person, say of age 54 and with income 250, will buy product P. We simply plug these figures into the two functions and get $f_0(54.250) = 24.023$ and $f_1(54.250) = 21.800$. Since $f_0(54.250) > f_1(54.250)$, we predict that the person belongs to group 0, that is s/he will not buy the product.

Let us consider observation number 1 in the above example. This observation truly belongs to group number 0 and has also correctly been classified into group number 0. The squared distance from this observation to the *group centroid* (mean point) of group 0 in the plane where x_1 and x_2 are coordinates is 0.06104, which is a small figure. The estimated probability of this observation belonging to group 0 is therefore a large figure, namely 0.969. On the other hand, the squared distance from this observation to the group centroid of group 1 is 6.94746, which is a large figure. The estimated probability of this observation belonging to group 1 is therefore a small figure, namely 0.031. The estimated probabilities are

Table 11.9 True and predicted group membership

Observation	True group	Pred group	Group	Squared distance	Probability
1	0	0	0	0.06104	0.969
			1	6.94746	0.031
2	0	0	0	3.028	0.997
			1	14.613	0.003
3	1	1	0	5.9264	0.074

based upon the assumption that the independent variables follow a multivariate normal distribution. If a unit is classified into a group other than the one where it truly belongs, the unit is said to be *misclassified* and is marked in the computer output as shown in Table 11.9.

Notice also that we should be careful not to be too impressed by a high proportion of correctly classified units, that is by a high hit ratio. Suppose we have two groups, one consisting of 20 units and the other consisting of 80 units. If we arbitrarily classify all units into the larger group, we automatically get a hit ratio of 80 per cent! In any case, the hit ratio recorded in analyses such as the one above is usually too optimistic because we classify the very data that we have used to compute the discriminant functions. A sound recommendation, which ought to be followed if we have a sufficiently large sample, is to divide the sample randomly into two groups, often called the *analysis sample* and the *holdout sample*. The analysis sample is used to compute the discriminant functions, while the holdout sample is used to test the validity of the functions.

11.3.5 Logistic regression analysis

Several alternatives to the two-group discriminant analysis exist. One is *logistic regression*. In logistic regression the probability of an event occurring is predicted. Probability values can be any value between zero and one. To define a relationship bounded by zero and one, logistic regression uses an assumed relationship between the independent and dependent variables, the accumulated logistic distribution (resembling an S-shaped curve). The procedure that calculates the *logistic coefficients* compares the probability of an event occurring with the probability of its not occurring. The *odds ratio* can be expressed as:

$$\frac{Prob_{(event)}}{Prob_{(not\ event)}} = e^{B_0} + e^{B_1 X_1} + \ldots$$

The estimated coefficients B_0, B_1, ... are measures of the changes in the ratio of the probabilities (the odds ratios). They are expressed in logarithms. To be assessed more easily, they need to be transformed back, that is take the antilog of the values. In logistic regression analysis both metric and categorical variables can be included. Some computer programs (e.g. BMDP) automatically transform categorical variables into 'design' variables (very much like dummy variables). A variable with n categories is transformed to $n - 1$ variables.

Example

In some countries, such as Norway, subsidies to and taxes for businesses vary across regions. A study was conducted to examine whether the response rate of a mailed questionnaire to municipal authorities was influenced by type of municipality (central, peripheral), subsidy region (three categories), and the level of income in the municipality.

The two categorical variables were transformed as follows:

	Code	Design variables (1)	(2)
Type of municipality (M)	1	−1	
	2	1	
Subsidy region (S)	1	−1	−1
	2	0	1
	3	1	0

The two subsidy regions design variables are here termed $S1$ and $S2$. The estimated values are shown in Table 11.10.

The Bs correspond to the unstandardized regression coefficients, SD = standard deviation, and B/SD gives approximate t-values. Inspection of Table 11.10 shows that level of income and subsidy region yield most predictive power. Now we can estimate the odds for the two responses (that is answered or not answered the questionnaire), as follows:

$$\ln \frac{P(Y = 1)}{P(Y - 0)} = 5.980 - 0.261M - 0.911S1 - 0.371S2 - 0.179INC$$

The odds for a central municipality (−1) in a low subsidy region (code 1 corresponding to −1 for the two design variables $S1$ and $S2$) are thus:

$$\ln \frac{P(Y = 1)}{P(Y - 0)} = 5.980 - 0.261(-1) - 0.911(-1) - 0.371(-1) - 0.179INC$$

Table 11.10 Logistic regression

Variable	B	SD	B/SD
M	−0.261	0.183	−1.426
S1	−0.911	0.194	−4.695*
S2	−0.371	0.188	−1.973
INCOME	−0.179	0.039	−4.590*
Constant	5.980	1.193	5.013*

* $p < 0.001$.

The number of municipalities in the present study is 399, of which 270 responded to the questionnaire, while the remaining 129 did not. By using the proportional by-chance criterion, 224.2 of the cases would have been correctly classified. In the present case, 291 cases were correctly classified, that is an improvement from 56.5 per cent to 73.3 per cent ($p < 0.001$).

Logistic regression in some way can be seen as having more 'logic' in predicting group belongingness than two-group discriminant analysis, as the independent variables can be considered 'stimulus'-variables. It is also somewhat more robust against violation of statistical assumptions.

> **Logistic regression is preferable to discriminant analysis when the independent variables are not multivariate normal.**

11.4 Data reduction, structure and dimensions

In business research we are often confronted with intercorrelated data where we seek structure and underlying dimensions. For example, in marketing, consumers are often asked to rate products and stores along semantic scales (i.e. bipolar scales), for example:

good	−3	−2	−1	0	1	2	3	bad
inexpensive	−3	−2	−1	0	1	2	3	expensive

The various scales may be intercorrelated, and the firm (researcher) will often be interested to know whether they can be reduced to a small(er) number of independent, that is uncorrelated dimensions. Factor analysis is useful to handle such problems.

11.4.1 Factor analysis

Factor analysis is a generic name given to a class of multivariable statistical methods whose primary purpose is to define the underlying structure in a data matrix. It addresses the problem of analysing the structure of interrelationships (correlations) among a large number of variables by defining a set of *common* underlying dimensions, termed *factors*. With factor analysis one can identify the separate dimensions of the structure, and then determine the extent to which each variable is explained by the various dimensions. Factor analysis is an interdependent technique in which *each* variable is simultaneously considered in relation to all others. Thus, in factor analysis we do not distinguish between independent and dependent variables. A distinction can be made between *exploratory* and *confirmatory* factor analysis. In the first case the purpose is to explore, that

189

is to discover some underlying but unknown structure. In the second case the purpose is to examine or test an assumed structure.

Conducting factor analysis

Burnout is often envisaged as a unique type of stress syndrome, characterized by emotional exhaustion, depersonalization and diminished personal accomplishment. Over the years substantial research has been conducted to define and measure the construct. Today, burnout is often defined as a three-dimensional concept, including the following components: emotional exhaustion, depersonalization or dehumanization, and diminished personal accomplishment. The focus in past research has been on job-related burnout. This research has primarily been conducted among employees in the service professions, for example nurses and teachers.

A study was conducted to examine whether the same three conceptual dimensions were also valid in the off-shore oil industry, which a work environment assumed to be stressful and dangerous (Hellesøy et al., 2000). To capture the burnout construct a questionnaire case containing multiple items was prepared. Table 11.11 shows the findings.

Inspection of Table 11.11 shows that 14 items (variables) are included. Here four *factors* are extracted. The factors are labelled 'Alienation', 'Focus loss', 'Depression' and 'Worry'. Now we will explain the table: h^2 are the commonalities, that is the amount of the variance in the variables extracted by the factor analysis. For example, for item number 1 we see that 65 per cent of the variance

Table 11.11 **Factor analysis: an example**

	h^2	Alienation	Focus loss	Depression	Worry
1 Feel lonesome even together with other people	0.65	0.74			
2 Feel everything is a great effort	0.41	0.41			
3 Never feel close to another person	0.41	0.70			
4 Feel that nobody cares or understands	0.46	0.59			
5 Difficulties in remembering	0.36		0.51		
6 Difficulties in deciding	0.45		0.61		
7 Difficulties in concentrating	0.71		0.76		
8 Become easily irritated	0.47			0.57	
9 Feel depressed	0.63			0.51	
10 Feel easily hurt	0.47			0.51	
11 Feel tense	0.53			0.52	
12 Worries about home when away	0.62				0.77
13 Worrying about home affects work	0.57				0.69
14 Difficulties in sleeping due to worry	0.58				0.50
Percentage of common variance	45.8	34.9	4.6	4.1	2.2
Percentage of trace	100.0	76.2	9.0	9.5	4.8

in that item is extracted. When we move to the next column, we observe the number 0.74 on the factor term 'Alienation'. This is a *factor loading*, which is the correlation between the original variable and this factor. When squaring this factor loading we obtain $0.74^2 = 0.55$. Simple calculation shows that this loading counts for most of the extracted variance in item number 1, that is $0.55/0.66 \times 100 = 83$ per cent.

In Table 11.11 we have only included the highest reported loading for each item. This has been done to ease the reading of the table. The various items also load on factors other than shown in the table. When squaring the loadings or the various factors for each item we get:

$$(\text{loading})^2 + \text{--------------} + (\text{loading})^2 = h^2$$

When inspecting the extracted factors we see *four* factors. These factors are interpreted and labelled by the researchers. (Here we also observe the factor 'Worry' captured by items 12, 13 and 14. This factor represents an additional dimension to the burnout construct discovered in the actual research context.)

When moving to the penultimate line we see 'Percentage of common variance'. This can be explained as follows. A distinction can be made between three types of variance: common, unique and error variance. Common variance is shared between the variables included; unique variance refers to variance that is specific for the individual variable. Error variance is variance due to unreliability in the data gathering, measurement error, etc. In factor analysis only common variance is accounted for. Here we see that our factor analysis takes 45.8 per cent of the total variance into account, and that $(100.0 - 45.8) = 54.2$ per cent of the total variance is not taken into account. Inspecting the same line further we observe that the factor 'Alienation' counts for 34.9 per cent of the variance, or, as can be seen from the last line, 76.2 per cent of the extracted variance (trace).

We also see that the amount of variance extracted decreases rapidly as we read across the extracted factors. This is due to the following. First the linear combination of variables that accounts for the most variance is extracted. Then a linear combination of factors that account for the second largest portion of the variance is extracted, and so on. If the factors are *orthogonal* (as here) they are mathematically independent of each other. In factor analysis the factor solution is often *rotated* to make it more easily interpretable. *Varimax* is the most popular orthogonal rotation method. Factors may, however, be correlated. *Oblique* rotation identifies to what extent each of the extracted factors is correlated.

In factor analysis one also meets the term *eigenvalue* (not shown in Table 11.11). It represents the amount of variance accounted for by a factor (and this represents what is shown in the second to last line of the table). In the above factor analysis we have examined the relationships between variables. This is termed R-type factor analysis. We could also examine the similarities between individuals, termed Q-type factor analysis.

11.4.2 Principal component analysis

A somewhat similar technique to factor analysis is *principal component analysis*. Principal component analysis takes the total variance (and not only common variance as in factor analysis) into account. A prime objective of principal component analysis is to transform a set of interrelated variables into a set of unrelated linear variables. Both factor and principal component analysis are widely used. For further discussion, see e.g. Hair et al. (1998).

11.5 Additional methods

So far in this chapter we have shown examples of ways of analysing data. Many more methods of analysis are available, however. A brief overview of some other multivariate techniques is given below.

11.5.1 Cluster analysis

The objective of *cluster analysis* is to discover natural groupings of the units in a sample. Each resulting group is called a *cluster*. A beginner may easily confuse cluster analysis with discriminant analysis. One very important difference is that in discriminant analysis the groups and the group memberships of the various units are known before the analysis starts. In cluster analysis, by contrast, we do not have any groups at all at the outset. On the basis of the data for the n units in the sample, groups are created.

In business studies, grouping or clustering of units is often useful and can help in generating hypotheses to be tested later. One example is to group customers into clusters that are market segments consisting of similar customers. Another application is to group brands of a product into clusters consisting of similar brands. The grouping is based upon similarities or distances (dissimilarities) in an n-dimensional space.

11.5.2 Multidimensional scaling

The basic idea of *multidimensional scaling* or MDS can be illustrated as follows. Suppose we are given a table listing the distances between all pairs of capitals for all the countries in Europe. This table could, for instance, be arranged as a symmetric matrix with zeros along the main diagonal. Only the upper or lower triangle of the matrix is needed. Using only this information, we are asked to construct a map of Europe showing the locations of all the capitals. In principle, customers can express their attitudes regarding the distances between various brands by telling which pairs of brands are very similar and which are not so similar. This way we obtain data comparable to the distances between cities.

The basic objective of MDS in this example is to map the brands in a multi-dimensional space in such a way that the relative positions of the brands reflect the perceived distances between the brands.

11.5.3 Canonical correlation analysis

Canonical correlation analysis is a technique for identifying and quantifying the associations between a set of *x*-variables on the one hand and a set of *y*-variables on the other. Multiple and simple correlation analysis can be considered as special cases of canonical correlation analysis where one or both sets contain a single variable. If we consider a variable related to a commodity such as a car and a variable related to the person buying the car we will, except for price and income, often find only a small correlation coefficient. Still, we have a definite feeling that persons with specific characteristics buy special kinds of cars. In such situations, canonical correlation analysis may be useful.

11.5.4 Multivariate analysis

Multivariate analysis of variance, often referred to as *MANOVA*, is a generalization of the usual, univariate analysis of variance, ANOVA. The new aspect of MANOVA, compared with ANOVA, is that instead of comparing *k* group means for only one dependent variable, *k* group means for *several* dependent variables can be compared simultaneously. As an example, suppose we want to compare prices for *p* different products in *k* different cities on a certain day based upon random samples of *n* price observations for each product in each city. For each product we could, for instance, take a random sample of *n* stores from each city. Our data matrix would then consist of *pkn* observations altogether. Using ANOVA to test the hypothesis of equal population means in the *k* cities, we would have to perform *p* different analyses: one for each product. With MANOVA, a single analysis would be sufficient. Using the concept of a vector (a mathematical term for writing a set of numbers), MANOVA can be used to test the hypothesis that the *k* *p*-dimensional vectors of population means for the prices are the same for all *k* cities. Such a vector of population means is called a *centroid*. While with ANOVA we are testing that *k* population means are equal, with MANOVA the more general hypothesis is that *k* population centroids are equal. Conceptually, the two procedures are similar. To perform one MANOVA is in most cases a more powerful procedure than conducting *p* univariate ANOVAs. Group differences that are not revealed using several ANOVAs may be found using MANOVA. The reason is that MANOVA takes into account the correlations between the dependent variables (the prices in our example). Interpretation of results may also be more meaningful using MANOVA. If the dependent variables are uncorrelated, there is nothing to gain by using MANOVA.

11.5.5 Structural equation modelling

Today, *structural equation modelling (SEM)* has become a popular and important way of analysing data. Structural equation modelling is a technique that allows separate relationships for each set of dependent variables. In its simplest sense, structural equation modelling provides the appropriate and most efficient estimation technique for a series of multiple regression equations estimated simultaneously. It is characterized by two basic components: the *structural* model and the *measurement* model. The structural model is the path model, which relates independent variables to dependent variables. The measurement model allows the researcher to use several variables (indicators) for a single independent or dependent variable (see the discussion on measurement in Chapter 6). Theory plays an important role in structural equation modelling, and such modelling is seen as an important way to test theories.

There is a vast literature on data analysis in general and multivariable analysis in particular. An excellent introduction to multivariable analysis for readers with a limited background in mathematics and statistics is found in Hair et al. (1998).

Notes

1. For an excellent introduction to an overview of non-parametric statistics, see Siegel and Castellan (1988). Non-parametric tests are available in statistical software programs.
2. Even though the theoretical values for a correlation coefficient are between +1 and –1, the observed values for correlations between dichotomous variables will be lower. More precisely, the correlation between two variables with distributions (50, 50) and (30, 70) cannot reach unity.

Further reading

Churchill, G.A. and Iacobucci, D. (2002) *Marketing Research: Methodological Foundations*, 8th edn, Fort Mason, OH: Thomson Learning (Chapters 15–17).

Questions

1. What is a hypothesis?

2. What does a correlation coefficient tell?

3. What is regression analysis? In which research situation is it useful?

4. In a multiple regression analysis, while using income, product experience and family size as dependent variables, the observed R square (R^2) is 0.35. What does this tell us? Explain your answer.

5. What is factor analysis? In which situation is it useful?

Exercises

1. You have the following data:

   H_0: $m = 200$, $S = 30$, $n = 64$, and $x = 218$. Conduct a test at the 0.05 significance level.

2. Assume you have the following data:

   H_0: $m = 2.450$, $S = 400$, $n = 100$, and $x- = 2.300$. Conduct a test at the 0.01 significance level.

3. What is the difference between regression analysis and correlation analysis?

4. What is a 'dummy' variable? When is it used and how is it interpreted?

CHAPTER 12

Qualitative data analysis

Quality, not quantity is my measure.

(Douglas Jerrold)

Qualitative research imposes specific analytical challenges. This chapter addresses important characteristics of qualitative research and qualitative data. Strategies and procedures to handle the analytical challenges are also dealt with, as well as validity and reliability issues in qualitative research.

12.1 Characteristics of qualitative research

Previously we have emphasized that a key purpose of qualitative research is to understand and gain insights (see section 2.5). Qualitative research is particularly relevant when prior insights about the phenomenon under scrutiny are modest, implying that qualitative research tends to be exploratory and flexible because of 'unstructured' problems (due to modest insights). Even though qualitative research may allow for tests of hypotheses, the main emphasis is usually on gaining insights and constructing explanations or theory. In the terminology of Popper (1961) qualitative research is in particular relevant in the 'context of discovery' (see sections 5.2, 8.2).

Ambiguity partly prevails with regards to what distinguishes 'qualitative' and 'quantitative' research. Qualitative research approaches are multiple and no agreed-upon classification of the various approaches or methods exists (see Box 12.1). Van Maanen (1979: 520) also claims that

> [the] label qualitative methods has no precise meaning in any of the social sciences. It is at best an umbrella term covering an array of interpretative techniques which seek to describe, decode, translate, and otherwise come to terms with the meaning, not the frequency, of certain more or less naturally occurring phenomena in the social world.

As noted above qualitative research tends to be more explorative and unstructured, with emphasis on understanding, while quantitative research tends more to emphasize descriptions and testing of derived hypotheses.

In qualitative research data collection and analysis are often conducted simultaneously in an interactive way where collected data are analysed, initiating new questions, and initiating further data collection. In 'traditional quantitative' research, data collection and analysis are usually sequential. The reason for the continuous data collection and analysis is caused by modest a priori understanding of the problem. As more data (evidence) are collected and analysed the problem becomes gradually clarified. An analogy is the effort of a detective trying to find the person guilty of a crime.

12.2 Qualitative data

Data are carriers of information. To become information they must, however, be interpreted. The distinction between quantitative and qualitative data is not an easy one – and disagreements prevail. A common observation is that in qualitative studies the researcher easily becomes overwhelmed by the masses of data. One reason for this is that when the research problem is badly (modestly) understood many data are collected, of which many may be irrelevant. Thus redundancy of data is often the case. Miles (1979: 590) has even termed qualitative data as 'attractive nuisance'. Quantitative data are usually associated with numbers. As noted above numbers possess specific characteristics that make them very useful for analytical purposes. They can be seen as an efficient way to represent information and meanings. The following example illustrates this.

Example

Assume that a researcher is interested in knowing whether women and men differ in their interest for sports cars. Here we have two rather well-understood concepts, that is gender (woman, man) and interest (degree of). Let us further assume that the researcher collects a sample and gathers information on gender and degree of interest in sports cars, and codes this information in the following way: woman = 1, man = 2, and almost no interest = 1 ------ great interest = 7. By correlating the two variables the following correlation emerges: $r = 0.57$. This finding shows that men are more likely than women to be interested in sports cars. The correlation coefficient makes sense – and gives insights because clear understanding of the concepts and the problem is present.

Often the research problem is less well understood and the underlying concepts may be ambiguous. Assigning numbers to something we do not know and understand makes no sense. In such situations qualitative data may be useful to gain insights and understand concepts. Qualitative data come in many forms, such as pictures, texts and verbal reports. Such data are rich, full, earthy, holistic and 'real' (Miles 1979: 590). Such data are in many ways closer to the problem/phenomenon studied.

In a famous study Burns and Stalker (1961) were interested to understand why some firms were very innovative while others were not, in spite of the firms belonging to the same industry, being of approximately the same size and located in the same region. In this case they had adequate information about the dependent variable, innovativeness, that is, the extent to which the firms introduced novel products and patents. Their insights regarding why the difference in innovativeness between firms occurred were, however, highly limited. Detailed study of a sample of highly innovative and non-innovative firms revealed that the two groups of firms differed greatly in organizational structure and flow of information (see Box 12.1). They termed the highly innovative firms as 'organic' and the non-innovative as 'mechanic'. These terms are summary 'labels' of the characteristics shown in Box 12.1.

When going back to our two examples above, it is easily seen that in the first (gender – interests in sports cars) we derive meanings from numbers (the positive correlation coefficient reflects that men are more interested in sports cars than women); that collection results in numerical and standardized data (e.g. woman = 1, man = 2; no interest = 1 ------ great interest = 7); and that analysis in this case is conducted by using statistics ($r = 0.57$).

Inspection of our second example (see Box 12.1) shows that meanings are expressed through words; the non-standardized collected data here are classified into two broad categories, 'organic' and 'mechanistic'; and the analysis is conducted through conceptualization. The two 'labels' organic and mechanistic are used as 'shorthand' to capture the differences in organizational structure and

---

Box 12.1   'Mechanic' and 'organic' forms of management system

Management system

'Mechanic'	'Organic'
– specialized differentiation of functional tasks	– contributive nature of special knowledge and experience to common tasks
– abstract nature of individual tasks	– 'realistic' nature of individual task set by the situation adjustment and continuous redefinition of individual tasks
– immediate superiors	
– precise definition of rights and obligations	
– translation of rights and obligations into responsibilities	– spread of commitment
– hierarchic structure of control, authority and communication	– network structures of control, authority and communication
– vertical interaction	– lateral direction of communication
– instructions by superiors	– information and advice rather than instructions

Source: Burns and Stalker (1961: 120–1)

flow of information for the two groups of firms, innovative and non-innovative respectively.

12.3 Analytical procedures

A key – if not *the* key – purpose of analysis is to understand and gain insights from the collected data, or as stated by Marshall and Rossman (1995: 111), 'data analysis is the process of bringing order, structure and meaning to the mass of collected data'. As noted above, in qualitative studies the research is often over-whelmed by the mass of data. A key characteristic of analysis is the dividing up or breaking down of some complex whole into its constituent parts (i.e. from the Greek, *ana-*, 'up, throughout', and *lyein*, 'to loose'). Through analytical operations the researcher dissects, reduces, sorts and reconstitutes data. Researchers use analysis to manipulate data to gain understanding, clarify problems and test hypotheses. No single, agreed-upon approach to qualitative data analysis exists. However, it is possible to give some rather general and helpful advice. For example, in their recognized 'source book' Miles and Huberman (1994) distinguish between the following components in qualitative data analysis (see Figure 12.1):

- data reduction
- data display
- conclusion drawing/verification.

Data reduction refers to the process of selecting, focusing, simplifying, abstracting and transforming the data that appear in writing up field notes or transcriptions.

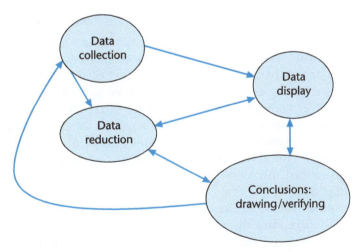

Figure 12.1 Components of data analysis: interactive model
Source: Miles and Huberman (1994: 23)

For example, to be manageable and to give meaning, lengthy transcripts from focus group interviews must not only be read, the researcher must also focus, simplify and abstract to create meaning from the mass of words.

In this phase the researcher generates categories and identifies themes and patterns. As categories and patterns between them in the data are gradually uncovered, understanding or explanation of the phenomenon studied may emerge. However, the researcher should be extremely careful and critical in this phase, because other explanations are in most cases possible. This is important, because the key purpose is to arrive at valid explanations (see Kirk and Miller, 1986, for an excellent discussion).

Data display is an organized, compressed assembly of information that permits drawing conclusions and taking action. Data display can be in the form of a data matrix, figures and so on. For example, a study of a strategy process may display the major events and/or actors in that process.

In the following section such activities will be dealt with in greater detail. We first describe various analytical activities, and then turn to interpretation, which is at the heart of qualitative research.

12.3.1 Analytical activities[1]

Here we distinguish between:

- categorization
- abstraction
- comparison
- dimensionalization
- integration
- iteration, and
- refutation.

Categorization is the process of classifying units of data. Qualitative researchers categorize data during the process of coding. The essence of categorization is identifying a chunk or unit of data (e.g. a passage of text of any length) as belonging to, representing or being an example of some more general phenomenon. Categorization involves naming, or giving labels to, instances of the phenomenon found in the data. A passage categorized with a specific label may be a few words or many pages long. A passage may also exemplify different categories of interest to the analyst and thus have many labels. Usually some part of the text, for example a transcribed interview, will contain no meaningful information and remain uncategorized.

Codes serve as shorthand devices to label, separate, compile and organize data. Coding of qualitative data differs somewhat from the coding of quantitative data, for example survey data (see section 10.1.2). When handling quantitative data it is mostly a way of managing data, while in qualitative data analysis – in particular in situations where the analysis departs from inspection of the collected data (see section 12.5) – coding is an important first step in arriving at understanding and generating theory.

Several approaches to coding exist. Probably the most elaborate is that developed by Strauss and Corbin (1990) drawing on the 'grounded theory' approach (see section 12.5). These authors distinguish between three types of coding: open coding, axial coding and selective coding.

- *Open coding* – 'the process of breaking down, examining, comparing, conceptualizing and categorizing data' (1990: 61); this process of coding yields concepts, which are later to be grouped and turned into categories.
- *Axial coding* – 'a set of procedures whereby data are put back together in new ways after open coding, by making connections between categories' (1990: 96). This is done by linking codes to contexts, to consequences, to patterns of interaction, and to causes.
- *Selective coding* – 'the procedure of selecting the core category, systematically relating it to other categories, validating those relationships, and filling in categories that need further refinement and development' (1990: 116). A *core category* is the central issue or focus around which all other categories are integrated. It is what Strauss and Corbin call the storyline that frames your account.

The three types of coding are really different levels of coding, and each relates to a different point in the elaboration of categories in grounded theory.

Qualitative researchers do not generally specify the unit of analysis (although it is done in some cases). Rather they categorize a chunk of data on the basis of its coherent meaning – its standing on its own – and not by an arbitrary designation of grammar. It is also quite common in qualitative research for initial categories and codes to be changed and refined during the research process.

Abstraction builds on categorization. It surpasses categorization in that it collapses more empirically grounded categories into higher-order conceptual constructs. Abstraction goes beyond the identification of patterns in the data. It groups previously identified categories into more general conceptual classes. Abstraction includes both incorporating more concrete categories into fewer, more general ones, and recognizing that a unit of data is an empirical indicator of a more general construct of interest. For example, a researcher studying consumers' purchasing behaviour has, based on transcribed interviews, made categories for 'reading of advertisements', 'brochures', 'store visit', and 'asking for advice', and then related these categories to a more general and abstract one – 'information search'.

Abstract constructs encompass a number of more concrete instances found in the data that share certain common features. The theoretical significance of a construct partly depends on its relationship with other constructs. The reason is that most research is relational. For example: Is *amount of search* in a purchase situation related to the *importance of the purchase*?

Comparison explores differences and similarities across incidents within the data currently collected and provides guidelines for collecting additional data.

Comparison begins in the initial stage of the analysis as one categorizes and abstracts data. While categorizing, the investigator notes general similarities in the specific empirical instances in the data and labels them as representing the same category. As the analysis proceeds, the investigator may conduct comparisons in a systematic way.

Example

A researcher is studying purchasing behaviour in a business firm. Among other things s/he is observing various search and evaluation activities for the purchase of the same products. To examine whether search and evaluation activities are related to purchase experience, s/he makes the following comparison:

	Purchase product A:	
	First	*Last*
Bid	Yes	No
Price evaluation	Yes	No
Brochures	No Yes	No
Advertisements	No Yes	No

Here we see that more search/evaluation are conducted in the first then in the last purchase. This may indicate learning and simplification of purchases through experience.

Glaser and Strauss (1967) pioneered the *constant comparative* method as an analytical procedure in which the analyst compares incidents in the data with other incidents appearing to belong to the same category, exploring their similarities and differences. As the analysis proceeds and categories develop, the investigator compares incidents in the data with appropriate emergent categories.

Comparison processes also guide subsequent data collection. As investigators identify categories, constructs and preliminary propositions, and conceptual linkages from the initial analyses, they may define subsequent individuals or groups to sample that maximize or minimize differences between them on variables of interest. This procedure allows them to control for, or manipulate, similarities and differences in conditions, outcomes, or information characteristics in a way that is analogous to that in experimental and survey designs.

Example

A researcher is doing a detailed tracking of budgeting in small, privately owned restaurants and notes that the restaurants do not prepare formal budgets (as prescribed in the textbooks). S/he wonders whether this is something special for this industry, and proceeds to collect the same information from other small, privately owned service firms. Depending on the observed findings s/he may proceed to include other types of firm, for example larger firms or firms from manufacturing industries. This way of proceeding is an example of purposive or theoretical sampling (see section 9.5).

Dimensionalization involves identifying properties of categories and constructs. Once a category has been defined the researcher may explore its attributes or characteristics along one or more dimensions. The properties represent conceptual dimensions that vary empirically in the data across the incidents depicting the constructs. Strauss and Corbin (1990: 72) offer the following hypothetical example:

Category	*Properties*	*Dimensional range* (applied to each incident)
Watching	frequency	often --------- never
	extent	more --------- less
	intensity	high --------- low
	duration	long --------- short

In this example the category 'watching' is described by four properties, each one dimensionalized along a continuum.

Dimensionalization is important for theory construction in the following ways. By systematically exploring empirical variations across incidents representing a construct, the researcher can clarify and enrich the conceptual meaning. Identification of properties and their dimensions can also help the researcher to explore and define relationships across categories and constructs.

Integration is important in efforts to build theory based on data, and departs by noting in the data that certain conditions, contexts, strategies and outcomes tend to cluster together. Integration requires the mapping of relationships between conceptual elements.

Iteration involves moving through data collection and analysis in such a way that preceding operations shape subsequent ones. In doing so the researcher does not perform specific research stages in a sequential order, but moves back and forth between stages. An example is simultaneous data collection and data analysis as emphasized above. This is in contrast to quantitative research, where the various stages tend to be performed sequentially.

Refutation involves deliberately subjecting one's emerging inferences – categories, constructs, propositions or conceptual framework – to empirical scrutiny. To do so the researcher may make use of a negative case or negative incident to disconfirm the emerging analysis. A main reason for trying to disconfirm is to omit the so-called 'confirmation bias' (Bazerman, 1998).

NB: It is important to note that assumptions and hypotheses are not tested by seeking supporting evidence, but by seeking information that allows for disconfirmation.

Example

In their well-known book *In Search of Excellence* Peters and Waterman (1982) made an effort to come up with characteristics for excellent firms, such as that

203

successful firms were headed by managers who walked around talking to the employees. In their study they only included – at that time – successful firms, which makes it impossible to conclude whether the suggested criteria hold true. To hold true the probability of success should be higher when a given characteristic is present, $P(S/c_i)$, compared with when the characteristic is not present, $P(S/\bar{c}_i)$.

12.3.2 Data reduction

The above analytical operations – categorization, abstraction, comparison, dimensionalization, integration, iteration and refutation – provide a way of managing analysis of qualitative data. Even though the researcher cannot programme these operations in a mechanical fashion, s/he can proceed *systematically*. One way of doing this is to read through all the data before rereading records for each case. Alternatively the researcher can read and retract the record for each case before going to subsequent cases. Also, as one categorizes, abstracts, compares and integrates one can move through the data horizontally (e.g. grouping indicators of categories), or vertically (e.g. grouping records of cases), or both sequentially. *Tabulations* can be helpful in promoting systematic comparisons, for example listing incidents that represent a construct across cases.

The purpose of proceeding systematically is to stimulate a complete analysis, and minimize potential distortion from selective use of the data.

Record. In analysing qualitative data the researcher is strongly encouraged to *keep records* of the analysis in process in the form of memos, journals, charts and other documents. Records may be of two types: those that condense, summarize and integrate data displays and documents that *facilitate* the analysis, and records that *preserve* the construction of inference. Such records can be memos about insights and ideas, notes and summaries.

Report. Both in quantitative and qualitative research it is common to report the procedures applied for collecting and analysing data. A reason for doing so is that others should in principle be able to arrive at the same conclusions, be able to *reproduce* the findings, or more realistically be able to follow and evaluate the underlying logic. Spiggle (1994) suggests that the following should be reported in qualitative research:

- the volume of the text used to produce the analysis, and how many cases, sites or locations were studied;
- how many times the text was read, and in what order rereading occurred;
- whether and how previous interpretations are modified;
- procedures used to ensure systematic and thorough analysis;
- specific iterates, data collected and cases selected for study on the basis of prior analysis;
- procedures for and to what extent negative evidence is sought and used to modify emergent interpretations.

12.4 Interpretation

Analytical procedures are applied to manipulate data. Through interpretation the researcher makes sense of the collected (and manipulated) data. Compared with data analysis, interpretation tends to be more intuitive, and subjective. Interpretation may occur in many ways, and involves the use of some 'lenses', that is, some conceptual or theoretical 'glasses'. A key point is that data make sense by using some concepts, perspective or theory. One example is the use of metaphors. A metaphor requires us to suspend our ordinary frame of reference of viewing some aspect of the world 'as is', and, instead, view it 'as if'. In using a metaphor as a lens we seek correspondence, similarities and identities between domains. One domain is compared with or seen in terms of another. The comparison involves a mapping of elements of one domain on to those of the other. Metaphors not only play an important role in research, but are also of crucial importance for how people make sense of their observations and experiences (for an excellent discussion, see Lakoff and Johnson (1980)). An interesting example is Alvin Toffler's use of the wave metaphor – that is, a phenomenon belonging to our physical world, the ocean – to grasp dramatic changes in our society – and to imagine future changes as well (Toffler, 1980).

Grasping the meanings of others. In qualitative research the investigator often attempts to understand informants by grasping a concept, an experience or an idea in *their* terms. In doing so the researcher grasps their (the informants') meaning by 'translating' their sayings into her/his own insights and understanding. This implies seeking correspondence between the informants' and the researcher's experiences and understanding.

Seeking patterns in meaning. Often the researchers represent the meaning and experiences of informants as forming coherent patterns. They do this by aggregating them into larger wholes, identifying unified themes by which the individual informants construct their worlds and more generalized patterns that characterize their sample.

12.5 Strategies for qualitative analysis

From the above discussion it is apparent that there are several approaches for analysing qualitative data. A distinction can be made between whether the research departs from existing theory (deductive), or whether the analyses mainly depart from the observations/data (inductive).

12.5.1 Departure from theory

Also in qualitative research the investigator may – and often does – depart from some theory. This may sound strange. However, even when conducting exploratory, discovery-oriented research with a focus on understanding and con-struction of explanations, the investigator often holds prior assumptions and 'hunches' about critical factors and relationships. By taking such assumptions and hunches into account, the research may benefit from theorizing at the out-set, which can be helpful to get some direction for how to proceed (cf. Zaltman et al., 1982). Two things should be noted. First, the a priori assumptions and hunches should guide and direct, not dictate, the research. Second, even though some a priori theory may exist, it is assumed that a priori insights should not allow for complete structuring and explanation of the research problem. If so, the research could probably benefit from structured tests of hypotheses (see section 5.2).

Example

Firms make use of technologies, and these can be described in various ways. One way is the flexibility of a firm's production technology, that is, how many types of input can produce a specific output, and how many outputs the technology allows for by using specific input. In a study a researcher asked whether techno-logical flexibility influences firms' buying strategies. Here the researcher believed that technological flexibility did influence firms' buying strategies, but not exactly how, and therefore conducted a discovery-oriented qualitative study.

Inspection of Figure 12.2 shows that problem recognition occurs very differently in the two firms. In Alpha, information about expected increases in the prices is the stimulus for the purchasing department to start the search for raw materials. It should also be noted that in this firm no alternative for the type of raw mater-ials used exists. In Beta, the buying process is triggered by a sales order. In this firm, multiple alternatives for raw materials were perceived to be possible. Is it possible to explain the two apparently different buying strategies reflected in Figure 12.2?

The actual study focused on the role of technological flexibility, here con-ceived as bindings between input and output possibilities. In Alpha, the per-ceived technological possibilities of changing to other combinations of input and output factors were few. Thus the 'proactive' behaviour in Alpha can be seen as a way of 'buffering' against environmental changes. In Beta, a high degree of technological flexibility allows for 'reactive' behaviour. Its flexibility allows for immediate adjustments (Grønhaug, 1999).

NB: Going back to section 12.4 it should be noted that pattern matching assumes some a priori theoretical frame (Yin, 1994).

12.5.2 Departure from data (observations)

The opposite strategy is to start from the data and let inspection of the data result in explanation. In its extreme form this is what has been termed *grounded theory*, that is 'theory derived from data, systematically gathered and analysed' (Strauss

Figure 12.2 Problem recognition – raw materials (last purchase)

and Corbin, 1990: 121). An important point is that theory is needed in any type of research. To make sense of data (observations) theory is needed. In fact the quality of qualitative research is highly dependent on the investigator's ability to observe, conceptualize and theorize. As noted above, qualitative research implies intensive interplay between data (observations) and theory (see section 2.5).

Over the years the original grounded theory (Glaser and Strauss, 1967) has been modified. It has also been criticized. One objection is that theory-neutral observations are hardly feasible, and what we 'see' when conducting research is influenced by multiple factors, one of which is what we already know about the social world being studied. (For more detailed discussion of criticism of grounded theory, see Bryman, 2001: 395–7.)

12.5.3 Analysing case studies

One way to analyse data collected through case study methods is to look for commonalities and differences, for example in situations where there are many cases. As stated by Boyd et al. (1985: 51):

> In one study to improve the productivity of the sales force of a particular company, the investigator studied intensively two or three of the best sales representatives and two or three of the worst. Data was collected on the background and experience of each representative and then several days were spent making sales calls with them. As a result, a hypothesis was developed. It was that checking the stock of retailers and suggesting items on which they were low were the most important differences between the successful and the poor sales representatives.

As illustrated by the above example, we can find answers to our questions by comparing different cases. In some cases the best and worst comparisons are most suitable. In the same manner we could compare performance of several units/branches of a company by comparing them with each other. Campbell (1975) and Yin (1994) refer to 'pattern matching' where information from several cases could be related to a priori assumptions. If we could find a systematic pattern we could accept or confirm our assumption or proposition. We do not need statistical testing to come to the conclusions (Ghauri, 2004). The requirement is that the pattern has to be sufficiently systematic.

> For the purpose of analysis or drawing conclusions, the cases that display contrast or an extreme situation (e.g. performance or failure) are most useful. This is because it is easier to find differences or determine what distinguishes two extreme cases than to compare and find differences between two average or normal cases (Churchill, 1991: 143).

In the case of descriptive case studies, this does not mean that the purpose is to collect and present only the facts. As put by Ferber et al. (1964: 153):

> Facts do not lead anywhere. Indeed facts, as facts, are the commonest, cheapest and most useless of all commodities. Anyone with a questionnaire can gather thousands of facts a day – and probably not find much real use for them. What makes facts practical and valuable is the glue of explanation and understanding, the framework of theory, the tie-rod of conjecture. Only when facts can be fleshed to a skeletal theory do they become meaningful in the solution of problems.

In descriptive research, the researcher has to work with specific research problems, propositions or hypotheses. While exploratory study is characterized by flexibility, descriptive study can be considered more rigid. It requires a clear specification of the who, what, why and how of the research problem. For further details of specific techniques for data analysis for descriptive studies the reader should look into Miles and Huberman (1994).

12.6 Quantifying qualitative data

According to the present authors, quantification can be relevant in qualitative research. This may be the case, for example, when the researcher wants to capture the frequency of certain events.

Example

To gain insights into whether computer models influence strategic decision making, a study was conducted where a management team was asked to solve a strategic task with and without a computer tool. When solving the task the team was taped and video-taped. A part of the analysis was to examine the concepts used (because concepts held and used relate to what is captured). Table 12.1 reports

Table 12.1 **Concept list**

Concept list	Number of concepts		Number of concepts	
	Mentioned		Used in discussions	
	Before	After	Before	After
Management of the Norwegian shelf	7	1	7	1
Goals	2	0	2	0
Role of the authorities	5	1	5	1
Producer economic results	4	7	2	7
Profit	1	1	1	1
Price	1	1	1	1
Income	0	2	0	2
Cost	2	3	0	3
Transportation costs	1	1		1
Production costs	1	1		1
Marginal costs		1		1
Supply (production)	18	13	17	13
Producer behaviour	4	3	4	3
Actors	8	7	8	7
Gas fields	1	1	0	1
Volumes	5	2	5	2
Production capacity	1	1	1	1
Production volume	1	1	1	1
Surplus/scarcity	1		1	
Seasonal variation (winter sale)	1		1	
Take back gas clause	1		1	
Demand (consumption)	9	16	7	16
Actors	5	13	3	13
Import quota	0	1	0	1
Growth	2	1	2	1
Substitutes	2	0	2	0
Volumes	0	1	0	1
Trade pattern – changes	0	3	0	3
Norway 1/Norway 2		1		1
Norway 1 and 2/other producers		1		1
Market share		1		1
Pipelines	1	4	0	4
Landing node	1	1		1
Capacity		1		1
Utilization		1		1
Shadow price		1		1
Number of superordinate categories	5	6	4	6
Number of concepts	39	44	33	44

Source: Fuglseth and Grønhaug (2003). Copyright © 2003, with permission from Elsevier concepts mentioned and used before (without) the computer and after (with the computer aid). In this case the researchers knew that managers hold concepts, but not what concepts they hold and use.

Also, assume that an identified concept is gradually refined and defined. Over time quantitative measures to capture the underlying phenomenon empirically may be developed (see Chapter 6). Hypotheses may as well be tested statistically in qualitative research.

Example

An anthropologist observes a specific behaviour among a group of people, and advances the assumption (hypothesis) that this is due to so and so. When the specific condition occurs nothing happens. The researcher drops the initial hypothesis and advances a second one, and so on. At his nth trial to advance a hypothesis, the observation is as expected. Moreover, every time the expected condition is present, the specific behaviour is observed. Assume that the researcher has observed the expected behaviour in five subsequent situations when the specific condition is present. With no prior information, this implies the probability for such an outcome by chance is: that $P(B = 5) = 0.031$, $p = 0.5$, $n = 5$, that is, gaining such an observation by chance is a little higher than 3 per cent.

12.7 Validity in qualitative research

In earlier chapters we emphasized the importance of validity, and that validity is also required in qualitative research (see sections 5.5, 6.3–6.5). Validity concerns are challenging to handle. In qualitative research the following types of validity are often emphasized.

- descriptive
- interpretative
- theoretical
- generalizable.

Descriptive validity refers to the degree to which the actual description holds true. For example, is the description of a strategy process or the buying process in Figure 12.2 correct: that is, does it capture the buying process in Alpha and Beta as it took place?

Interpretative validity refers to how good the interpretation is. Is the expressed interpretation the correct one? For example, is the explanation regarding technological flexibility suggested above valid?

Theoretical validity refers to the adequacy of our suggested 'theory' on explanation. For example, based on a substantial research effort, a researcher suggests an explanation (a theory) of how firms cope with external uncertainties. Does the suggested theory hold true?

By *generalizable validity* we mean to what extent the findings from a study can be generalized to other settings. For example, the suggested explanation of how firms cope with external uncertainties was *based* on observation among small firms in one industry. Can the explanation be generalized to hold true also for large firms or firms in other industries?

Validity claims: It is not enough only to talk about validity. Validity must also be *demonstrated*. For example, in a study you claim that 'a power game was going on in the company'. The term 'power game' must be explained (on conceptual definitions, see Chapter 3). Moreover, evidence that the claimed power game really was going on must be reported. Validity claims are responses to the question: How can I trust you?

12.8 Use of computers in qualitative research

Analysis of qualitative data is tedious and time consuming. However, over the years various software programs have been designed to facilitate data analysis. For example, known by the acronym CAQDAS (Computer Assisted Qualitative Data Analysis Software), a number of programs have been developed over the past 15 years. A well-known computer program for qualitative research is QSR NUD*IST (see also Chapter 11).

Weitzman and Miles (1995) published a comprehensive and useful guide to computer programs for qualitative data analysis. They categorize the programs into four basic types:

1. text retrievers: these programs are useful for finding words, phrases, etc., in one or several data files;
2. text-based managers, designed to organize, sort and make subsets of text systematically;
3. code and retrieve programs: these are useful for dividing text into segments by theme or category and assigning codes to these;
4. conceptual network builders, helpful in building networks and examining semantic relationships between codes.

The various programs are rather general, being useful for several of the above tasks. Such programs are designed to do what the researcher might wish to do manually. Software packages are particularly useful where there is a large quantity of data requiring coding, annotation, linking, search and retrieval, development of data display, and so on.

12.8.1 A word of warning

To make proper use of such programs, the researcher must of course know how to analyse data and have command over how to use the program. Probably even more important is to have an intimate personal knowledge of the data, so that

211

appropriate trigger codes and responses can be inserted at the outset of data inter-pretation. Such knowledge can best come from personal involvement in the entire process, from data collection through to analysis.

12.9 Case studies and triangulation

Triangulation refers to the combination of methodologies in the study of the same phenomenon. Through triangulation we can improve the accuracy of judgements and thereby results, by collecting data through different methods or even by collecting different kinds of data on the subject matter of our study. The discussion on validity (in Chapter 5) is particularly relevant here. Some-times to enhance the validity of our research we need to collect or analyse data through triangulation. In cases where correctness or precision is important, it is quite logical to collect information through different methods and angles. The following story illustrates what we mean.

Three blind men were asked to describe an elephant by touching or feeling only a part of it. We can well imagine what they could have described by touch-ing different parts of an elephant such as a foot, an ear or a trunk. This illustrates that, in many cases, one method alone cannot be enough to explain or describe a phenomenon, and we need to use a multi-method approach to get the whole reality.

The use of multi-methods or triangulation is not new and can be traced back to Campbell and Fiske (1959), who argued that to ensure validation one should use more than one method. The main advantage of triangulation, however, is that it can produce a more complete, holistic and contextual portrait of the object under study. In the case study method this is particularly important as you need to check and validate the information you receive from various sources. For example, you can check the performance of a firm or a project, claimed by the interviewee, from annual accounts or archives or by interviewing another manager or company auditors.

Moreover, it is quite useful to use qualitative methods in a pilot study to build hypotheses or propositions and then to use quantitative methods to test these hypotheses. We can call this a two-step study. There are some problems with triangulation. For example, sometimes it can be difficult to judge if the results from different methods are consistent or not. A second problem arises when the different methods come up with contradictory results. Sometimes it is possible that the researchers prefer or emphasize one method over another: for example quantitative versus qualitative. However, all research methods have advantages and disadvantages when it comes to different research problems. Our conclusion is that triangulation or the use of a multi-method approach on the same study object can be useful even if we do not get the same results. It can lead us to a better understanding or to new questions that can be answered by later research.

Triangulation is particularly useful in international business research to check for the method bias. Using multiple methods to examine the same phenomenon and checking for consistencies enhances our confidence in the analysis and results. Here we could compare the data and results obtained through an experiment and through interviews. Convergence of results obtained through these different methods will enhance the reliability and validity of our results. We could also compare results obtained through qualitative methods with statistical analysis.

Note

1. This section builds on Spiggle (1994).

 ## Further reading

Ghauri, P. (2004) 'Designing and conducting case studies in international business research', in Marshan-Piekkari, R. and Welch, C. (eds), *A Handbook of Qualitative Research Methods for International Business*, Cheltenham: Edward Elgar, pp. 109–24.

Miles, M.B. and Huberman, A.M. (1994) *Qualitative Data Analysis*, 2nd edn, Thousand Oaks, CA: Sage.

Sinkovics, R.R., Penz, E. and Ghauri, P.N. (2005) 'Analysing textual data in international marketing research', *Qualitative Market Research: An International Journal*, 8(1), pp. 9–38.

Sinkovics, R.R., Penz, E. and Ghauri, P.N. (2008) 'Enhancing the trustworthiness of qualitative research in international business', *Management International Review*, 48(6), pp. 689–714.

Questions

1. What do you consider to be key characteristics of qualitative research?

2. Explain what is meant by coding. Also explain the role of coding in analysing qualitative data.

3. What is meant by suggesting that qualitative data are an 'attractive nuisance'?

4. What do you think are the main advantages and disadvantages in departing from theory in qualitative research?

5. How can triangulation make our research more reliable?

Exercises

1. You wonder whether young women and young men differ in their evaluations and behaviours in their purchase of a new car. Suggest how you would design a study to explore your research problem. Also explain what data you will gather and how to do this to solve your research problem.

2. Assume you decide to gather information through un(modestly)-structured interviews. Prepare, conduct and tape-record one such interview. Transcribe the interview, read it, code and analyse it.

CHAPTER 13

Cross-cultural research

13.1 The international dimension

In cases of international or cross-cultural research we need to take extra care in each and every stage of the process. The research involving unfamiliar environmental and cultural differences may complicate the understanding of the research problem. The researchers often fail to anticipate the impact of local cultures on the question asked. This also has to do with deciding the scope and limits of the problem. In some cultures a broader scope is necessary to cover the necessary variables. For example, concepts such as 'supermarket' have different meanings in different markets. In Japan a supermarket usually occupies two or three stories and sells groceries, daily necessities and clothing on respective floors. Some even sell furniture and electronics, stationery and sporting goods (Ghauri and Cateora, 2006). The availability of data/statistical information on exports or imports of a particular product may also be different. Even if it is available, in some countries it might not be up to date or reliable. Many countries do not have government agencies that collect and maintain up-to-date data. In some countries private firms collect and sell data. Or the researchers have to collect primary data themselves. It is not possible to use data gathered in one market in another market. This is important for researchers as well as managers doing research in different markets, as illustrated by Box 13.1.

Comparability of data is, however, the main issue in international/cross-cultural research. It is not just due to the availability but also due to the manner in which data are collected and analysed. The researchers have to be extra careful in categorization and measurement of cross-cultural data. The international dimension of the research process, explained earlier, is added in Figure 13.1.

As illustrated in the figure, the researcher has to be careful and adjust her/his approach at each and every stage of the research process when doing international/cross-cultural research. It is appropriate to eliminate items/concepts that are found to be biased in one or more countries involved in the research. However, we still have to be careful so that a meaningful comparison between the countries can be made. This will increase the probability that the results obtained are comparable and equivalent (Craig and Douglas, 2000).

Box 13.1 Marketing research in Egypt

The 'Habits and Practices' study by Procter & Gamble consisted of home visits and discussion groups (qualitative research) to understand how the Egyptian housewife did her laundry. The study wanted to discover her likes, dislikes and habits (the company's knowledge of laundry practices in Egypt had been limited to automatic washing machines). From this study it was determined that the Egyptian consumer goes through a very laborious washing process to achieve the desired results. Among the 95 per cent of homes that washed in a non-automatic washing machine or by hand, the process consisted of soaking, boiling, bleaching and washing each load several times. Several products were used in the process; bar soaps or flakes were added to the main wash, along with liquid bleach and bluing to enhance the cleaning performance of the poor quality of locally produced powders. These findings highlighted the potential for a high-performing detergent that would accomplish everything that currently required several products. The decision was made to proceed with the development and introduction of a superior-performing, high-suds granular detergent.

Once the basic product concept (i.e. one product instead of several to do laundry) was decided on, the company needed to determine the best components for a marketing mix to introduce the new product. The company went back to focus groups to assess reactions to different brand names, to get ideas about the appeal and relevant wording for promotions and to test various price ranges, package design and size. Information derived from focus group encounters helped the company eliminate ideas with low consumer appeal and to focus on those that triggered the most interest. Further, the groups helped refine advertising and promotion wording to ensure clarity of communication through the use of everyday consumer language.

At the end of this stage, the company had well-defined ideas garnered from several focus groups, but did not have a 'feel' for the rest of those in the target market. Would they respond the same way as the focus groups? To answer this question the company proceeded to the next step, a research programme to validate the relative appeal of the concepts generated from focus groups with a survey (quantitative research) of a large sample from the target market. Additionally, brand name, price, size and the product's intended benefits were tested in large sample surveys. Information gathered in the final surveys provided the company with the specific information used to develop a marketing programme that led to a successful product introduction and brand recognition for Ariel throughout Egypt.

Source: Ghauri and Cateora (2006: 151)

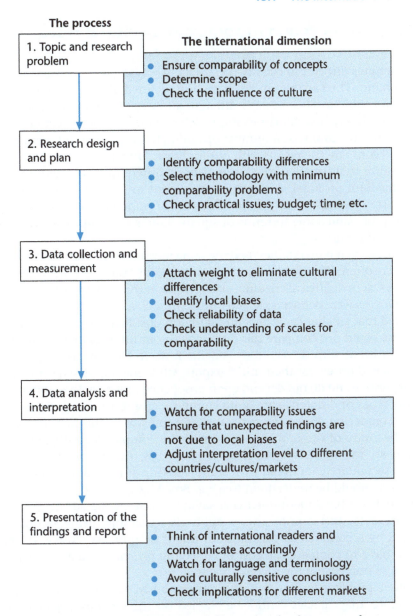

Figure 13.1 Managing the international dimension in the research process

Source: Based on Ghauri and Cateora (2006: 149)

13.2 Data collection in some cross-cultural research

It is sometimes difficult to classify these data in ways that are consistent with the study at hand. The variables might have been defined differently or the measurement unit could have been totally different and would, therefore, make the comparison absolutely invalid. For example, when studying the export behaviour of smaller firms, we could use a number of studies undertaken in different countries and could compare the results with our findings. After a closer look, however, we might realize that 'smaller firms' were defined differently. To determine the size (small, medium or large), different measurement units were used. Some studies defined size in terms of sales, some in terms of number of employees, some in terms of profit and some in terms of square metres of occupied space, as in the case of retailing firms.

Moreover, even if two studies used the same measurement unit, the terms of definition were often different. In a study in Norway, for example, firms with 200–499 employees were defined as medium sized, while in the USA firms with fewer than 500 employees were defined as smaller firms. In such a comparison, if the US study concluded that smaller firms depend highly on unsolicited orders for their initial export, we could not compare this finding with our findings in Norway by saying that, 'Consistent with the US study, smaller firms in Norway also depend heavily on unsolicited orders for their initial export, while medium-sized firms are much more aggressive and do not depend upon unsolicited orders for their initial exports.'

These types of difference are quite common, and researchers using secondary data or comparing and supporting their findings with the help of these data should be aware of the problems and make the comparison with some caution. One way to ameliorate the situation is to discuss the differences and the relevance of secondary data to our own study, looking at the validity of comparison and how it should be understood (see e.g. Box 13.2).

Although we have mentioned cost saving as one of the advantages of using secondary data, this cannot always apply. For example, using secondary data compiled by a commercial organization might be quite expensive. In this case you will have to compare the cost of collecting primary data as compared with the price of purchasing the secondary data.

Another problem is that it is the responsibility of the researcher that data are accurate; inaccuracies cannot be blamed on the secondary source. It is the researcher's responsibility to check whether findings presented by another researcher are based on primary or secondary data. This can be checked by internal consistency of the report being consulted. It is therefore important always to check the original source of data. It is only the original source that can provide us with the required information on the quality of data as it describes the process of data collection and analysis. Also, while referring to secondary data, you have to consult and refer to the original source and not what you have collected from an intermediate or third-hand report.

| Box 13.2 | Difficulties in making cross-cultural comparisons using official statistics |

Jackie Davis (2001) carried out an international comparison of labour disputes and stoppages through strike action in 23 OECD countries between 1990 and 1999 using statistical data collected at a national level. However, the article is careful to point out the limitations of such an analysis for the following reasons:

- *Voluntary notification.* In most of the countries governments rely on employers notifying them of any disputes, which they are then able to confirm through media reports.
- *Fail to measure full effects.* None of the countries records the full effects of stoppages at work, for example measured in terms of lost working time in companies not involved in the dispute but that are unable to work because of a shortage of materials caused by the strike.
- *Different thresholds for inclusion.* In the UK, disputes involving fewer than ten employees or lasting less than one day are excluded from the recorded figures. In other countries the thresholds for inclusion are particularly high. For example, in the USA, records include only disputes involving more than 1000 workers. This can make comparison of strike rates between countries particularly difficult.
- *Exclusion of certain industrial sectors.* Some of the countries exclude the effects of disputes in certain sectors: for example, Portugal omits the public sector and general strikes.
- *Changes in the way figures are recorded.* For example, France has changed the way it records lost working days, thus making it difficult to make comparisons over time.
- *Indirectly involved workers.* There are differences between the countries in recording those workers who are unable to work because others at their workplace are on strike. Half of the countries, including France, the Netherlands and New Zealand, attempt to include these workers in the statistics, but the other half, including Italy and Japan, do not.
- *Dispute rates affected by a small number of very large strikes.* Some countries can appear to have very high labour dispute rates in one particular year because of one strike involving a large number of workers. In France, for example, there was a strike in 1995 involving all of the public sector.

These differences lead some countries, such as the USA or Japan, to record a lower number of working days lost through labour disputes than say the UK or Germany simply because of the different methods used for compiling statistics in the individual countries. This means that cross-cultural comparisons using nationally collected statistics need to be made with a degree of caution.

Source: Davis (2001); Bryman and Bell (2003: 227). Reproduced under the terms of the Click-Use Licence.

13.3 Collecting cross-cultural data

Before collecting primary data, however, you need to consider a number of issues. First you need to define the relevant unit of analysis, that is who should be the right person/group/organization to be consulted/studied. This is particularly important in an international research setting, as the complexity of environmental and contextual factors may have a major impact on the topic/area of research. According to some views, cross-cultural research can be viewed as a quasi-experiment in which data is collected from different contexts that may or may not be equivalent (Campbell and Stanley, 1966; Craig and Douglas, 2000).

The unit of analysis and a particular research question may lead to different research design and data sources. Here the comparability of data collected from different countries/cultures also needs to be evaluated. The data source, and the information collected, should represent the same meaning and interpretation. The data collected from different countries should also be equally reliable and accurate. Diversity in culture, language and methods of communication between the respondents and also between the researchers (if more than one researcher is involved) can lead to misunderstandings and misinterpretations (see Craig and Douglas, 2000; Andreasen, 1990 for further reading and Lonner and Adamopoulos, 1997).

In cross-cultural and international research projects/studies we need to handle this issue and develop equivalent or comparable measures/interpretations of the data to be collected. In literature, we find two different approaches to handling this issue. The *'emic'* approach believes that cultures are different and issues related to one culture should be understood through the particular cultural context. Consequently our questions and interpretations should be adjusted to the specific culture to get the correct understanding (Pike, 1966).

The *'etic'* approach advocates constructing measures that are 'culture free' and can be used in cross-cultural studies without posing equivalence or comparability problems (Triandis, 1972). In this situation, constructs and measures development in one country can be used without any or minimum adjustment to cultural differences. These two approaches present two extremes, and many authors recommend that while doing cross-cultural research you need to raise this issue and try to use an etic approach as far as possible, by preparing constructs and measures that are comparable. This can also be achieved by using already established constructs and measures (Wind and Douglas, 1982; Schwartz, 1992; Craig and Douglas, 2000).

In many situations a combination of emic and etic approaches is advisable (Berry, 1989). Here it is suggested that you first conduct research in your own culture and then apply the construct or measurement instrument to study behaviour in the other culture (imposed etic). Behaviour is then studied in the other culture within its own context, using an emic approach in both cultures. These two observations are then brought together towards an etic approach and are

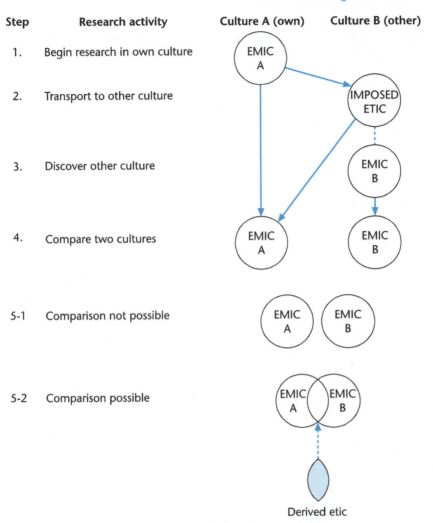

| Step | Research activity | Culture A (own) | Culture B (other) |

Figure 13.2 Steps in operationalizing emic and etic approaches
Source: Based on Berry (1989), reproduced with permission of Ralph Berry

interpreted in a comparable manner. A derived etic approach is thus possible based on common aspects and features. This is further explained in Figure 13.2.

For data collection involving multi-culture or multi-context study, it is important to understand the differences between culture and behaviour. Quite often researchers collect and interpret data according to their self-reference criteria (SRC) (Ghauri and Cateora, 2006) while collecting data in a culture very different from their own. Qualitative data collection methods can be useful in such cases, as they often use unstructured questions that can be changed, translated and reformulated more easily.

Qualitative research allows researchers to explore and probe deeply into attitudes towards product classes, brands, trends and behaviour. It also helps to reduce the psychic distance between the researcher and the respondent, especially in cross-cultural research (Craig and Douglas, 2000). In this type of research qualitative research provides better understanding of a given context and underlying motivations, values and attitudes. Data collected from a small number of carefully selected samples on relevant issues can be sufficient in this case (Patton, 1990).

In cross-cultural research, behaviour can be observed quite easily, for example shopping behaviour in supermarkets, department stores or bazaars. The researcher can observe whether bargaining takes place or not, how long each transaction takes, the conditions of sales and customers' reactions, the reaction of customers to special offers or promotions and so on. The observation can be made personally by the researcher or by placing a video camera in the supermarket. This type of research can provide useful insight into how people purchase a certain product in different cultures or how different environments, cultures and promotions influence the buying behaviour of customers. The data collected from different countries/cultures can easily be compared (Craig and Douglas, 2000).

Observations, however, are often criticized because their interpretation can be rather subjective. In international research it is particularly problematic if the researcher who is going to interpret the data is not familiar with the cultural conditions in which the data is collected. This can, however, be handled through collection of data by several researchers familiar with different cultures, and through interpretation of data through a common and systematic analytical framework.

In international or cross-cultural research it is important that the instrument is adapted to the specific culture in which it is used and not to just one of the cultures in the study. The design and administration of the instrument needs adaptation, according to the education levels and other background of respondents. The formulation of questions, the questionnaire as a whole and the response format often influence comprehension and response accuracy in different cultures (Malhotra, 1996; Schwartz and Sudman, 1996; Craig and Douglas, 2000).

Concepts such as 'supermarket', 'household', 'occupation', etc. may have different meanings in the USA, Sweden, India or China. All these need to be explained so that they are correctly understood and interpreted. The response format should encourage correct and clear answers.

We should check and ensure that everybody *understands the question in the same manner*: in other words, that everybody draws the same meaning from the questions. This is particularly important in questions or questionnaires that are translated from one language to another. One way to deal with this is to have an expert translate the questions, for example from English to Norwegian, and then have another expert translate the text back from Norwegian to English. The researcher can then clearly see if there has been any change in the meaning.

The discrepancies should be corrected with the help of experts from both sides. There are several methods to handle the language issue in international research. For more details, see Ghauri and Cateora's (2006) chapter on international marketing research.

13.4 Analysis of cross-cultural data

Multi-country or multi-cultural data can be involved in quantitative and qualitative research. Analysis of data in these situations becomes more complex due to the existence of multiple units of analysis. In this case the analysis can be conducted in different phases: first within-country analysis and then cross-country analysis. In international research the purpose might be not only to understand each country/market involved but also to assess the extent to which strategies or decisions can be standardized across different markets (Craig and Douglas, 2000).

In qualitative research this issue is particularly important, as one way of handling cross-cultural differences is to collect data through less-structured research. In international business research the focus shifts from within country to between countries variables. Thus country becomes the unit of analysis, and it becomes very important that variables chosen in each country are representative of the country. Figure 13.3 explains the unit of analysis discussion.

In cross-cultural or international business research equivalences of the unit of analysis need to be considered. Moreover, it should be clearly defined and

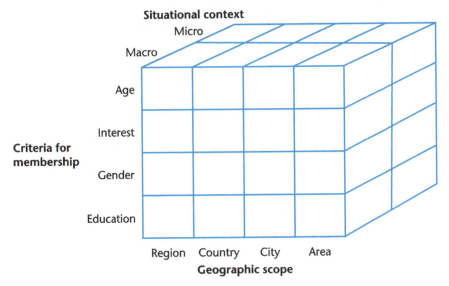

Figure 13.3 Defining unit of analysis

Source: Based on Craig and Douglas (2000). Copyright © John Wiley & Sons Limited. Reprinted with permission explained so that it is not mixed up and is distinct from other units. Figure 13.3 explains that we need to consider three distinct aspects (Craig and Douglas, 2000: 142–3): the *geographic scope* of the unit, the *criteria for membership* in the unit, and the *situational context*, meaning the particular socio-cultural setting.

Geographic scope helps us to define geographic boundaries of the unit we intend to study. In international business the most commonly used unit is country, and most secondary data is collected on a country-by-country basis. Increasingly, however, research is being done on a regional basis, such as the European Union, NAFTA or ASEAN. Sometimes we also undertake research in cities and/or in particular industries (e.g. airlines, banking or retailing) in a certain country or due to the size of the countries/companies (e.g. measured as GDP, revenue or number of employees).

Criteria for membership has to be determined for the unit to be studied. Whether it is individuals or organizations we need to decide some criteria for their inclusion. For individuals it could be age or gender, and for organizations it could be businesses or non-profit organizations. For organizations, we could include criteria such as size, industry, origin, internationality, etc.

Situational context can range from broad socio-cultural settings (macro-context) to a specific situation (micro-context). At the macro level our geographic unit is a country, and we should identify country characteristics that might influence the behaviour of the respondent. In the same manner, if we are studying cities, we need to differentiate between rural and urban areas. Moreover, whether we conduct the study in business settings or in social (e.g. at home) settings might have some influence on the data collected.

This means that we need to analyse data within each country and across different countries. Moreover, we need to examine the structure or relationship between variables. Craig and Douglas (2000: 292–3) present this issue as illustrated by Figure 13.4.

Difference in	Within-country analysis	Cross-country analysis
Level		
Structure		

Figure 13.4 Cross-country data analysis

Source: Based on Craig and Douglas (2000: 293). Copyright © John Wiley & Sons Limited. Reprinted with permission

There are two phases in data analysis. In the first phase we analyse data within each country. In the second we examine and compare data between the countries involved, to find out similarities and differences. In the first phase, the relationship between different variables is studied (e.g. factors influencing consumer behaviour). In the second stage we compare the findings from different countries. In qualitative research, the observations in each country might be based on subjective judgement and experience. While comparing data from different countries we can apply relatively objective techniques to find out the similarities and differences.

Here we can focus either on level of variables or on the structure of variables. For level issues, we need to find out whether there is a significant difference in a certain variable in the countries compared. If there is a difference then the researcher tries to find out why there is a difference. In structure issues we try to find out whether there is a difference in the relationship between two variables between the countries compared, for example whether high income and gender influence a certain consumer behaviour for a certain product. This type of analysis is more complex, and the complexity increases with the number of variables. Analysis in this case demands more sophisticated techniques and clear definition of the unit of analysis that is consistent across countries (Douglas and Craig, 1997; van de Vijver and Leung, 1997).

The level of variables between countries can be analysed using cross-tabulation and other statistical techniques. Techniques such as multiple regression and analysis of variance are useful ways to analyse data in international business research.

13.5 Enhancing trustworthiness of cross-cultural research

Driven by globalization and relocation of companies' activities all over the globe, there is an increasing emphasis on comparative international research and how to make it more trustworthy or reliable. One way of enhancing trustworthiness and standards of qualitative research is to follow steps suggested in Table 13.1. Cross-cultural perspectives that were used in many other disciplines such as psychology and ethnography are now adopted and extended by management scholars. In quantitative research there are established methods to handle and analyse cross-cultural data and its dealing with equivalence and comparability issues, as objectivity and validity in data collection is easier to enforce.

For qualitative data collection and analysis it is important to establish conformability, credibility and trustworthiness. Some researchers claim that CAQDAS, computer assisted methods such as N*VIVO, can assist researchers in enhancing this trustworthiness. N*VIVO facilitates coding and categorization and can assist in preparing matrix graphs. However, if you are planning to use N*VIVO for your data collection and analysis, we suggest you look at Sinkovics et al. (2005 and 2008).

Table 13.1 Enhancing the trustworthiness of qualitative research in international business – linking standards and stages

How to enhance the quality of interview-based qualitative research? – Standards

Standards → ↓ Stages	Credibility/Validity	Dependability/Reliability	Transferability/ Generalizability	Confirmability/Objectivity	Enhanced outcome – Logic and transparent analysis and report documentation. (*Marshall, 2001*) Research report (*see Lee, 1999*)
'Getting started' Construct bias • Theoretical basis • Literature review • Problem definition	• Build on established theory • Use of pre-established dimensions (*Potter, 1996*)	N/A	• Functional and conceptual equivalence • Equivalence of research topic (e.g. pre-testing definition of concept) (*Craig and Douglas, 2005; Salzberger et al., 1999; Sinkovics et al., 2005*)	Alertness to and coherence of • background assumptions • theory, construct • 'leading' literature • problem overrepresented • definition of behaviours (*Potter, 1996*)	1. Study derived from formal theory, semi-developed conceptual structure, or general topic 2. Study served to generate new theory, extend or elaborate existing theory, or not generate a new theory 3. References: key, 'critical', accurate 4. Can contractions be explained? 5. Study's problem is sufficiently important
Research design Method bias	• Build on established theory • Build and extend proven research design (*Creswell, 1997*)	N/A (only applicable after data collection)	N/A (only applicable after data collection)	N/A (only applicable after data collection)	6. Hypotheses: appropriate level of analysis; falsifiable; central to theoretical, conceptual or applied basis; adequately operationalized; derives from key construct
Sample and context	Theoretical sampling and testing of external validity (*Creswell, 1997; Salzberger et al., 1999*): • Confirmation and disconfirmation of responses and contexts	Evidence of a committed study (e.g. number of interviews) (*Lee, 1999; Sinkovics et al., 2005*)	Analytic generalizability (ecological validity) (*Kvale, 1996; Lee, 1999*)	• Ethics: the way participants were treated in general • Communication with participants • Encounters with participants (*Strauss and Corbin, 1994; Strauss and Corbin, 1998*)	7. Subject selection (probabilistic, convenience, theoretical sampling) 8. Information was given to subjects before, during, after study 9. Subjects' social and emotional states before, during, after study 10. Researchers' rapport with subjects before, during, after study

Data collection and Data preparation	Construct validity: • Use multiple sources of evidence: interviewees' comments, researchers' observations, use of documents • Establish 'chain of evidence': documentation, archival records, interviews, direct observations, participant-observation and physical artefacts (Yin, 2003)	• Description • Use protocol to ensure repeatability (Maxwell, 1997; Yin, 2003)	Equivalence of • Methods (training of interview situation • Units (selection of companies and managers) • Administration (Salzberger et al., 1999), through training sessions (see Welch et al., 2002)	• Researcher participated but is still detached enough to make good observation • Data collection and analysis occur in alternating sequences (analysis drives collection) • Interpretation: what was said – what was meant (Strauss and Corbin, 1994; Strauss and Corbin, 1998)	11. Data (kinds of data, how much) 12. Data recorded 13. Data transcription (language issue) 14. Specific steps in data collection 15. Specific questions 16. Interview agenda 17. Fit of collected data to researchers' general topic, theory 18. Rich descriptions of the phenomenon's context (value-free note taking)
Stimulus bias Data analysis	Internal validity: • Accuracy, completeness • Search for negative incidents • Check for plausibility of rival hypotheses (Maxwell, 1997)	• Derivation of coding scheme from data (grounded approach) • Application of formalized steps of organizing, coding, searching and modelling (Strauss and Corbin, 1994; Yin, 2003)	• Equivalence of data by following a common coding scheme (Salzberger et al., 1999) • Description allows replication (Lee, 1999)	Confirmability: • Objectivity through external audit • Participant should react to data and interpretation of researcher • 'Devil's advocate' (Maxwell, 1997)	19. Analysis involves global interpretation or formalized analysis 20. How were categories defined? 21. How were defined categories imposed on data? 22. Fit of researchers' interpretation with what is already known
Discussion	External validity, transferability, applicability • How generalizable are findings to another setting of people, etc. • Establishing domain to which the study's findings can be generalized (Lee, 1999)	Research report is logical, transparent and consistent – invites replication (Lee, 1999)	Comparison with conflicting and similar literature (Lee, 1999)	Truth • Accuracy of particular findings (Lee, 1999) Enhanced outcome – Logic and transparent analysis and report documentation. (Marshall, 2001)	23. Results clearly and concisely summarized 24. Implications follow data 25. Limitations concisely stated 26. Contributes to the body of knowledge clearly and convincingly 27. Alternative explanation

Note: Please note that we purposefully use both quantitative and qualitative terminology in the headings of the respective columns, in order to link quality criteria, which were originally suggested without reference to particular research methodologies (see Nunnally, 1978).

Source: Sinkovics et al., 2008: 696–98 with kind permission from Gabler Verlag and Dr Rudolf Sinkovics.

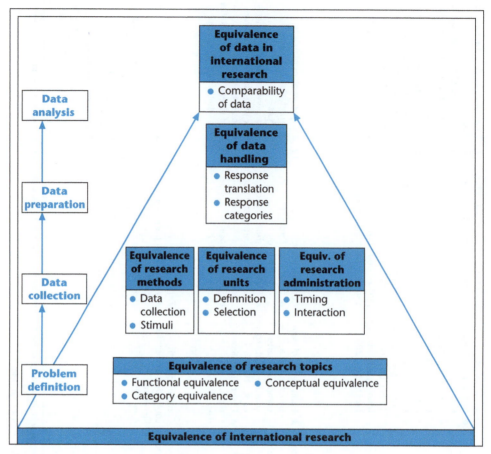

Figure 13.5 Ensuring the equivalence in cross-cultural research
Source: Salzberger *et al.* (1999: 23–28).

For cross-cultural research however, you have to be careful right from the start and at each and every stage of the research process as suggested by Figure 13.5. The question of equivalence, that the respondents have understood your questions in the same way in each and every country/culture and have responded in the same way across cultures, is the responsibility of the researcher. This has to be dealt with right from the start, at the problem definition stage. In the same way, at the data collection stage if you are collecting data/information from several countries, the methods of data collection, the unit of study you have chosen and the timing have to be comparable.

It is quite common for a researcher to conduct the data collection in the home country and then decide to collect data from another country after a year using the same questionnaire. The equivalence and comparability of data in this case is highly questionable. Also, the method of data collection is important; for example, was the researcher present at the time of data collection or not? Later when data is sorted and prepared for analysis, through data reduction and categorization, it is important to obtain the real meaning. Dictionary translation is often not very helpful as this does not explain the intensity or the seriousness of the response. This has to be considered throughout the data analysis stage.

Further reading

Ghauri, P.N. and Firth, R. (2009) 'The formation of case research in international business', *Der Markt: Journal for Marketing*, 48: 29–40.

Grisar-Kassé, K. (2004) 'The role of negative personal experiences in cross-cultural case study research: failure or opportunity', in Marshan-Piekkari, R. and Welch, C. (eds) *A Handbook of Qualitative Research Methods for International Business*, Cheltenham: Edward Elgar, pp. 144–61.

Richards, T.J. and Richards, L. (2000) *Using N*VIVO in Qualitative Research*, 2nd edition, Bundoora: QSR International Pty.

Sinkovics, R., Penz, E. and Ghauri, P.N. (2008) 'Enhancing trustworthiness of qualitative research in international business', *Management International Review*, 48(6): 689–714.

Questions

1. Is cross-cultural research different from research in the same cultural setting? Discuss.

2. What is meant by the equivalence of the unit of analysis? Explain with examples.

3. Explain the two concepts emic and etic. How can we handle these issues in cross-cultural research?

4. How can a cross-cultural research project be most meaningful? What adjustments are necessary to accommodate cultural differences?

Exercises

1. A firm wants to go to a new market and is analysing Russia or India to enter. Do you think the firm can collect demographic data on the two markets and compare it to see which market is more suitable? Advise the company how it can enhance the comparability of the data collected in the two markets.

2. Discuss the emic and etic approach of data collection for a multi-country research project that you have to undertake. Select three countries of your choice and explain how you can use these approaches.

3. You are working on a qualitative research project through interviewing several firms to understand how companies evaluate a new market to enter. Suggest ways that can help you to enhance reliability of your results.

CHAPTER 14

Writing the final report

After completing the data collection and data analysis, we have to put the research problem, the data collected and the findings into a logical, consistent and persuasive report. Fortunately, as with research proposals and methodology, research reports conform to a fairly standard format. In many cases an oral presentation is also made to present your findings and research. We deal with both of these aspects.

14.1 Purpose and importance of a written presentation

Before starting to write the final report, we should consider its purpose and to whom it is addressed. Research reports typically start with an executive summary providing the important points from the report. After the summary, a preface is normally written where we explain the course of the study and thank individuals and organizations who have been helpful in data collection, funding, etc.

If the purpose of presenting a report is a Master's thesis, it may look different from a report that is presented to a company/manager on a specific issue. In the latter case, the report can be very concise and to the point, so that the manager can easily comprehend it and use the results in decision making. On the other hand, if the report is a thesis or project work, it has to be more detailed and written in a systematic manner. In this case all the details regarding problem formulation, data collection, the method of analysis and conclusion should be presented. In fact, a report written to 'sell' an idea to management should also be very detailed and convincing, with regard to concepts used, comparison with present systems/ideas and the benefits of the new system/ideas (Sekaran, 1992). We believe that a report needs to be detailed, argumentative and convincing in both cases. Another type of report is an academic paper written with the purpose of getting it published. We will deal with this type of report separately.

You must also realize that your report, project work or thesis will be assessed according to the criteria set by your institution or supervisor. Before working on the final report, you must revisit these criteria. Several authors (Bloom et al., 1971; Easterby-Smith et al., 1991; Saunders et al., 2000) provide educational objectives for different levels of research and report. For lower levels, your report should demonstrate understanding and knowledge of the topic. At a higher level, your report should demonstrate not only that you have knowledge of the topic but also that you can apply it to a concrete problem, having analysed the situation. At a still higher level, in addition to the above you have to demonstrate that you can synthesize, evaluate and analyse to draw conclusions.

The process of writing up a report is complex and sometimes tedious work. The report should be concise, and the findings and arguments presented in a convincing and consistent way. It is also important to present the research methodology and results in such a way that the reader can judge the validity and relevance of the findings.

> **A report needs to be argumentative and convincing, whether it is to be submitted to a company or as an academic thesis.**

We should give an account of our methods' *weaknesses and strengths* and the necessary details so that readers can make their own judgements on the validity and reliability of our study and findings. We should convince the reader that we have, first of all, done our job as a researcher, investigating a certain problem area with systematic data collection and data analysis, presented in a logical, easy-to-read and understandable report. Second, we must show that we have followed the technically correct and consistent method expected of a qualified report, that our hypotheses and/or conclusions are properly supported by existing literature and empirical evidence, and that there is a logical congruence between different parts of the report. We should also be concerned that our report gives due credit to earlier studies we have used and that we refer to all the sources in a proper manner. These two aspects are very important in qualified report writing and are therefore treated separately in this chapter.

14.2 Guidelines

14.2.1 Audience

The best reports are those that are written with a particular audience in mind. The contents, the length, the terminology used, the focus and the presentation of data and results all depend upon the audience. In writing a report for a company/manager the tone should be concise and efficient and the writing and usage of terminology should be according to their background, considering how much they already know about the topic. In this case, an executive summary becomes very important, as it provides a summary of the report in a direct and brief manner. Managers can then go into the report fully or into only those parts of it they feel appropriate.

In the case of a thesis, you need to check the rules and regulations of your particular school or supervisor. The guidelines provided later in this chapter on the structure of the report are the most commonly used. The audience influences the overall presentation, as some audiences are distracted by extensive use of tables and figures and by footnotes. In this case, you have to decide which tables and figures are necessary in the text and which should go into appendices, where those who are interested can look at them. The restriction on number of pages also influences the above. Quite often there is a maximum page limit but no minimum page limit, which shows that a concise report is more useful than an extensive one. In any case, the audience determines the type, the level and the complexity of the report. Researchers must make every effort to acquaint themselves with the specific preferences of their audience. They should not consider these preferences unalterable, but any deviation from them should be made with reason and not from ignorance (Boyd et al., 1989; Churchill, 1999).

14.2.2 Good communication

It goes without saying that the report should be readable. Scholars often suggest that the report has to be clear, concise, coherent, focused, lively, exciting, meaningful and without pedantry (Sekaran, 1992; Rubin and Rubin, 1995). The main idea is that the text should provide a clear explanation and should entice the readers, making them interested and curious to read the whole report. The assumptions and methods should be clearly stated and explained. There should be a natural and smooth flow from one part of the report to the next. Many researchers use a pedantic writing style to impress the reader with their sophisticated concepts and terminology. In our opinion, such a report does not communicate well. The reader should flow through the report without any hindrance or being stuck in understanding difficult terminology.

The format of the report enhances its readability; the use of headings and subheadings takes the reader through the report step by step. The reader should understand what you are saying and where you are going. As a good communicator, you can 'programme' the reader's mind in a way that he or she reads your report as you want it to be read or as you believe readers would like to read it. Do not expect your reader to read between the lines; you have to use direct and simple language.

> You can 'programme' a reader's mind as to how he or she reads your report.

14.2.3 Language and flow

It is not easy to write clear and simple sentences. As Elliot (1980: 18–19) says:

> Think what you want to say. Write your sentence. Then strip it of all adverbs and adjectives. Reduce the sentence to its skeleton. Let the verbs and nouns do the work. If your skeleton sentence does not express your thought precisely, you have got the wrong verb or noun. Dig for the right one. Nouns and verbs carry the guns in good writing; adjectives and adverbs are decorative camp followers.

233

Using difficult language and terminology does not really impress the reader but influences the readability of the report adversely. Good writing does not mean setting obstacles for the reader to overcome.

Sentences and paragraphs should be kept fairly short. The flow of arguments should run logically through the report. A concept or a terminology should be explained when first mentioned in the report.

In our opinion, the fewer the words the better the report. Several short sentences are better than one long sentence. Do not torture the reader by explaining your difficulties in collecting data or interviewing prominent business executives; just say what you have done and how you have collected your data. If you are using a concept to explain a certain situation, use the same concept every time you want to explain that situation. In verbal language, when we explain a certain situation we repeat facts and stories to make sure that the listener has heard and understood what we mean. This is not necessary in written language, and you should always avoid repeating things. Reports and theses are never judged according to their length or weight.

Normally we do not start a sentence or a paragraph with 'But', 'Because' or a number. If it is necessary to start a sentence with a number, it should be expressed in words: for example 'Fifty per cent' instead of '50 per cent'. Whatever rules are used, the most important aspect is to be consistent in writing, spelling (for example UK English versus US English), terminology, usage of headings, and figures and tables.

> **Using difficult language and terminology does not really impress the reader.**

The report, especially the descriptive part, should be written in the first person. Some people believe that impersonal language presupposes objectivity and suggest writing in the third person. We, however, advise that the third person observer/ researchers be referred to as 'I' or 'we' and that participants or respondents, etc., be referred to as 'we' or 'them'.

14.2.4 Form and style

The question of form and style is often more a question of likes and dislikes or individual styles than a matter of rules. However, the following are common mistakes and should be avoided (Grønhaug, 1985: 71):

- *Telegraphic style.* This means that a report is written in sentences which are not connected to each other with any logical consistency.
- *Long and complicated sentences.* Reports are sometimes written in long sentences that are not comprehensible unless we read them several times. Writing short and concise sentences is, however, a good way of writing reports.
- *Usage of terminology and differences between spoken and written language.* When using textbook or other terminology, you should be sure that the reader will

understand their use in the same way. It is quite common for students to use a spoken language form in their report. In report writing you should follow the rules of writing and avoid using a spoken or slang version.

- *Shortage of tables, figures or other illustrations.* You should try to simplify, highlight and complement the important and interesting parts of the report with figures and tables or other illustrations. It is important to point out that these tables and figures should not replace the text. They are used to complement or further explain the text or the point being made.

Our experience as researchers is that we have to write and rewrite reports at least four or five times before they are in a final shape. This is the working draft, and after writing this you should go through the material again, along with the data and findings, to see if there is something that has been missed and which should be included in the report. Then read the draft again and start correcting it as you read. Add the information you think is missing and delete the information you feel is irrelevant or repetitive. At the same time, check that the information is correctly placed; if it is not, reshuffle the text. This process is repeated three to four times before you have an almost-ready report. Finally, you should check the language and ideally have someone else read the report. It is quite common that, having read and re-read the report several times, you become blind to drawbacks or mistakes.

Before submitting the report, have someone else read it through.

The appearance is very important. It does not matter how well written a report is if it does not look good; it leaves a bad impression on the reader. Here the title page, the margins and the structure of the report are very important. It is easier to read double-spaced reports than single-spaced ones. It is common practice to use double spacing and indent the first word of each paragraph. In the case of single-spaced reports, double-space between the paragraphs to mark the new paragraphs. Regardless of whether the report is single-spaced or double-spaced, the following documents should always be typed single-spaced: letters, displayed quotations, footnotes (but use double spacing between them), tables and figures (Murphy and Hildebrandt, 1988).

14.2.5 Headings

The headings serve as an outline of a report and should be clear, meaningful and consistent. We often number headings to highlight different heading levels, but numbers are not essential. It is possible to use different styles or type to make these levels explicit. The most important aspect is not to use too many levels of headings as the reader should be able to differentiate easily between different levels of headings and subheadings.

14.3 Structure of the report

The following outline is a commonly used format for a research report. The chosen format is, however, dependent upon the reader for whom the report is prepared. Our common format is as follows:

1. Title page
2. Table of contents
3. Executive summary
4. Introduction and problem statement
5. Theoretical background
6. Methodology
7. Findings or empirical study
8. Conclusions and recommendations
9. Footnotes
10. Bibliography or references
11. Appendix.

14.3.1 Title page

The title page should indicate the topic of research and the name(s) of the researcher(s) (authors). Second, it should indicate the name of the organization where the report has been prepared and for what programme, if appropriate; for example, 'MSc Thesis for King's College London'. If it is a research project ordered or demanded by a company or any other organization, the company's or organization's name should also appear on the title page. Moreover, if the project has received any financial help from an institute other than the school or university, this name should also appear on the title page.

14.3.2 Table of contents

The table of contents lists the contents of the report with page numbers. Here, the headings and subheadings are presented. The reader should be able to differentiate the headings and subheadings both in the table of contents and in the report (see Figure 14.1). The table of contents should also include tables and figures with page numbers.

14.3.3 Executive summary

A summary provides the important aspects of each part of the report. It is often stated that a summary should be *self-sufficient* because most of the readers, especially business executives, often read only the summary (Churchill, 1999). The summary thus should highlight the whole report. However, it should be based on the main report and should not include any new material. The data

	Page no.
PREFACE	i
SUMMARY	ii
1. INTRODUCTION	1
1.1 Purpose of the study	3
1.2 Research problem	3
1.2.1 Research questions	4

Figure 14.1 **An example of a table of contents**

we have collected, presented and analysed in our report are often buried in the middle or at the end of it and have to be brought forward in the summary so that the reader can quickly and without any trouble perceive the message of the report (Bolsky, 1988).

The length of a summary depends upon the complexity of the original material. Normally we should reduce material in a summary to, at the most, 5 per cent of the report's full length or to a couple of pages. An ideal length is two to three pages.

14.3.4 Introduction and problem statement

An introduction to a research report should present what the study is about and what the purpose of the study is. This background will provide the reader with the necessary information to understand and comprehend the rest of the report. The objectives and the purpose of the study should be clearly mentioned in this section. After reading this section, the reader should have complete information on what the report deals with, why we are studying a particular problem and what can be expected in the rest of the report. Here all the unfamiliar terms should be clarified and the concepts of the research problems defined. Some account of what has already been done in this research or problem area is presented. This section should also explain how the report is organized, so that the reader's mind is programmed accordingly.

14.3.5 Theoretical background

Here the theoretical background to the problem area as well as to the study design is presented. If we are using hypotheses or a priori assumptions there has to be proper reasoning with the help of previous studies and findings. Depending upon the research orientation, as covered in Chapters 2 and 3, the importance of theory and its use is different. It is therefore important to be consistent in our report and we should check this section with our research orientation and design.

14.3.6 Methodology

In this section we inform the reader of our research design, whether it is exploratory, descriptive or causal, and why a particular design is chosen. We should state the design requirements and how they are met. Different research designs require different methods, as explained in Chapter 5. The research designs, exploratory, descriptive or causal, would also suggest whether we should use qualitative or quantitative methods for our data collection and analysis. This then influences the structure of our report. We have to ensure these consistencies.

We should also inform the reader about our primary and secondary sources of data along with arguments and justifications. When discussing the primary sources, we should explain how we collected information and discuss our population and sampling, and in the case of in-depth case studies, how the cases were selected and why. When writing about data collection, we have to explain what we have done, how we did it and why we have used this particular method. We should also explain which methods of data analysis have been used: if statistical methods, why these particular methods; if qualitative methods, then how we operationalized different concepts, from where the models came, and what types of conclusion could be drawn through this type of analysis.

14.3.7 Findings

The empirical study, what we have found out from our data collection, is presented here. This section is often a major part of the report as the findings are presented in detail with supportive tables and figures. Here we have to refer back to our research questions or hypotheses and present our findings in accordance with these in a systematic, structured and logical manner. The findings, tables and figures should follow a systematic, chronological or psychological order. The most important job is to prune out irrelevant information and findings.

How to arrange and present the findings of our study is a difficult issue. There are no rules for this, but we should refer to the purpose of the study and the report when it comes to what we want to communicate and to whom. We suggest that researchers should be systematic and choose one of the following methods of presentation:

- *By order of occurrence.* Here you present the findings chronologically. This is particularly suitable when you are working with case studies or when you have a process or longitudinal approach: for example, when explaining the process of negotiations and factors influencing this process (see, for example, Ghauri, 1983).

- *By criteria or topics.* You may use your own headings – for example from the questionnaire or problem statement – as a format to present the findings. You may have some criteria on what affects what – for example independent and dependent variables – which can be used as headings to present the findings. You might number your research questions or hypotheses 1, 2, 3 . . . and then discuss each of these in the same sequence.
- *By order of location.* You can present your findings from different parts of the country or world in different sections and use these as headings: for example findings from the south, east or central parts of the country, or findings from different countries or continents.
- *By order of importance.* Quite often it is advised that you present findings in order of importance. The most important and interesting findings should be presented first, followed by the less important issues. When listing criteria, you can list them according to their importance.

14.3.8 Conclusions

In this section evaluated facts are discussed, but these evaluations should only be made from the data presented in the earlier sections; the author's biases and desires should not influence these conclusions. You should state your conclusions systematically for each study objective, research question or hypothesis. The best way is to refer back to the objectives or research questions and check whether or not you have provided conclusions for each of these. If the data collected and the analysis do not provide enough information or support required to draw conclusions, you should clearly state that. It is important to be specific and concise. We suggest the following format for conclusions:

'Based on our findings our conclusions are: . . .'

or

'We have found that: . . .'

Recommendations for future research or implications for business executives should be based on the findings and conclusions. There should be a logical congruence between conclusions and implications or recommendations. If recommendations or implications are given throughout the report, for example while presenting findings, these should be summarized and highlighted in this section. We suggest the following format:

'The implications of C1 are: . . .'

14.3.9 Footnotes

As mentioned earlier, the value of a report also depends upon argumentation and sources. Proper credit to these sources is given in two ways: the bibliography

239

or references listed at the end, and the footnotes or references given throughout the paper. The footnotes specifically and individually document the facts and opinions referred to in the report (Berry, 1989).

In most reports and theses, footnotes are used primarily for three reasons:

1. footnotes giving credit to the source or earlier study we have used;
2. footnotes directing the reader to another section of the same report, also referred to as cross-references;
3. footnotes to explain, discuss or provide additional information on a particular concept or issue.

In research reports a separate reference list or bibliography is provided. In that case we only need to mention the surname of the author and year of publication or source in footnotes or bracketed within the text at the appropriate point, as in this book.

The type of information that should be documented is a difficult question. A fact that a reader already knows need not be documented: for example, the year when the Second World War ended. However, facts that are not common knowledge have to inform the reader how we arrived at a certain point. It is also important for the sake of intersubjectivity. For example, the result of a study on the buying behaviour of a certain segment needs to be documented with the year of the study because the buying behaviour might change at different times. The behaviour can change due to awareness about environmental pollution, oil crises or any other major incident.

Whenever we bring in and use a paraphrase or quotation it has to be documented with a footnote, together with the page number in the book. This goes for articles or any other source we have used: for example, 'Grønhaug (1985: 18)'.

The most important rule is to use the same method throughout the report; different forms should not be mixed up in the same report. When using the form where footnotes are presented at the end of the report, these should come before the list of references or bibliography. Some authors advise using different forms for different types of footnotes: for example, footnotes where we only want to document and mention the source might be gathered at the end, while footnotes where we need to explain or discuss a concept should be mentioned at the bottom of the page (Berry, 1989). It is advised that one consistent method should be used for all types.

There should also be internal consistency. For example, if footnotes are given at the bottom of the page, they should be consistently separated from the main text with double spacing (double the spacing in the text). The footnotes themselves should be in single spacing, while giving double space between two footnotes. The margins and numbers should also be consistently at the same place, not only on the same page but throughout the report. For cross-referenced footnotes or references to other parts of the same report, you should avoid referring to later pages, as the reader is not yet aware of what is coming. On the other hand, it is acceptable to refer to previous pages: for example, 'see p. 10'.

14.3.10 Bibliography and references

Bibliographies are lists of books (and other material) on a particular subject and should include *at least* all the sources that have been cited in the report. A list of references, on the other hand, includes *only* those sources cited and should not include books and other sources consulted but not used. All references should be listed in alphabetical order with authors' surnames coming first. If there is no author, the issuing organization's name should come first in the alphabetical order: for example the European Commission or, in the case of an *editorial* in a periodical, *The Economist*. In the case of a reference to an *article* in a periodical, the author's name should come first.

The most popular format is to place the first word of the first line (e.g. surname) at the left-hand margin, while the rest of the lines are indented by several spaces. Remember, however, that for footnotes, especially those at the foot of the page, the opposite system is often used: the first word of the first line is indented, while the rest of the lines start at the left-hand margin. This system is used for each and every source. The bibliography or references, like footnotes, should be typed in single spacing while giving double spacing between two references. Where there is more than one author in a source, it is possible to reverse the names of all authors. However, it is quite common to reverse just the first author's name for the sake of alphabetical order and mention the rest of the authors with their first name (or initials) first. Both systems are correct, but for the sake of consistency you should use only one system in the same report.

The titles of books, names of journals, periodicals and newspapers and titles of published government reports are often underlined, italicized or typed with capital letters. In the case of edited books, if the references come from a chapter written by another author, the reference should start with the author's name and not with the editor's name, and the title of the edited volume or book should be underlined or italicized. The title of articles and chapters from edited books and journals should be indicated by quotation marks (' ') and be typed exactly as the original. If the title is in a different language, such as Dutch or Norwegian, it should be mentioned in the original language. Some common examples of references are provided here:

Buckley, P. and Ghauri, P. (eds) (1999), *The Internationalization of the Firm*, 2nd edn, London: Thomson.
Ghauri, P.N. and Usunier, J.-C. (1996), *International Business Negotiations*, Oxford: Elsevier.
Grønhaug, R. and Haukedal, W. (1989), 'Environmental imagery and strategic action', *Scandinavian Journal of Management*, vol. 4, nos 1–2: 5–17.

Dunning, J. (1980), 'Towards an eclectic theory of international production: some empirical tests', *Journal of International Business Studies*, Spring/ Summer, 1: 9–31.

United Nations Center on Transnational Corporations (1985), *International Accounting and Reporting Issues*: 1984 review, New York: United Nations Publications.

As mentioned earlier, there are several methods and styles that are correct in listing the bibliography. The most important thing, however, is to use one form throughout a report and not to mix up different styles.

For the format and structure of the report, also check the rules of your institution.

14.4 Oral presentation

Often you have to present your report in front of not only your supervisor but also company executives or members of an evaluation committee: people who have not been involved in your project. As in writing a report, the first important issue is to know your audience, as that will decide the level of your presentation. It should not be too technical or academic in nature, especially if people from outside (companies, etc.) are present.

The presentation has to be organized in the same manner as the written report. First, the main objectives and the specific research questions should be presented, as well as why these questions are interesting or worth your study. You should relate your study to earlier work on the topic, and demonstrate how your study differs from that work. You should also state your limitations and constraints.

Second, you have to explain 'how' you have done the study: how you have collected the information and how you have analysed it. Here again you should explain your limitations and constraints. This will adjust the expectation level of the audience as well as help them to make their own judgement as to the reliability of your study and its conclusions.

Finally, the findings and conclusions can be presented in a simple and straightforward way. These conclusions should be discussed in cases of unexpected results and other surprises. The conclusions should also be related to your objectives and research questions. If you have not been able to answer all your questions, this should be explained. In the case of a research project regarding specific company problems, you need to also present your recommendations or solutions and argue why, in your opinion, these are the best solutions or recommendations.

The most important issue, however, is the presentation itself: how you are going to use PowerPoint presentations, etc. We recommend that you use a minimum amount of text, preferably just points, and then talk about it. Technical or difficult terminology and concepts should be avoided and, if used, should be explained. Use of illustrations, tables and figures is a good strategy to support your arguments, though figures and tables with lots of numbers and characters should be avoided. If used, the part of the table/figure explaining your point should be highlighted. Use of graphics and charts facilitates understanding. Listeners in this case can easily see the whole picture and make comparisons more quickly and easily. Otherwise, they will have to make such evaluations themselves, which is often difficult, if not impossible, during the presentation.

Use simple and direct language when presenting, speak slowly and articulate your words properly – say the whole words. Do not rush through the presentation, in order to say a lot of things. If possible, make copies of your slides and distribute them. Time management is one of the most important aspects of your presentation. Rehearse your presentation so that you can explain the issues clearly without the need to rush. Do not forget that one of the major purposes of the presentation is for the audience to ask questions. You have to plan question and answer time into your presentation. In the case of a 30-minute presentation, we suggest you divide your time as follows:

- 5 minutes to present the objectives and the research question; also, to relate your study to earlier work and explain its importance;
- 5 minutes to present how you have carried out the study, your information sources and arguments;
- 10 minutes to present the findings and conclusions;
- 10 minutes for questions and answers.

Rehearse your presentation and, while presenting, speak slowly and clearly.

14.5 Writing for publication

If you are writing a report with an intention of getting it published in a journal, the report needs a separate structure. The first thing to consider is the journal you are aiming at. Most journals demand a certain format for the papers submitted to them with regard to length, headings, use of footnotes and references and the emphasis on methodological rigour. The starting point is thus first to decide where you want to publish your paper and look through its criteria and format requirements.

Most academic journals look for well-focused research that can contribute something to existing knowledge in the particular field. Many journals also value contributions towards managerial practice, so-called managerial implications. In business studies, the knowledge developed by researchers is rather more quickly applied to practice than in many other fields. The research, whether developing theories or testing existing ones, contributes considerably towards the furthering of knowledge. This is the main objective of most academic journals: to further knowledge in their respective field.

Considering the above, a report written for publication needs first to establish the objective of study and emphasize the gap it will fill or the new knowledge it will lead to. Second, it has to be related to existing knowledge in the field. Third, the methodology needs much more argumentative explanation to convince the reader that, for the particular research problem, this is the most appropriate method. Here the discussion on internal validity, for example of the measurement instrument, and external validity, for example the generalizability or managerial implications, is much more important than in other reports (Huff, 1999).

A report written for publication need not have headings and paragraphs on all the above issues, but nevertheless the argument in the methodology section and on measurement should satisfy all concerns regarding them. A paper/report written for publication is normally written with the following headings:

- Introduction, which introduces the topic and explains the research problem and objective;
- Literature Review, either as a separate section or while building/presenting hypotheses and propositions;
- Method/Model/Measurement, where you have to explain how you have done the study (data collection and data analysis) with all the argumentation mentioned earlier;
- Findings, where the results are presented according to the method chosen (quantitatively or qualitatively);
- Discussion and Conclusion, where the conclusions are drawn out of the findings and unexpected or drastic results are discussed.

Finally, with or without a heading, the contributions (theoretical as well as practical) of the study are presented in a convincing manner. A reference list is attached at the end, following the formatting instructions of the journal or the publisher.

Once the report is ready it should be read by at least a couple of colleagues, especially your supervisor if you have one. The colleagues should have some experience of reviewing papers for the journal being considered, or for similar journals. The criticisms and comments given by these colleagues should be taken seriously and the paper should be revised before you send it to the journal.

 ## Further reading

Birkinshaw, J. (2004) 'Publishing qualitative research in international business', in Marshan-Piekkari, R. and Welch, C. (eds), *A Handbook of Qualitative Research Methods for International Business*, Cheltenham: Edward Elgar, pp. 570–84.

Miles, M.B. and Huberman, A.M. (1994) *Qualitative Data Analysis*, 2nd edn, Thousand Oaks, CA: Sage (Chapter 12).

Perry, C. (1998) *A Structured Approach to Presenting Theses: Notes for Students and their Supervisors*; retrieved 25 August 2004 from: http://www.scu.edu.au/schools/gcm/ar/art/cperry.html.

Rousseau, D.M. (1995) 'Publishing from a reviewer's perspective', in Cummings, L.L. and Frost, P.J. (eds), *Publishing in the Organizational Sciences*, Thousands Oaks, CA: Sage, pp. 151–63.

? Questions

1. What are the differences in writing a company report and a thesis?

2. What are the most important issues to be considered while writing the final report for a research project?

3. Is writing for publication different from writing up the thesis? How?

Exercises

1. Pick up a Master's thesis from the library and prepare a 15-minute presentation.

2. Pick up a Master's/PhD dissertation and write a two-page executive summary.

3. Working in groups of two, read each other a report and give critical comments regarding the structure of the report and the language flow.

References

ACR News (1995) 'Where's the big idea?', *ACR News*, December, p. 13.

Addison, J.T. and Belfield, C.R. (2000) 'The impact of financial participation and employee involvement on financial performance', *Scottish Journal of Political Economy*, 47(5), pp. 571–83.

Andreasen, A.R. (1990) 'Cultural interpretation: A critical consumer research issue for the 1990s', *Advances in Consumer Research*, 3, pp. 185–96.

Bazerman, M. (1998) *Judgment in Managerial Decision Making*, 4th edn, New York: Wiley.

Becker, H.S. (1970) *Sociological Work*, Chicago, IL: Aldine.

Bem, J. (1979) *Désir et savoir dans l'oeuvre de Flaubert: 'La tentation de Saint Antonine'*, Lyon: La Bacconnière.

Bennett, R. (1986) 'Meaning and method in management research', *Graduate Management Research*, 3(3) (whole part).

Berry, R. (1989) *How to Write a Research Paper*, 2nd edn, Oxford: Pergamon Press.

Beza, T. (1984) *Psaumes mis en vers Français* (1551–62), Geneva: Droz.

Bloom, B.S., Hastings, J.T. and Madaus, G.F. (1971) *Handbook on Formative and Summative Evaluation of Student Learning*, New York: McGraw-Hill.

Bolsky, M.I. (1988) *Better Scientific and Technical Writing*, Englewood Cliffs, NJ: Prentice-Hall.

Bonoma, T.V. (1985) 'Case research in marketing: opportunities, problems, and a process', *Journal of Business Research*, 12, pp. 199–208.

Boyd, W.B. and Westfall, R. (1970) 'Interviewer bias once more revisited', *Journal of Marketing Research*, 7, pp. 249–74.

Boyd, W.B., Westfall, R. and Stasch, S.F. (1985) *Marketing Research: Text and Cases*, 6th edn, Homewood, IL: Irwin.

Boyd, W.B., Westfall, R. and Stasch, S.F. (1989) *Marketing Research: Text and Cases*, 7th edn, Homewood, IL: Irwin.

Braithwaite, R.B. (1955) *Scientific Explanation: A Study of the Function of Theory, Probability and Law in Science*, Cambridge: Cambridge University Press.

Brewer, J. and Hunter, A. (1989) *Multimethod research: A Synthesis of Styles*, Sage Library of Social Research, 175, Beverly Hills, CA: Sage.

Bryman, A. (1988) *Quantity and Quality in Social Research*, London: Routledge.

Bryman, A. (2001) *Social Research Methods*, Oxford: Oxford University Press.

Bryman, A. and Bell, E. (2003) *Business Research Methods*, Oxford: Oxford University Press.

Buchler, J. (ed.) (1955) *Philosophical Writings of Peirce*, New York: Dover.

Buckley, P.J. (1983) *The Growth of International Business*, London: Allen & Unwin.

Burns, T. and Stalker, G.M. (1961) *The Management of Innovations*, London: Tavistock.

Burrell, G. and Morgan, G. (1979) *Sociological Paradigms and Organizational Analysis*, London: Heinemann.

Campbell, D.T. (1975) 'Degrees of freedom and the case study', *Comparative Political Studies*, 8(2), pp. 173–93.

Campbell, D.T. and Fiske, W. (1959) 'Convergent and discriminant validation by the multitrail-multimethod matrix', *Psychological Bulletin*, 56, pp. 81–105.

Campbell, D.T. and Stanley, J.C. (1966) *Experimental and Quasi Experimental Designs for Research*, Chicago, IL: Rand McNally.

Cannell, C.F., Miller, P.U. and Oksenberg, L. (1981) 'Research on interviewing techniques', in S. Leinhardt (ed.), *Sociological Methodology*, San Francisco, CA: Jossey-Bass, pp. 389–437.

Chalmers, A.F. (1982) *What is this Thing called Science?*, 2nd edn, Philadelphia, PA: Open University Press.

Churchill, G.A. (1979) 'A paradigm for developing better measures of marketing constructs', *Journal of Marketing Research*, 16, February, pp. 64–73.

Churchill, G.A. (1991) *Marketing Research: Methodological Foundations*, 5th edn, Chicago, IL: Dryden Press.

Churchill, G.A. (1995) *Marketing Research: Methodological Foundations*, 6th edn, Fort Worth, TX: Dryden Press.

Churchill, G.A. (1999) *Marketing Research: Methodological Foundations*, 7th edn, Fort Worth, TX: Dryden Press.

Coase, R.H. (1937) 'The nature of the firm', *Economica* 4(16), pp. 386–405.

Cohen, M. and Nagel, E. (1934) *An Introduction to Logic and Scientific Method*, New York: American Advertising Association.

Colley, R.A. (1961) *Defining Advertising Goals for Measured Advertising Results*, New York: American Advertising Association.

Conant, J. (1951) *Science and Common Sense*, New Haven, CT: Yale University Press.

Cook, T.D. and Campbell, D.T. (1979) *Quasi-Experimentation: Design and Analysis Issues for Field Settings*, Chicago, IL: Rand McNally College Publication Co.

Cooper, D. and Schindler, P. (2001) *Business Research Methods*, Boston, MA: McGraw-Hill.

Cooper, H.M. (1984) *The Integrative Research Review: A Systematic Approach*, Beverly Hills, CA: Sage.

Coutrot, T. (1998) 'How do institutional frameworks affect industrial relations outcomes?', *European Journal of Industrial Relations*, 4(2), pp. 177–205.

Cowley, J.C.P. (2000) 'Strategic qualitative focus group research: define and articulate our skills or we will be replaced by others', *International Journal of Market Research*, 37(7), pp. 903–30.

Craig, C.S. and Douglas, S.P. (2000) *International Marketing Research*, 2nd edn, New York: Wiley (Chapter 12).

Creswell, J.W. (1997) *Qualitative Inquiry and Research Design: Shoosing Among Five Traditions*, London: Sage Publicaitons.

Data Mining (1997) 'Plumbing the depths of corporate databases', *Computer World*, 21 April, p. 12.

Davis, J. (2001) 'International comparison of labour disputes', *Labour Market Trends*, April, pp. 195–201.

Denzin, N.K. and Lincoln, Y.S. (1994) eds, *Handbook of Qualitative Research*, Thousand Oaks: Sage.

References

Douglas, J. (1976) *Investigating Social Research*, Beverly Hills, CA: Sage.

Douglas, S.P. and Craig, C.S. (1997) 'The changing dynamic of consumer behavior: implications for cross-cultural research', *International Journal of Research in Marketing*, 14(4), pp. 379–95.

Easterby-Smith, M., Thorpe, R. and Lowe, A. (1991) *Management Research*, London: Sage.

Eisenhardt, K.M. (1989) 'Building theories from case study research', *Academy of Management Review*, 14(4), pp. 532–50.

Elliot, J. (1980) 'How hard it is to write easily', *View Point: the Ogilvy & Mathew Magazine*, 2, pp. 18–19.

Ferber, R., Blankertz, D.F. and Hollander, S. Jr. (1964) *Marketing Research*, New York: Ronald Press.

Field, A. (2000) *Discovering Statistics Using SPSS for Windows*, London: Sage.

Forcese, D.P. and Richer, S. (1973) *Social Research Methods*, Englewood Cliffs, NJ: Prentice-Hall.

Fowler, F.J. and Mangione, T.W. (1990) *Standardized Survey Interviewing: Minimizing Interviewer-Related Error*, Newbury Park, CA: Sage.

Frankfort-Nachmias, F. and Nachmias, D. (1996) *Research Methods in the Social Sciences*, 5th edn, London: Edward Arnold.

Fuglseth, A.M. and Grønhaug, K. (2003) 'Can computerized market models improve strategic decision making?', *Journal of Socio-Economics*, 32, pp. 503–20.

Ghauri, P.N. (1983) *Negotiating International Package Deals*, Stockholm: Almqvist & Wiksell.

Ghauri, P.N. (2004) 'Designing and conducting case studies in international business research', in Marshan-Piekkari, R. and Welch, C. (eds), *A Handbook of Qualitative Research Methods for International Business*, Cheltenham: Edward Elgar, pp. 109–24.

Ghauri, P. and Cateora, P. (2006) *International Marketing: European Edition*, London: McGraw-Hill.

Ghauri, P.N. and Firth, R. (2009) 'The formation of case research in international business', *Der Markt: Journal for Marketing*, 48, 29–40.

Gibbons, M., Limoges, C., Nowotny, H., Schwartzman, S., Scott, P. and Trow, M. (1994) *The New Production of Knowledge*, London: Sage.

Gill, J. and Johnson, P. (1991) *Research Methods for Managers*, London: Paul Chapman.

Gill, J. and Johnson, P. (2002) *Research Methods for Managers*, 3rd edn, London: Paul Chapman.

Glaser, B.G. and Strauss, A.L. (1967) *The Discovery of Grounded Theory: Strategies for Qualitative Research*, Chicago, IL: Aldine.

Grønhaug, K. (1985) 'Problemer i empirisk forskning', in NHH/RSF, *Methoder og perspectiver i okonomisk-administrativ Forskning*, Oslo: Universitetsforlag.

Grønhaug, K. (1999) 'Technological flexibility and organisational buying strategies', *European Journal of Purchasing and Supply Management*, 51, pp. 13–22.

Grønhaug, K. and Haukedal, W. (1989) 'Environmental imagery and strategic action', *Scandinavian Journal of Management*, 4(1/2), pp. 5–17.

Guba, E.G. and Lincoln, Y.S. (1989) *Fourth Generation Evaluation*, Newbury Park: Sage.

Hair, J.F., Anderson, R.E., Tatham, R.G. and Black, W.C. (1998) *Multivariate Data Analysis*, 5th edn, Harlow and Englewood Cliffs, NJ: Prentice-Hall.

Hammersley, M. and Atkinson, P. (1995) *Ethnography: Principles in Practice*, London: Routledge.

Hawkins, S.W. (1988) *A Brief History of Time: From the Big Bang to Black Holes*, Toronto: Bantam Books.

Hellesøy, O., Grønhaug, K. and Kvitastein, O. (2000) 'Burnout: conceptual issues and empirical findings from a new research setting', *Scandinavian Journal of Management*, 16, pp. 233–47.

Holland, R. (1999) 'Reflexivity', *Human Relations*, 52(4), pp. 463–85.

Huff, D. (1954) *How to Lie with Statistics*, New York: Norton.

Huff, S.A. (1999) *Writing for Publication*, Thousand Oaks, CA: Sage.

Jankowicz, A.D. (1991) *Business Research Projects for Students*, London: Chapman & Hall.

Jerrold, D. quotation from Henry, L. (1995) *Best Quotations for all Occasions*, New York: Fawcett Premier.

Jones, M.O. (1988) 'In search of meaning: using qualitative methods in research and applications', in Jones, M.O., Moore, M.D. and Snyder, R.C. (eds), *Inside Organisations: Understanding the Human Dimension*, London: Sage, pp. 31–48.

Keller, K.L. (1998) *Strategic Brand Management*, Englewood Cliffs, NJ: Prentice-Hall.

Kent, R.K. (1989) *Marketing Research in Action*, London: Routledge.

Kerlinger, F.N. (1964) *Foundations of Behavioural Research: Educational and Psychological Inquiry*, London: Holt, Rinehart & Winston.

Kirk, J. and Miller, M.L. (1986) *Reliability and Validity in Qualitative Research*, Sage University Paper Series on Qualitative Applications in Social Sciences, No. 01, Newbury Park: Sage.

Kornhauser, A. and Lazarsfeld, P.F. (1955) 'The analysis of consumer actions', in Lazarsfeld, P. and Rosenberg, M. (eds), *The Language of Social Research*, pp. 392–403, Glencoe, IL: Free Press.

Kotler, P. (1997) *Marketing Management*, 9th edn, Englewood Cliffs, NJ: Prentice-Hall.

Kuhn, T. (1970) *The Structure of Scientific Revolutions*, 2nd edn, Chicago, IL: University of Chicago Press.

Kvale, S. (1986) *Interviews: An Introduction to Qualitative Research Interviewing*, Thousand Oaks: Sage.

Lakoff, G. and Johnson, M. (1980) *Metaphors We Live By*, Chicago, IL: University of Chicago Press.

Lave, C.A. and March, J.G. (1993) *An Introduction to Models in the Social Sciences*, 2nd edn, New York: Harper & Row.

Layder, D. (1993) *New Strategies in Social Research*, Cambridge: Polity Press.

Lazarsfeld, P. (1959) 'Latent structure analysis', in Koch, S. (ed.), *Psychology: A Study of a Science*, vol. 3, New York and London: McGraw-Hill.

LeCompte, M.D. and Goetz, J.P. (1982) Problems of Reliability and Validity in Ethnographic Research, *Review of Educational Research*, 52/1: 31–60.

Lee, T.W. (1999) *Using Qualitative Methods in Organizational Research*, Thousand Oaks: Sage.

Light, D. Jr. (1979) 'Surface data and deep structure: observing the organization of professional training', *Administrative Science Quarterly*, 24(4), pp. 551–9, Ithaca, New York: Johnson Graduate School of Management, Cornell University.

References

Lofland, J. (1971) *Analyzing Social Settings*, Belmont, CA: Wadsworth.

Lonner, W.J. and Adamopoulos, J. (1997) 'Culture as an antecedent to behaviour, in Berry, J.W., Poortinga, Y.H. and Panday, J. (eds), *Handbook of Cross-cultural Psychology*, vol. 2, Boston: Allyn & Bacon, pp. 43–83.

Maanen, J. van (1979) 'Reclaiming qualitative methods for organizational research: a preface', *Administrative Science Quarterly*, 24(4), 520–6.

Maanen, J. van (ed.) (1983) *Qualitative Methodology*, Newbury Park, CA: Sage.

Maanen, J. van (1995) 'Style as a theory', *Organizational Science*, 7(4), pp. 641–52.

Maanen J. van and Kolb, D. (1985) The Professional Apprentice: Observations on Fieldwork Roles in Two Organizational Settings, *Research in the Sociology of Organizations*, 4, New York: JAI Press.

Malhotra, N. (1996) *Marketing Research: An Applied Orientation*, 2nd edn, Englewood Cliffs, NJ: Prentice-Hall.

March, J.G. and Simon, H.A. (1958) *Organizations*, New York: Wiley.

Marshall, C. and Rossman, G.B. (1995) *Designing Qualitative Research*, 2nd edn, London: Sage.

Marshan-Piekkari, R. and Welch, C. (2004) *A Handbook of Qualitative Research Methods for International Business*, Cheltenham: Edward Elgar.

Martin, C. (1988) *Computers and Senior Managers: Top Management's Response to Interactive Computing*, Manchester: NCC.

Maxwell, J.A. (1997) Designing a Qualitative Study, in Bickman, L. and Rog, D.J. (eds), *Handbook of Applied Social Research Methods*, London: Sage, 69–100.

McGrath, J.E. (1982) 'Dilammatics: the study of research choices and dilemmas', in McGrath, J.E. and Kulka, P.A. (eds), *Independent Calls in Research*, Beverly Hills, CA: Sage, pp. 69–102.

Meer-Kooistra, J. van der (1993) *Coordineren, Motiveren en verrekenen, Wisselwerking tussen omgeving, onderneming en mensen*, Groningen: Wolters-Noordhoff.

Merton, R.K. (1967) *On Theoretical Sociology*, New York: Free Press.

Merton, R.K., Fisk, M. and Kendall, P.L. (1956) *The Focused Interview: A Manual of Problems and Procedures*, New York: Free Press.

Miles, M.B. (1979) 'Qualitative data as attractive nuisance: the problem of analysis', *Administrative Science Quarterly*, 24(4), pp. 590–601.

Miles, M.B. and Huberman, A.M. (1994) *Qualitative Data Analysis*, 2nd edn, Thousand Oaks, CA: Sage.

Mintzberg, H. (1979) 'An emerging strategy of "direct" research', *Administrative Science Quarterly*, 24(4), pp. 582–9, Ithaca, New York: Johnson Graduate School of Management, Cornell University.

Mishler, E.G. (1986) *Research Interviewing*, London: Harvard University Press.

Morgan, G. (ed.) (1983) *Beyond Method*, London: Sage.

Moser, B. and Kalton, G. (1971) *Surveys, Methods and Social Investigation*, London: Heinemann.

Murphy, H.A. and Hildebrandt, H.W. (1988) *Effective Business Communications*, 5th edn, New York: McGraw-Hill.

Naegel, E. (1961) *The Structure of Science*, New York: Harcourt, Brace & World.

Orbell, J. (1987) *A Guide to Tracing the History of a Business*, Aldershot: Gower Press.

Patton, M.Q. (1990) *Qualitative Evaluation and Research Methods*, 2nd edn, Newbury Park, CA: Sage.

Peters, T.J. and Waterman, R.H. (1982) *In Search of Excellence: Lessons from America's Best Run Companies*, New York: Harper & Row.

Pettigrew, A. (1985) 'Contextual research: a natural way to link theory and practice', in Lawler, E.E., Mohrman, A.M., Mohrman, S.A., Ledford, G.E., Cummings, T.G. and Associates (eds), *Doing Research that is useful for Theory and Practice*, San Francisco, CA: Jossey-Bass, pp. 222–74.

Pfeffer, J. (1993) 'Barriers to the advance of organizational science: paradigm development as a dependent variable', *Academy of Management Review*, 18(4), pp. 599–620.

Pfeffer, J. (1995) 'Morality, reproductibility and the persistent of styles of theory', *Organization Science*, 6(6), pp. 681–93.

Phillips, B. (1966) *Social Research: Strategy and Tactics*, New York: Macmillan.

Piaget, J. (1950) *The Psychology of Intelligence*, London: Routledge & Kegan Paul.

Pike, K. (1966) *Language in Relation to Unified Theory of Structure of Human Behaviour*, The Hague: Mouton.

Polanyi, M. (1958) *Personal Knowledge*, Chicago, IL: University of Chicago Press.

Popper, K.R. (1961) *The Logic of Scientific Discovery*, New York: Science Edition.

Porter, M.E. (1980) *Competitive Strategy*, New York: Free Press.

Potter, W.J. (1996) *An Analysis of Thinking and Research about Qualitative Methods*, Lea's Communication Series, Mahwah: Lawrence Erlbaum Associates.

Reeves, T.K. and Harper, D. (1981) *Surveys at Work: A Practitioner's Guide*, London: McGraw-Hill.

Reichardt, C.S. and Cook, T.D. (1979) 'Beyond qualitative versus quantitative methods', in Cook, T.D. and Reichardt, C.S. (eds), *Qualitative and Quantitative Methods in Evaluation Research*, Beverly Hills, CA: Sage, pp. 7–32.

Revans, R.W. (1971) *Developing Effective Managers*, London: Longman.

Roethlisberger, F.J. and Dickson, W.J. (1939) *Management and the Worker*, Cambridge, MA: Harvard University Press.

Rose, A.M. and Peterson, W.A. (1965) *Older People and their Social World: The Subculture of the Aging*, Philadelphia, PA: Davis.

Ross, N.P. and Harris, S. (1994) 'What are the ethical responsibilities of model builders?', in Wallace, W.A. (ed.), *Ethics in Models*, Oxford: Pergamon Press, pp. 161–6.

Rubin, H.J. and Rubin, I.S. (1995) *Qualitative Interviewing: The Art of Hearing Data*, Thousand Oaks, CA: Sage.

Salzberger, T., Sinkovics, R. and Schlegelmilch, B. (1999) 'Data equivalence in cross-cultural research: a comparison of classical test theory and latent trait theory based approaches', *Australasian Marketing Journal* 7(2), pp. 23–38.

Saunders, M.N.K., Lewis, P. and Thornhill, A. (2000) *Research Methods for Business Students*, 2nd edn, Harlow: Prentice-Hall.

Saunders, M.N.K., Lewis, P. and Thornhill, A. (2003) *Research Methods for Business Students*, 3rd edn, Harlow: Prentice-Hall.

Scase, R. and Goffee, R. (1989) *Reluctant Managers*, London: Unwin Hyman.

Schuman, H. and Presser, S. (1976) *Questions and Answers in Attitude Surveys: Experiments on Question Form, Wording, and Context*, New York: Academic Press.

Schwartz, N. and Sudman, S. (eds) (1996) *Answering Questions: Methodology for Determining Cognitive and Communicative Processes in Survey Research*, San Francisco: Jossey-Bass.

Schwartz, S.H. (1992) 'Universals in the content and structure of values', in Zane, M. (ed.), *Advances in Experimental Social Psychology*, 25, New York: Academic Press.

Scott, C. (1961) 'Research on mail surveys', *Journal of the Royal Statistical Society*, 24(124), pp. 143–205.

Sekaran, U. (1992) *Womanpower: Managing in Times of Demographic Turbulence*, London: Sage.

Selltiz, C., Wrightsman, S. and Cook, S.W. (1976) *Research Methods in Social Relations*, 3rd edn, New York: Holt, Rinehart & Winston.

Siegel, S. and Castellan, N.J. (1988) *Nonparametric Statistics for the Behavioral Sciences*, 2nd edn, New York: McGraw-Hill.

Silkoset, R. (2004) *Collective Market Orientation in Co-producing Networks*, Oslo: BI Norwegian School of Management (doctoral dissertation).

Simons, R. (1987) 'Accounting control systems and business strategy: an empirical analysis', *Accounting, Organisation and Society*, 12(4), pp. 357–74.

Sinkovics, R.R., Penz, E. and Ghauri, P.N. (2005) 'Analysing textual data in international marketing research', *Qualitative Market Research: An International Journal* 8(1), pp. 9–38.

Sinkovics, R., Penz, E., Ghauri, P. (2008) 'Enhancing the trustworthiness of qualitative research in international business', *Management International Review*, 48(6), pp. 689–714.

Spiggle, S. (1994) 'Analysis and interpretation of qualitative data in consumer research', *Journal of Consumer Research*, 21 (December), pp. 491–503.

Stewart, D.W. and Shamdasani, P.N. (1990) *Focus Groups: Theory and Practice*, Newbury Park, CA: Sage.

Strauss, A. and Corbin, J. (1990) *Basics of Qualitative Research: Grounded Theory Procedures and Techniques*, Newbury Park, CA: Sage.

Strauss, A. and Corbin, J. (1994) 'Grounded theory methodology: an overview', in Denzin, N.K. and Lincoln, Y.S. (eds), *Handbook of Qualitative Research*, Thousand Oaks, CA: Sage, pp. 273–85.

Strauss, A.L. and Corbin, J. (1998) *Basics of Qualitative Research: Techniques and Procedures for Developing Grounded Theory*, 2nd edn, Thousand Oaks, CA: Sage.

Sudman, S. (1976) *Applied Sampling*, New York: Academic Press.

Sudman, S. and Bradburn, N.M. (1989) *Asking Questions*, San Francisco, CA: Jossey-Bass.

Svatko, J.E. (1989) 'Working with consultants', *Small Business Reports*, 14(2), pp. 58–68.

Tesch, R. (1990) *Qualitative Research Analysis Tools and Software Tools*, New York: Falmer.

Thompson, J.D. (1967) *Organizations in Action: Social Science Bases of Administrative Theory*, New York: McGraw-Hill.

Toffler, A. (1980) *The Third Wave*, London: Pan.

Tranfield, D. and Starkey, K. (1998) 'The nature of social organisation and promotion of management research: towards policy', *British Journal of Management*, 9(4), pp. 341–53.

Triandis, H.C. (1972) *The Analysis of Subjective Culture*, New York: Wiley.

Utterback, J.M. (1994) *Mastering the Dynamics of Innovation*, Boston, MA: Harvard University Press.

Vijver, F. van de and Leung, K. (1997) *Methods and Data Analysis for Cross-Cultural Research*, Thousand Oaks, CA: Sage.

Watson, T.J. (1994) *In Search of Management: Culture, Chaos and Control in Managerial Work*, London: Routledge.

Weidersheim-Paul, F. and Eriksson, T. (1998) *Att Utreda och Rappportera*, Malmo: Liber.

Weisberg, H.F. (1992) *Central Tendency and Variability*, Quantitative Applications in the Social Sciences, 83, Newbury Park, CA: Sage.

Weiss, R.S. (1968) 'Issues in holistic research', in Becker, H.S. Blanche, G. and Weiss, R.S. (eds), *Institutions and the Person*, Chicago, IL: Aldine, pp. 342–50.

Weitzman, E. and Miles, M. (1995) *Computer Programs for Qualitative Data Analysis: An Expanded Sourcebook*, 2nd edn, Thousand Oaks, CA: Sage.

Welch, C., Marschan-Piekkeri, R., Penttinen, H. and Tahvanainen, M. (2002) Corporate Elites as Informants in Qualitative International Business Research, *International Business Review*, 11/5: 611–628.

Whitehead, A.N. (1911) *An Introduction to Mathematics*, London: Williams & Norgate.

Whitley, R. (1984) 'The scientific status of management research as a practically oriented social science', *Journal of Management Studies*, 21(4), pp. 369–90.

Wind, Y. and Douglas, S.P. (1982) 'Comparative consumer research: the next frontier', *Management Decisions*, 4, pp. 24–35.

Yin, R.K. (1994) *Case Study Research: Design and Methods*, Thousand Oaks, CA: Sage.

Yin, R.K. (2003) *Case Study Research*, 3rd edn, London: Sage.

Zaltman, G., Lemasters, K. and Heffering, M. (1982) *Theory Construction in Marketing*, New York: Wiley.

Zaltman, G., Pinson, C.R.A. and Angelmar, R. (1977) *Metatheory and Consumer Research*, New York: Holt, Rinehart & Winston.

Zikmund, W.G. (1997) *Business Research Methods*, 5th edn, Fort Worth, TX: Dryden Press.

Index